THE 2000
TOUR DE FRANCE

THE 2000 TOUR DE FRANCE

ARMSTRONG ENCORE

JOHN WILCOCKSON
WITH CHARLES PELKEY AND BRYAN JEW

FEATURING THE DIARIES OF TYLER HAMILTON,
FRED RODRIGUEZ AND CHANN McRAE

VELOPRESS
BOULDER, COLORADO

THE 2OOO TOUR DE FRANCE: **ARMSTRONG ENCORE**

Copyright © 2000 Inside Communications

International Standard Book Number: 1-884737-79-X

Library of Congress Cataloging-in-Publication Data applied for.

Printed in the USA

Distributed in the United States and Canada by Publishers Group West.

1830 North 55th Street
Boulder, Colorado 80301-2700 USA
303/440-0601; fax 303/444-6788; e-mail velopress@7dogs.com

To purchase additional copies of this book or other VeloPress books, call 800/234-8356 or visit us on the Web at www.velopress.com.

Photography by Graham Watson
Design by Paula Megenhardt

CONTENTS

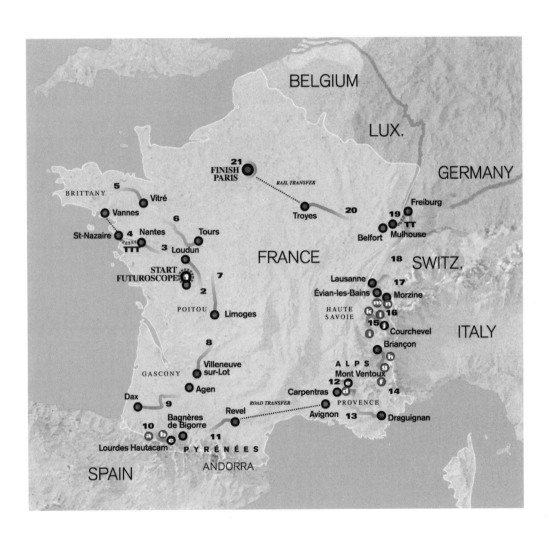

BELGIUM

LUX.

GERMANY

BRITTANY

5

Vitré

Vannes

St-Nazaire 4 Nantes

3 Loudun

START
FUTUROSCOPE

2

POITOU

7

Limoges

6

Tours

FRANCE

21
FINISH
PARIS

RAIL TRANSFER

Troyes

20

Freiburg

19

Belfort Mulhouse

18 SWITZ.

Lausanne 17

Évian-les-Bains Morzine

16

HAUTE
SAVOIE

15

Courchevel

Briançon

ITALY

8

GASCONY

Villeneuve
sur-Lot

Agen

Dax

9

Bagnères
de Bigorre

Revel

ROAD TRANSFER

Carpentras

PROVENCE

A L P S

Mont Ventoux

12

14

10

Lourdes Hautacam

11

P Y R É N É E S

ANDORRA

Avignon 13 Draguignan

SPAIN

Preface

Defending champion and cancer survivor Lance Armstrong was again the hero of the Tour de France, but the year 2000 edition also confirmed the qualities of the men who preceded him as winners of the world's greatest bike race: Jan Ullrich of Germany and Marco Pantani of Italy. At the same time, a whole new generation of riders emerged at the 87th Tour de France, including eventual third-place finisher Joseba Beloki, fellow Spaniard and fifth-place finisher Roberto Heras, and Colombia's new King of the Mountains, Santiago Botero.

This book takes a comprehensive look at the 2000 Tour. The first part—Road to the Tour—features a 1991 interview with Armstrong that reveals many of the qualities that went in to shaping the young American as a future champion. Then come interviews with the man who created Armstrong's team, Thom Weisel, and the team's young Belgian directeur sportif, Johan Bruyneel, who spearheaded Armstrong's two Tour challenges. Also included in this first section are profiles of the other leading Americans who contested the Tour, and a detailed story of the enigmatic Pantani and the travails that he had to contend with before even getting to the Tour's start line in July 2000.

The second part of the book describes and explains every important development and nuance of the 3662.5-kilometer race—from David Millar's opening time trial win in the surreal theme park of Futuroscope in west-central France to the final sprint victory by Stefano Zanini on the Champs-Elysées in Paris. The main story is complemented by the race diaries of three American riders: Armstrong's U.S. Postal Service teammate Tyler Hamilton, and two Tour rookies on the No. 1 Mapei-Quick Step team of Italy, Fred Rodriguez and Chann McRae.

The final section of the book reflects on the impact of Armstrong's repeat victory and how his achievements match up to the great Tour de France riders of the past. It also outlines the details and development of the American-built Treks ridden by Armstrong and his team, as well as the Cannondale and Specialized bikes supplied to the Saeco and Festina teams, respectively. Another chapter examines the state of the Tour two years after it was dragged into a damaging drugs scandal.

Helping to bring the text to life is the 16-page section of photographs by British photographer Graham Watson, and the course profiles for each of the Tour's 21 stages.

Acknowledgments

Covering the Tour de France is a logistical minefield as well as a challenging journalistic assignment. That's why the shared passion and companionship of fellow travelers is at the top of the list of priorities. In this respect, I would like to thank Bryan Jew, senior writer at *VeloNews*, for his great stories on the American riders, skilled driving and unending patience, despite this being the first Tour he had followed; Charles Pelkey, technical editor at *VeloNews*, for his important contributions on the technical and drugs aspects of the Tour; Rupert Guinness, sportswriter at *The Australian*, for his good humor and friendship; and David Walsh, sportswriter at *The Sunday Times* of London, for helping put into perspective an exercise as crazy as a 23-day bicycle race around France in mid-summer.

Besides riding the Tour, Tyler Hamilton, Fred Rodriguez and Chann McRae managed to find time in their busy schedules to write (or call in!) their diary contributions almost every day, bringing this book a new perspective.

No less appreciated are the insights and definitive photography of Graham Watson, who was awarded La Medaille de Reconnaissance du Tour de France, for completing his 20th Tour as a professional photo-journalist; the expert copyediting of Rivvy Neshama, whose daily feedback and constant encouragement helped remind me why we are married; the patience and optimism of the book's designer Paula Megenhardt; the organizational support of Amy Sorrells and Rick Rundall at VeloPress; and the cooperation of the book's managing editor, Lori Hobkirk.

—*John Wilcockson*

PART ONE

—— ❋ ——

THE ROAD TO THE TOUR

A Diamond in the Making

Ever since Lance Armstrong came into cycling as a junior racer in the late 1980s, he has made heads turn, eyes pop and ears prick. The young Armstrong was never shy to state his opinion, always ready to learn, and hugely ambitious. He has certainly mellowed over the past decade, but much of what makes him a leader and a champion today was apparent when he was still an amateur cyclist in 1991, when he gave the following interview to VeloNews. Even then, a year before he turned professional, the Texan was talking about his enthusiasm for the "rock and roll" European pro scene, losing weight, working with his coach Chris Carmicheal, winning races....

Twenty years old and a full-time cyclist for only the past two seasons, Lance Armstrong has already made an indelible mark on both U.S. and European racing. And as he swaps the neon-bright colors of Subaru-Montgomery for the blue-and-red of Motorola in 1992, the reigning U.S. amateur road champion has his sights set on even greater things.

"This season, I had two goals—the Tour DuPont and the world championships," stated Armstrong. "They both sucked. So, I'm not making any more goals."

However, speaking from his new apartment in downtown Austin, Texas, during an hour-long interview, Armstrong revealed a kinder, gentler side to his often brash, some say arrogant, character. Discussing his contract with Motorola, he said, "I can stay amateur up to the Olympics—that is, if I make the team. I'm not a certainty to go to the Olympics. I'm on an even scale with the rest of the U.S. amateurs; but I will train and race as hard as I can to make the team. If I do go to Barcelona, I won't come back (to America). I will turn pro the next day, and ride the rest of the season in Europe."

The well-built Texan went on to qualify his seemingly tepid view of racing in the Olympics, by saying, "I am excited about the Olympics—but I am really excited about riding as a pro with a team like Motorola. They're the best."

Armstrong's fast-track path toward a career in European professional racing has been as startling as it is unusual. He didn't come into the sport like Greg LeMond—who'd discovered bike racing when he was 15, and immediately showed highly developed, natural skills. Nor did Armstrong have a cycling background. He was brought up in Plano, Texas, by his mother Linda ("She's worth five parents!"), without ever having known his father. And, being in the bailiwick of the Dallas Cowboys, his first contact with sports was football. "I tried it for a while, but I was not very good," he admitted.

Armstrong found more success when he became involved with a local swimming program at age 12. "I worked my way up in the team," he explained. "I was pretty good on a state level, and best at long-distance freestyle races, at 500 yards, 1000 yards and 1650 yards. I don't have any natural speed, and even in cycling, my sprint is a little weak."

Besides swimming, the 13-year-old, junior high school student hung out a little at bike shops, and one day spotted a poster for the IronKids triathlon program. This fit into his idea of a really challenging pursuit, and the following year, he reached the IronKids national finals. "I came in second," Armstrong remembered. "I was very disappointed—pretty bummed out—to get beaten."

But getting beaten simply heightened his interest in the new sport, and, by the time he was 15, he was running, riding and swimming as a full-time triathlete. "I did have a bike, which was pretty reasonable, but I did my first race in tennis shoes and toe clips. I wasn't doing a lot of cycling … mainly weekend rides with other triathletes. Just hammering."

Despite his lack of scientific training, Armstrong soon became a formidable triathlete. At age 16, he won Triathlete magazine's Rookie of the Year Award, mainly as a result of his finishing fourth in the 1987 national sprint championship, at North Miami Beach, Florida, "It's just a 53-minute sprint—which suits me fine," he stated. "And you make pretty good money."

After skipping the championship in 1988, he came back to win the national title in 1989, at age 18. And in his wake he left such standout triathletes as Mike Pigg.

Having proven himself as a likely world-class triathlete, Armstrong could have been expected to remain in the swim-bike-run sport, and gone on to a well-paid athletic career. Instead, some of his Dallas friends had already persuaded him to try mainstream cycling, in which he found immediate success.

In fact, prior to his late-season triathlon nationals victory over Pigg, the young Texan has ridden a number of U.S. Cycling Federation junior races—and had made it onto the national team that traveled to the world junior championships, in Moscow.

"I rode the trials because I thought it would be pretty neat to go to Russia as a 17-year-old," Armstrong recalled. "But I regret not going on the European junior trip beforehand—that was a big mistake."

Despite his lack of real preparation—"I didn't have a full-time coach; I just rode my bike as much as I could"—Armstrong made a lasting impression on the enthusiasts gathered around the Moscow road race circuit. Casting caution to the wind, the sturdy American rider made an early attack ... and spent most of the three-hour race off the front of the peloton.

Going into the last laps, Armstrong was joined by a lone Soviet rider, Darius Kiselius. "If we'd worked together, we may have stayed away," the American observed. "But he was always trying to get rid of me. And I was so blown that when he put the hammer down, I was gone. We were on the last lap, and I thought he'd win. I was caught by the pack, and just let them go—and a few kilometers later, the Russian came back, too. All he wanted to do then was trade (jerseys); I told him to get outta my face. I was bummed out."

The records show that Armstrong finished 73rd in the 1989 junior world's, 4:13 behind pack-sprint winner, Patrick Vetsch of Switzerland. Earlier that week, with Bobby Julich, Chann McRae and Keven Moncrief, Armstrong had taken fifth place in the 70km team time trial. It had been a noteworthy beginning to his international cycling career....

Those junior world's also started Armstrong's education in bike racing. Looking back two years, he reflected, "I started to realize that you can't just take off solo in that type of field." A month after the world's, in Colorado Springs, Armstrong won national junior titles in both the individual and team time trials. Then, in September, he set a national junior 20km time trial record of 25:03. And, despite the continuing pull of his triathlon career, Armstrong was hooked on cycling.

For the 1990 season, the new talent was signed by the Subaru-Montgomery team, under the management of former U.S. Cycling Federation national coach Eddie Borysewicz. "Eddie and I are not on the best of terms, now," admitted Armstrong. "But he deserves a lot of credit for helping me learn more about racing. I was totally under his coaching in 1990. Everyone has their pluses and minuses. Eddie is very good for early-season preparation.... He kept me out of the Tour of Texas, and told me to ride the PostGirot Tour of Sweden, with the national team, in June."

The seven-day Swedish race proved an eye-opener for Armstrong, who remembered, "We were sitting in the airport when these Europeans walked in. I was thinking that their faces were familiar; and then we saw it was the PDM, Toshiba and Buckler teams … Jean-François Bernard, Frans Maassen and Jelle Nijdam were all there. I was awestruck.

"When we started racing, it was just like pro racing: steady for 50km to 80km, and then really fast on the finishing circuits. I was amazed at the speed. And it didn't help that I always had bad positioning coming out of the corners. But I enjoyed it. I finished top 10 in the prologue, and then finished fifth in the time trial. I ended up eighth overall.

"I really fell in love with the sport there … with the whole 'rock and roll' business. It looked like a lot of fun. It's a big scene, and I wanted to be part of it."

Besides inspiring Armstrong, the Tour of Sweden also helped to solidify his name on the road-race team for the 1990 world's, which were held on a hilly circuit at Utsunomiya, Japan. Again, as he had done in Moscow 12 months earlier, the now 18-year-old American was soon on the attack. "I was not as un-smart as I was at the junior world's, but I got a little excited in that early break," he exclaimed. "There were about 10 guys up there, and I thought, 'This is my chance.' I can remember the Italians in the break and couldn't work out why there were going so slow. I was shouting at them to go faster—and I think they went on to finish first and second! I was lucky to hang on for 11th—but that was respectable.

"It helped me to remember something that (Shimano product manager and national masters champion) Wayne Stetina once told me: A bike racer is like a gas tank, and if you step on the gas too much, too soon, you end up on empty."

After that performance, Armstrong was keener than ever to make a career in pro cycling in Europe. Unfortunately, this didn't fully mesh with the 1991 plans of the Subaru-Montgomery team, that would again focus most of its season on U.S. domestic racing. And, ironically, it was in Europe that the sometimes strained relationship between the ambitious Armstrong and his coach, the headstrong Borysewicz, reached breaking point.

The event was the Italian pro-am stage race, the Settimana Bergamasca, in which

Armstrong was riding for the U.S. national team, while Eddie B was guiding the all-pro Subaru-Montgomery squad. The problems started when Subaru's Nate Reiss took the overall lead, holding it for a couple of stages, with Armstrong in second, only 18 seconds behind.

"It was a confusing situation," Armstrong admitted, "and I feel that Eddie B didn't handle it right. He wanted me to help Nate win. I didn't have any problem in not working, and I said, 'Look Eddie, I'm not going to work against him, but I'm not going to kill myself to make him win.' There was a huge conflict, and we never spoke after that."

Things came to head on a stage when Reiss made a bathroom stop. Armstrong took up the story: "The pros saw Nate stop, and they asked me to lead an attack. I said no, and so the Gis team, that had a guy in third, went to the front. I jumped on them, but didn't work with them.

"Nate ended up catching us, but then there was a lot of fighting. The Italians kicked Thurlow (Rogers's) bars, and he fell off his bike, and other Subaru riders kicked back. I was feeling good and got with the lead group, and Nate was getting dropped. I was totally justified in what I did—but the team didn't see it that way.

"After the stage—when I took the jersey—Eddie B launched into me. He said, 'We're not going to pay you, and we'll kick you off the team.' We couldn't work together after that."

After winning the Settimana Bergamasca, Armstrong did continue racing for Subaru, and he picked up a total of 15 wins through the season, a dozen of them in the U.S. But he also came under the influence of the current USCF road coach, and former 7-Eleven pro, Chris Carmichael. "I've got to learn to be smart," said the talented Texan, "and I started to learn that under Carmichael."

It was Carmichael who encouraged Armstrong in May's Tour DuPont, and master-minded the U.S. team's success in the Richmond criterium stage. Despite being sick after his win in Italy, Armstrong rode strongly on the stage: He bridged up to a break that contained Nathan Sheafor, and then helped Sheafor escape for the stage win, coming in third himself.

Armstrong's focus then turned to the world championships, preparations for which included the national championships in Salt Lake City. A week before the nationals, he traveled to Vancouver, Canada, for the well-known Gastown Grand Prix—and won. "I was really excited about Gastown, because it was just Jonas (Carney) and me against Coors Light, who had six guys. We had a great day and won $12,000—and then painted the town."

A week later, Armstrong rode away from the nationals field with Steve Larsen, and even left behind his future Motorola teammate, to win by 47 seconds. "I was really focusing on the world's at that time, and I didn't get to appreciate it ... until I bombed at world's."

In trying to explain his dismal performance at the world amateur road race championship, in Stuttgart, Germany, Armstrong said, "The worlds were really stressful. I didn't sleep for days before the race. Everyone was saying I was the favorite—mainly because of my performance in the Regio Tour, a week before the world's.

"That was a race in which the plan was just to ride. But on the first stage—over 15 laps of a hilly circuit—I got in a 20-man break, that became a 10-man break, then five men … and I won the stage. The field was five minutes back. I was just on that day, and could ride away from anybody. I felt awesome. If the world's had been that day, I would have won."

Taken out of context, such bold statements have sometimes gotten Armstrong into trouble. Asked about this perceived "arrogance," he replied, "I don't feel I'm arrogant or cocky. I think I have a lot of self-confidence. I've tried to tone down (my language), and I realize that I've got a long way to go in my career. I've only just started to scratch the surface.

"I am a little outspoken, but the sport has to have personalities. And in a race, I can get hot-headed. The only thing that counts is winning, and if something goes wrong, I get furious. I know I can't win all the time … and it takes a special person to be a winner."

Armstrong has already proven that he is a winner, even though he's only just "scratched the surface" of his talent. To fully develop that talent—through the Olympics and beyond—he realizes that one change will have to be a reduction in his body weight.

"I was big as a 15-year-old kid, having developed big shoulders and upper-body muscles from swimming. I'm still trying to get rid of that—but I don't think it'll come off until I'm riding 200km a day with the professionals.

"I love to eat—anything goes. I'm a food junkie. I weight 165 pounds now, but I'm climbing with the best on an amateur level. For my height—five feet 11 inches—I'll need to come down to 155 or 150 pounds. Eddy Merckx was a big guy, and he was the best. The ultimate rider."

Lance Armstrong still has a long way to go before he can be regarded as even a potential Merckx or LeMond. But with his straight-talking attitude and fierce ambition, the Olympic Games road race in August 1992 could be a great starting point.

The Midas Touch

Lance Armstrong's U.S. Postal Service team—previously Subaru-Montgomery—was founded by California financial wiz Thom Weisel. He continues to play a major part in the American team's success. In an interview at the start of the 2000 season, Weisel spoke about the team's origins ... and its continuing plans.

On entering Thom Weisel's palatial, big-windowed 37th floor office in San Francisco, you immediately notice two things: the view of the city's famous pyramid building arrowed toward the sky a few blocks away, and the memorabilia-bedecked walls around Weisel's car-sized desk. The pyramid is home to BancAmerica Montgomery Securities—a boutique investment corporation that Weisel founded in the 1970s, and sold in 1998 for $1.3 billion. The walls reveal another side of this multi-millionaire's lifestyle: bike-racing fan.

Weisel is incredibly successful. On leaving Montgomery after butting heads with the new owners, he decided to found his own firm. Thomas Weisel Partners, merchant bankers, emerged in early 1999, and now occupies the top three floors of this nearby financial district high-rise.

This is where Weisel—whose broad torso fills out a blue-and-white striped, mono-grammed shirt that has white collar and cuffs, complemented by a yellow tie—greets his visitor with a firm handshake and motions him to sit at a large, stylish, polished-wood round table. Weisel, 58, pulls up a matching chair, and then points out a news article in the business section of the morning's *San Francisco Chronicle*: CalPERS, the nation's largest public pension fund, has bought 10 percent of Weisel's company for $100 million, giving the new firm a billion-dollar valuation. It's a remarkable day for Weisel, who says, "The phone hasn't stopped ringing all morning ... the Los Angeles Times, TV stations."

You'd expect that the man who created this financial empire would line the walls of his penthouse suite with personal items—maybe framed certificates of his MBA from Harvard and BA in economics from Stanford. Not so. The walls are ablaze with images of the '99 Tour de France: a framed *maillot jaune* signed by winner Lance Armstrong; huge blowups of Armstrong climbing with the race leaders on Alpe d'Huez and the Col du Galibier; and a group shot of the U.S. Postal Service team. Weisel's team.

Today's top U.S. professional cycling squad started out as an idea Weisel had to improve the profile of cycling in this country. "I tend to look at things from the top down," says the genial CEO, who speaks in a direct, unhurried, almost gruff style that reflects his Midwestern roots. The rationale behind his team, he explains, is "trying to see where and how the whole industry, the whole sport is organized ... how the U.S. is doing, and whether we can improve it or not—[particularly] at the international level."

Ex-skier

Before turning his attention to cycling, after knee injuries forced him to quit ski racing and speed skating, Weisel had directed the U.S. Ski Team for 10 years, making it one of the most successful sports franchises in America. So he knew what it would take to create a successful cycling team. But first, he wanted to learn all he could about bike racing.

"I did a little bit of competitive cycling as a kid," he recalls. "I rode the track, but really used it as a training method for speed skating. I only competed in a couple of races ... but I had enough of a taste of it that it appealed to me. I think I was one of the few people that was a cyclist in Milwaukee, Wisconsin, in the '50s!"

When Weisel returned to the sport in the mid-1980s, he wanted to compete, and figured that the man who could best teach him the ropes was the 1984 U.S. Olympic team coach, Eddie Borysewicz. Nothing like starting at the top.

"I'll never forget," says Weisel, warming to the subject, and remembering the first time he met Mark Gorski, then the top U.S. track sprinter. "Eddie B took me down to an Olympic training camp in Texas [in 1987]. I'd get in a paceline on the track, and I didn't have a clue of what I was doing. And that's a dangerous place to be, you know. And I get to see these guys: 'What's this squirrel doing with us here?'

"Mark was the only guy that actually paid any attention to me and tried to help me, in terms of style and technique. And so we struck up a relationship, a friendship...."

With an Olympic gold medalist and Olympic coach as tutors, the then 45-year-old Weisel soon found success in masters racing. He won several age-group national championships in the sprint and kilometer time trial, and in 1990 took world masters titles in the same disciplines. "I also won two national criterium championships," Weisel adds proudly. "I'm too heavy now, and I was too heavy then, to go up hills very fast. But at least on the flat I could stay in there until I got to the end, and that's when I can unleash a little bit of a sprint."

Today, Weisel no longer has time to train and compete in bike races—"I'm just a weekend warrior"—but in the business world he's still racing, still overachieving. A few minutes into this interview, which starts precisely at the pre-arranged time of 1 p.m., a waiter wheels in a lunch trolley....

"Ah, that's great! I asked these guys..." Weisel then turns to his guest and asks, "Have you eaten lunch? If not, I'd be glad to serve you some. I'm just gonna grab a quick bite here while we're doing the interview. I've got a big, firm-wide meeting at 2 o'clock, and I haven't eaten since.... I got up at 3 o'clock California time, in New York, just to get here."

Life wasn't always this hectic. Talking about his early years in San Francisco, between mouthfuls of spinach salad, he remembers, "I had a tough time getting a job, out of business school, in this business. I wanted to be either in venture capital or investment banking, and frankly I could not find a job. I took a job for six months at Food Machinery Corporation, and then I ran into a couple of fellows that were starting their own brokerage firm, back in 1967. So I started, on day one, with a start-up, in the brokerage business. I was the only non-partner there.... Two years later, I was the second largest partner in that firm; and then two years after that I started the predecessor to Montgomery Securities."

By 1978, the other partners in the company had left, and Weisel says he changed the name to Montgomery, for the street in San Francisco's financial district, "and kept on going...."

Along with building his company and acquiring the accouterments of success—a nice home in Marin County, a private plane—Weisel put the U.S. Ski Team on a business footing, with multi-year sponsors and a fine-tuned organization. So when he turned to cycling, and decided to start a professional road team, he knew all the necessary ingredients.

As he chops his vegetable linguini, Weisel explains the origins of what was first called the Montgomery-Avenir Cycling Team: "I was fortunate enough to get to know Eddie B, and it just looked like to me there was a real need for another team [besides the European-based 7-Eleven squad]. And so having Eddie as the coach and running the athletes, and myself with organizational and marketing skills, I figured that made a lot of sense."

But his small domestic cycling team, which became Subaru-Montgomery in 1990, was a world away from Tour de France status. And wasn't that Weisel's dream? "That was a total dream," he chuckles. "Do you remember our teams back then? We didn't even go international for a couple of years, and when we did we were kind of a joke. So I knew what a long stretch that was. It was a dream of mine from the beginning, but a realistic dream for only the last five or six years."

Gorski Arrives

The man who helped make that dream become real was Gorski. "When he quit cycling," Weisel continues, "I offered him a job over at Montgomery, which he turned down. Decided to work at Wells Fargo Bank—I don't think that was a great decision.

"Mark went on to work at the (U.S. Cycling) Federation … and we ran into each other up in Napa one weekend at a race. He and I were sitting on the sidelines just chatting about what I wanted to do [with the team], and he came back and presented me a business plan a few days after that discussion, which led to me bringing him on."

Gorski has a slightly different account. He recalls not hearing back for a couple of weeks, and then getting a call from Weisel, who said in his up-and-at-'em style, "Read your proposal. Let's do it!"

That was in 1995, a year Gorski remembers well: "I started with Thom on May 15, and the plan was to find a major sponsor for the team. The last two in the running were UPS and the U.S. Postal Service. It was very intense, hours of back and forth, every day for at least a month … until we finally signed the Postal Service on September 30."

In its first year, 1986, the Postal team proved itself on the international front, ending the season ranked No. 23 in the world by the Union Cycliste Internationale—compared with the 10th place of the then top U.S. squad, Motorola. A lively rivalry was in the cards, but Motorola withdrew its backing that winter, and the team broke up when manager Jim Ochowicz was unable to snag a new title sponsor.

That reversal, ironically, was a boon for Weisel's team, which picked up a number of Motorola's European-seasoned team personnel and some of its riders, including George

Hincapie. Gorski also took on former Motorola racer Johnny Weltz as his team *directeur sportif*, and then made two inspired hirings: Russian Viatcheslav Ekimov and Frenchman Jean-Cyril Robin. These two riders would spearhead the Postal team's successful drive for a wild-card slot in the 1997 Tour de France.

That was a breakthrough, for sure, but of even greater importance in the team's evolution was the signing that winter of another two ex-Motorola men: Frankie Andreu and, on his recovery from cancer, Lance Armstrong. These developments—along with Armstrong's return to the top—have given particular pleasure to dealmaker Weisel.

"I must say that working with this team has been every bit, if not more rewarding than competing myself," he says. "Seeing all the pieces come together—and particularly how Lance was able to rise to the occasion out of phenomenal adversity—was one of the great pleasures of my whole life. And he's emerged as just an incredible leader, too, which is wonderful to see ... because, I mean, he was on our team 10 years ago. He was a pretty rough-and-tumble kid at that stage."

While Armstrong was putting together his 1999 Tour de France campaign, Weisel was putting together his new company. "Getting this firm launched," he reveals, after a swig of iced tea, "I was in the air 150 days last year. I had to raise the money, put together and hire 450 people. We did $22 billion in over 100 transactions. Raised the largest first-time private equity fund ever in the United States, a billion three. And about 20 percent of that money came from all over the world, including the Mideast. So I was in Kuwait and Abu Dhabi, all over Europe ... and [set up] offices in London, Boston and New York. It's a pretty hectic schedule right now."

Tour Fan

So how did this globe-trotting financier manage to fit in an extended trip to the Tour de France in 1999?

"They had cell phones," he says, with a smile. "I spent three or four hours a day keeping things going. But I wouldn't have missed that for anything. And this year, I plan on being there the whole time ... that's my vacation."

Looking back at the '99 Tour, Weisel says his biggest thrill was following the stage to Sestriere with the U.S. Postal team director Johan Bruyneel: "That was just totally amazing. When Lance rode away from those guys, I just couldn't believe my eyes. I was right behind him, and he was talking to us [on the team radio link]. First, Johan got on the blower and said, 'Hey Lance, you're pulling away from these guys,' 'cause he was in front and wasn't looking behind … and all of a sudden—bam!—he had a 100-meter gap. And then he really put an effort in … and opened up this enormous gap, 30 seconds. And he came back to us and said, 'How the f—k do you like those apples?!' You know, he loved that movie 'Good Will Hunting.'

"For him to have that kind of sense of humor, you know, when [winning] the most critical stage in the history of the Tour de France, I just…. That's what I mean about this guy. He's just off the chart.

"Another time, I can't remember exactly which stage—it might have been going up the Tourmalet—very early, all the major riders were switching their bikes. So we went to Lance, and Johan said, 'Zülle and all these guys are switching their bikes right now.' And he comes back to us and says, 'I can beat those guys on a mountain bike!' We were laughing for an hour after that."

The '99 Tour was a high point for the Postal team and American cycling; but to reach that peak, Weisel lived through plenty of hard times, often dipping into his own pockets to enable his team to survive. Did he ever have any doubts that propping up the team was worthwhile?

"No," he replies without a pause. "It took me 28 years to build Montgomery, and it wasn't always straight. There's lots of bumps along the road. I'm used to that as a business person. You've just gotta take what hand you're dealt … use it as a base-building and learn from it. And that sport [cycling] is complicated, and knowing how to navigate it—rider contracts, the selection process, how you're gonna get in the top 10—all this stuff takes a lot of time to figure out….

"Our goal has always been to win, and so we're not as driven by the same things that many of the sponsors of European teams are … [seeing] their team jersey on TV day in and day out, all year. For me, and I hope most of our sponsors, we think we're gonna get enough benefit by building a winning effort."

Going into more detail, Weisel adds, "I think that over the years the firm [Montgomery, and now Thomas Weisel Partners] has gotten tremendous cachet in our marketplace for sponsoring and being associated with winning efforts. There's a certain component, not large, of avid cyclists in our constituency—whether they're CEOs, or private equity guys, or money managers. In general, though, in terms of image marketing, it did a lot for us over at Montgomery and it's the same thing here, in terms of the image we're trying to build as a professional, winning organization."

In keeping with that professionalism, our interview, scheduled for 45 minutes, ends exactly on time. Before he addresses his colleagues at 2, Weisel has a quarter-hour to jot down some notes on a big yellow legal pad, and maybe time to answer some of those incoming phone calls. It's life in the fast lane. And it just keeps on getting faster.

Weisel Speaks Out:

✛ On his team's success: "We just aren't fielding a team of dreams. This is a professional, elite-run organization with clear-cut marketing goals as well as performance goals. And the money is going to be well spent. We don't have anybody siphoning off a big percentage of this like a lot of the European teams, where it's going in one person's pocket. We're trying to build a major sports activity here, and the fact that we were able to attract not only the Postal Service, but Visa and Yahoo! and the other sponsors is a testament to that."

✛ On USA Cycling and his goal to give it a "world class" board of directors, as he did for the ski federation: "I think people will rally behind an organization that's got a clear vision and gives a real value proposition for its constituents. What you're seeing is an organization that's in disarray, so people are taking things into their own hands in creating these [regional] entities; but I think you can bring everybody back together if it's well organized. There's no reason for people to join it right now."

✛ On helping American cycling grow: "The sport needs a couple of other things, and we might be able to be the catalyst for this. You've got a great role model [Lance Armstrong] that's fabulous. Now you've got to coalesce around that and build more high-quality events in this country, and a good consistent development program. Partly, that's leadership—as well as good fund raising. We'll try to examine all those and see where we can be helpful."

✛ On the chances of signing a new title sponsor if the Postal Service dropped out: "If we had to replace the Postal Service, I think we could do it."

Sunny Outlook

When Johan Bruyneel came on as the directeur sportif of the U.S. Postal Service team in late 1998, the Belgian immediately began to lay the groundwork for Lance Armstrong's '99 Tour de France victory. He spoke to VeloNews *from his Spanish home just prior to the 2000 season.*

For Johan Bruyneel, the hills above the Spanish coastal town of Moraira are his safe haven. There, he can find some degree of relief from the crazy world of directing a European professional cycling team. The U.S. Postal Service team boss sat down poolside, on the deck outside of his white stucco home, just kilometers from the Mediterranean coast in eastern Spain. As he looked out past the deck, at the mountains to the west and the blue waters to the east, he explained part of the appeal of his Spanish *casa*: "The good thing is, nobody can find me here."

True, it's a bit of a haul, winding up into the hills through a maze of little streets; but the reality is, Bruyneel can never totally escape from his job. "I'm always working," he admitted. "Always on the phone, fax, e-mail—always doing things. There's not a lot of time off."

If you have to work though, you couldn't ask for a nicer setting than the three-bedroom house where Bruyneel lives with his French wife, Christelle, and their golden retriever, Junior. Bruyneel has called this his home since 1993, mostly as a result of Spanish economics.

"The reason that I came here is a little bit, maybe, a coincidence. In '92, I came from Lotto to ONCE, and '93, there was a big devaluation of the peseta. So I had to do something not to lose too much money. That was to buy a property here. So I bought this piece of land and we built this house," explained Bruyneel, who retired from racing just a year before this interview.

"I lived in Belgium, but I knew this area from training. Sometimes we had a training camp here with the team, a little bit further towards Calpe. I knew the coast area from riding with the bike, and I like this area.

"I was used to Belgium, and it's totally different. In Belgium, most of the time it's gray, raining a lot of the time. You feel that in the humor of the people…. Here it's different … When you wake up, you have the sunshine, you see the ocean—the day starts totally different … As a rider, also, when you wake up in the good weather, you like to go out for training. In the northern countries, it's a little bit different. In northern Europe, you have to be really strong to be in the mood to train."

Now, though, Bruyneel's days are no longer filled with five-hour training rides. In fact, he hadn't ridden his bike in a year, he said, adding that he had put on at least 10 kilograms (22 pounds) in his first year as a team official. No, instead of hours on the bike, his days were now filled with the seemingly endless duties of a directeur sportif.

Almost on cue, Bruyneel's cell phone rang, and the visit with the 35-year-old Belgian was interrupted by team-related business. "The only way is to switch it off," he said, once he got off the phone. "That's the only way to relax."

But for the man whose little upstairs office contains a desktop computer, two laptops, a copy machine and fax, the lines of communication are rarely closed. There are so many details associated with the operation of a UCI Division I team, he can't afford to take much downtime. Already, in September, he was making plans for three Postal Service training camps—in Austin in December, California in January and Majorca in February—finalizing the details for the new team bus, dealing with personnel matters and planning out the early-season schedule.

As Bruyneel took his visitor up the tight winding staircase and into that little office, one of the first things that drew attention was the framed yellow jersey on the wall opposite the door. "That's mine. That's not Lance's," he was quick to point out, showing off the maillot jaune that he wore for one day in the 1995 Tour de France, after winning the seventh stage, while riding for ONCE.

The dark-haired Belgian clearly takes great pride in his accomplishments as a rider.

But in 1999, he found new rewards in his first campaign as a team director with the Postal Service. "I think the first thing is, you have the possibility to stay in the same environment that you have been in for a good part of your life," said the veteran of 12 professional seasons as a racer. "Then also there's the satisfaction if you prepare the whole season for a specific race—or you prepare all the people together and you do everything you can to be as good as possible as a group—and then at the end, if you can finalize that with a success, that's a big satisfaction."

For Bruyneel, that satisfaction came on the first day of the 1999 Tour de France: "For me, the biggest emotion was when [Lance Armstrong] won the prologue. It was a race, the Tour, that since the winter we had made it the main, or maybe the only objective of the team. Everybody's nervous. You know that the preparation has been good, the team is in very good shape, but you still have a lot of doubts. And then, the day of the prologue, when Lance wins the prologue and takes the yellow jersey, it's like, whew. It's like something—the stress falls off. And then, the emotion and satisfaction of that day, for me, has been the biggest satisfaction of the whole year. The feeling after the prologue was even stronger than after the three weeks.

"It was like I won myself. For me, it was the same—or maybe even stronger. I don't know. When you are a rider and you train for something, you want to win. And when you win, you are happy. But when you are a director, you feel like you have a lot more responsibility—not only for a big group of people, but also for results."

Along with that responsibility came a great deal of stress, which Bruyneel experienced in his first season as director. "The stress is there always," he said, "because you're on the road with a big group of, say, 20 people. Everything has to work as good as possible, and there's always little things and details: 'This is not going as it should be.' There's always more problems that are occurring. It's not possible that it's always perfect.

"After a race—then, for me, the real race starts, because you have to do so many things. You have to see how the staff is, how they did, what they need for the day after. You have to speak with each rider. Then you have to prepare the day after."

Bruyneel has made the transition from being a rider—totally focused on himself—to being a director, focused entirely on the group of people around him. And in the process, while dealing with a big staff was his most challenging learning experience, dealing with one strong-willed Texan was probably the most critical relationship of his first season.

"I think we ... I don't know why ... it's like ... I don't know how you say it in English," said Bruyneel. Fluent in five languages—French, English, Spanish, Flemish and

German—he now struggled for words to describe his dealings with Armstrong. "It's like, there was like a click. I don't know why, because Lance is a person, he is, aah, he likes to take his own decisions. I think, in the first year, I have been able to take that situation—I try sometimes to be the boss, and sometimes to be the colleague, and it has worked. I think Lance accepts that, and he knows that I'm open for his ideas, but that I don't always agree with him. It's up to me, and both of us, to try to find the best middle solution in that relationship."

For the 2000 season, Bruyneel will try to build upon that relationship, as the Postal team tries to live up to the high standard it set in 1999. The squad will be helped in that respect by an infusion of both youth and experience, provided by its eight new riders: Viatcheslav Ekimov, Patrick Jonker, Cédric Vasseur, Levi Leipheimer, Steffen Kjaergaard, Kirk O'Bee, Jamie Burrow and Stive Vermaut. In fact, Bruyneel believes that 2000 could be even better that the yellow-jersey season of 1999.

"It will be difficult to do better next year, that's for sure. But next year, we'll have a stronger team—on paper at least," he assessed. "We will have mainly the same objectives: a team around George [Hincapie] for the spring classics, and a team around Lance for the Tour."

So while Bruyneel "relaxed" at his Moraira home at the end of the season, he was already looking ahead to year No. 2 as team director. And despite the allure of his pool, the beach and the mountains, for this Postal Service boss, the work never ends. In the warm Spanish sunshine of late-September, the ball was already rolling toward the start of the new season....

First Class Accommodations

Lance Armstrong's preparations for the Tour de France begin as soon as the previous year's race ends. The first major step in his U.S. Postal Service team's 2000 schedule came in January at a West Coast training camp that brought the whole team together for the first time.

On a cool, misty California morning, a father and son waited anxiously in the parking lot of the San Luis Bay Inn resort. Just a few meters away, inside a big white tent, the U.S. Postal Service cycling team was getting ready for what looked like being another training ride in the rain. One by one the riders began to walk out, and then came the moment that the little boy was waiting for. The tall, lean figure of George Hincapie emerged from the side of the tent, and the little boy approached his hero and asked him for a "race." Hincapie obliged, and the two slowly circled the parking lot, the boy astride his little two-wheeler and Hincapie on his team-issue Trek. Moments later, the youngster was face-to-face with Postal's biggest star and the reigning Tour de France champ, Lance Armstrong. He, too, turned a lap with the delighted young fan. Then, as the team pulled out of the parking lot, father said to son: "You just beat the two best riders."

No doubt, the Postal Service team agrees. Hincapie and Armstrong are sure to be the focal points of the team's plans for the new season. Armstrong faces the daunting task of repeating his 1999 Tour de France victory, while Hincapie will focus on fulfilling his promise as a potential classics winner. But those goals were a long way's off when the team gathered in California for its 2000 training camp. In fact, in their luxurious surroundings in Avila Beach, on the state's central coast, the rough lifestyle of a professional cyclist in Europe seemed—except for the wet weather—a world away.

A year before, the squad's surroundings were more typical: riders doubled up in small rooms at a modest hotel in Buellton, California, right off of Highway 101. But when the Sunterra Resorts time-share company became a new team sponsor in 2000, some nice new benefits piled up. Things like each rider enjoying a spacious suite to himself, complete with a kitchenette and dining area, a well-furnished sitting room and a spacious master bedroom. Add to that the catered meals down in the marquee in the parking lot, and the riders had few concerns aside from the daily routine of ride, massage, eat and rest.

"It's definitely different than years past," said third-year man Christian Vande Velde, "where we always stayed in ... pretty crummy places, you know. This is great. You get more personal things done. You get to really focus on what you want to do, which is nice. It's a really good time to set your focus and set your goals."

With the California resort offering full amenities, including an 18-hole golf course and sweeping views of the Pacific Ocean, there wasn't much to complain about. "It's really luxurious," said the team's director of operations, Dan Osipow. "We're kind of worried it's a little bit too luxurious." In fact, the riders became a little bored by the hotel's isolation, and some went to the movies one afternoon to kill time.

But for the most part, the team was ready to focus on the task of preparing for the upcoming season. And while its main goals remained the same as the '99 season, the dynamics of the squad had changed. The team expanded from 16 to 19 riders, and the group assembled in Avila Beach featured eight new faces: Steffan Kjaergaard from Norway, Cédric Vasseur from France, Patrick Jonker from Australia, Jamie Burrow from Britain, Stive Vermaut from Belgium, Viatcheslav Ekimov from Russia, and the Americans Levi Leipheimer and Kirk O'Bee.

Vasseur, after seven seasons with French teams, noticed some differences as he rode with his new American entourage. "In France, the riders split up into small groups at training camp, but here all of us go out in one big group. I like that, because on a five- or six-hour ride you're always talking with a different teammate."

And for Postal, a bigger team means a different outlook: While the spring classics and Tour are still the priority, the squad can look for steady results all season long, without overtaxing its riders.

"I think it's a good thing," said 1999 USPRO champion Marty Jemison, "rather than just taking a 16-man team and really your focus is just on the Tour de France and getting the nine strongest guys out of that 16. Now having 19 means the pressure can be separated between obviously the Tour de France, but also other events. And I think that's good for a lot of guys."

Along with that seemingly small but significant increase in riders, Postal also saw a big boost in its number of support people. "We're dealing with much bigger numbers," said Osipow. "It's probably double last year, with 19 riders and 19 full-time staff. It's an astronomical logistical undertaking for us. January and July are probably the two most difficult months for us."

Adding to those logistics in California was an increase in the media presence at the 2000 training camp. American, British, French and German press were on hand, along with German, Belgian and American television crews, and a couple of American Internet sites. But for a team that's dealt with the media circus that goes with winning the Tour de France, the California scene was small by comparison.

"It's been pretty manageable," said Osipow. "It hasn't stopped for Lance over the winter, though. It's been pretty consistent. I thought there would be a little more media here, perhaps, but to be honest, we're at our capacity."

"You come to expect it," said Vande Velde. "But I'll take it any day. The more press is out there, the more [American] cycling is going to get into the mainstream."

Of course, the majority of the press was there for one reason: Armstrong. Everybody, it seemed, wanted the day-by-day details as he geared up for his defense of the Tour de France yellow jersey. And while the Texan was being evasive with the press—aside from a short press conference and a one-on-one interview with a French sportswriter from L'Équipe—his preparations looked to be right on target.

"He seems very relaxed," Frankie Andreu said of his long-time teammate. "He's fine, he's not so worried. But then, he has until July, and he knows it. It doesn't matter if he's fit right now, or a little overweight. He's just gonna take his time, and later on, I'm sure he'll get a bit more serious."

For Armstrong, the camp kicked off a build-up to the Tour that will look very similar to 1999's program: an early season heavy with races in Spain and highlighted by Paris-Nice, Milan-San Remo and the Amstel Gold Race; a mountain training camp in May; and then the short French stage races leading up to the Tour.

As for Hincapie, Postal's man for the classics, his plan was also similar to 1999's, but with some fine-tuning added by new assistant team director Dirk Demol, the 1988 Paris-Roubaix champion. The change in approach included careful advanced scouting prior to races like the Tour of Flanders, Ghent-Wevelgem and Paris-Roubaix. "Before, he was there and he did the race. That's all," said Demol. "But now, I'm going to work hard for him, make it easier, so he knows all the important places.

"He's 26, his best years come now. I think we have to count on him in the classics, but I think he's ready for that, for sure."

Those tests would come, but as the Postals put in their miles on the roads of California and relaxed in the luxurious setting in Avila Beach, they still seemed a long way off....

Dress Rehearsal

In the buildup to the Tour de France, Lance Armstrong and his closest teammates used a well-thought-out mix of endurance training, power training, reconnaissance rides and races, designed to bring them to the July 1 start line in top shape. One of the vital ingredients in 2000 was the Dauphiné Libéré stage race, mostly in the French Alps, and on some of the roads that would later be used at the Tour.

At the 1999 Tour de France, New Englander Tyler Hamilton proved himself as the faithful first lieutenant to Lance Armstrong—pushing himself to the brink to insure that the U.S. Postal Service team leader was in perfect position when the key moves were made in the high mountains; and riding brilliantly in the time trials to finish 13th overall. This year, at the Dauphiné Libéré, Armstrong got the opportunity for payback in a major way, giving Hamilton a tutorial on where to attack and how to defend on the way to a historic victory.

"Having Lance's support was amazing," said Hamilton, who won the eight-day race in southeast France by 31 seconds over upstart Spanish rider Haimar Zubeldia of the Euskaltel-Euskadi squad, with Armstrong taking third, another five seconds back.

The Dauphiné is always one of the key build-up races to the Tour de France, and the 52nd edition, June 4-11, was no exception. Among the seven stages was one to the top of Mont Ventoux—which would see the finish of stage 12 at the upcoming Tour—and another through the high Alps, from Digne to Briançon, which included the Allos, Vars and Izoard, the same three passes to be tackled in stage 14 of the Tour.

As in 1999, Armstrong and his Postal teammates made some early-season reconnaissance rides through the Alps—including the Dauphiné's key climbs—as part of their preparation for the Tour. But while the Tour remained the focus for the squad, the significance of Hamilton's Dauphiné victory shouldn't be underestimated.

"The Dauphiné is a big race, like the Tour of Switzerland or Paris-Nice," said Postal Service directeur sportif Johan Bruyneel. "It's the same high-category race—just under the three grand tours. So, winning the Dauphiné is a big achievement for Tyler and for our team."

Either way you look at it—as an hors-categorie UCI stage race or an important Tour de France preparation event—the Dauphiné demonstrated that Postal was on top of its game, with Hamilton taking two stage wins on his way to the overall title, while Armstrong had a stage win and a day in the leader's jersey besides his third-place overall.

While Hamilton and Armstrong would prove to be the race's main animators, Alberto Lopez de Munain struck the first blow for the Spanish Division II team, Euskaltel-Euskadi, winning the difficult prologue time trial in Grenoble. Just 3.6km long, the opening test ended with the infamous 1.5km climb, featuring 20-percent grades, to the Fort de la Bastille, perched almost a thousand feet above the city. It resulted in some sizable time gaps, with Lopez beating runner-up Armstrong by 11 seconds, followed by the previous day's Classique des Alpes winner José Maria Jiménez (16 seconds back) in third, his Banesto teammate Alex Zülle (in fourth) and Lopez's teammate Zubeldia in fifth. Hamilton was eighth fastest, 24 seconds down.

Despite the presence of Tour teams such as Banesto, ONCE-Deutsche Bank (with Laurent Jalabert and Abraham Olano) and Crédit Agricole (Bobby Julich and Jonathan Vaughters), Euskaltel would prove to be the biggest challenger to the Postal Service, with Zubeldia, fourth behind third-placed Armstrong at the Classique des Alpes, leading the charge.

Lopez de Munain would hold the leader's jersey through the first two road stages—won by Frenchmen Frédéric Guesdon (La Française des Jeux) and Fabrice Gougot (Crédit Agricole—but then the American contingent asserted itself in the stage 3 time trial.

On an undulating 35.7km course between St. Etienne and St. Chamond in the Loire region, Armstrong continued to flash the form that had him on the top of everyone's list as a "super-favorite" for the Tour.

Covering the course at an average speed of 45.652 kph, he beat out Zubeldia by 21 seconds to take the stage and move into the race lead ahead of the Spaniard. Ten seconds slower than Zubeldia, Hamilton took an excellent third place and moved into third overall. Of the other likely Tour contenders, Julich placed a strong sixth (1:23 behind Armstrong), Olano seventh (at 1:33), Zülle eighth (at 1:41) and Vaughters 10th (at 2:02).

While Armstrong was the star attraction after taking the lead, Hamilton would take center stage the following day on the Ventoux, the mountain steeped in Tour de France lore. In 1999, the famous climb was included in the Dauphiné, as a 21.6km time trial, and Vaughters put the Postal mark on the mountain, winning the stage and taking over the race lead, which he would eventually relinquish to Alex Vinokourov. This year, the Ventoux was the finishing touch of a 159km road stage that started in Romans.

The Postal team worked hard, both to chase a six-man break that gained as much as six minutes and to get Armstrong and Hamilton to the base of the climb in good shape. They succeeded on both counts, because the break's gap was cut to two minutes as the climbing began and the two Postal leaders slid easily into a strong chase group that also included Euskaltel's Ramon Gonzales, ONCE's Peter Luttenberger, Lotto-Adecco's Kurt Van de Wouwer, Vaughters, Zubeldia, AG2R's Andrei Kivilev, Julich, Jalabert and Zülle.

The chasers overhauled the remnants of the break with about 10km still to climb, while Jalabert and Julich dropped back. Vaughters then launched a series of attacks, further splintering the group, while race leader Armstrong, bonking, was among those who dropped back.

With 4km remaining, the group was down to five, including Hamilton, who later said: "Both Lance and Johan told me on the radio, if I feel good, to attack." That moment came about 2km from the finish.

Hamilton soloed to the biggest win of his career, followed by Zülle, Van de Wouwer and Vaughters. Armstrong crossed the line in 11th, 1:13 behind, which allowed sixth-placed Zubeldia to take over the race lead. "Lance is riding very well, but the overall was not the big objective for him," Bruyneel said.

After Hamilton's Ventoux win, the objective was now to put him in the blue-banded yellow jersey; and the following day, that mission was accomplished.

On a broiling hot day between Beaumes-de-Venise and Digne, a break of 10 riders led for most of the 201km stage. Among the leaders were Julich and Postal's Kevin Livingston—riding his first comeback race since breaking a collarbone in April. As on the previous stage, the break started to crumble on the closing climb. The narrow, steep Col de Corobin is only 8km long, but it would prove more decisive then the 20km Ventoux.

"Kevin started at a pretty good tempo, then Lance took over," related Hamilton, who said he was then guided by mentor Armstrong. "He pointed up and said to me, 'See that piece of road? That's where you go.'

"So I attacked there and got a very good gap. I was looking over my shoulder ... and I saw this Giro helmet behind with the Texas star on it. Lance was coming up, so I eased up a bit and he caught on.

"It was 16km from the top to the finish, and Lance went straight down without braking. He was like a motorcycle...."

Behind the Armstrong-paced duo, a 12-strong chase group developed, but there was no chance of catching the flying Americans, who hurtled into Digne together. "(Lance) told me he wanted me to win. 'This is for you,' he said. That felt pretty special," added Hamilton, who took his second consecutive stage win, and the race lead.

The sprint for third, 46 seconds back, was taken by Verbrugghe from a group that also contained Jalabert, Zülle, Vaughters and Zubeldia.

With a lead of 44 seconds over Zubeldia, Hamilton and his team had to stay on the alert on the remaining two stages.

They were not too concerned when a 12-man break developed early on the three-mountain stage 6 to Briançon, as most of the attackers were more than 20 minutes down overall. But on-and-off rain, combined with more than six hours in the saddle, made it a trying day.

On the mighty Izoard pass, two Spaniards—Iñigo Cuesta of ONCE and Pablo Lastras of Banesto—rode away from the break, with Cuesta going on to take a sole stage win. Some five minutes back, Armstrong led the pack to prevent any potential attacks by Zubeldia. "Lance set a pretty nasty tempo on the Izoard," said an impressed Hamilton. "There were only six or seven guys left at the top."

It seemed that the danger was over, but the race leader had a scare on the short finishing climb into the old walled city of Briançon. "I had a little problem with my jacket," Hamilton related. "The streets were wet and I slipped on a cobblestone ... lost my concentration a little bit." As a result, the 29-year-old American conceded 13 seconds to Zubeldia, and had just 31 seconds in hand entering the final 147km stage from St. Jean-de-Maurienne to Sallanches.

"It was nail-biting," Hamilton conceded, knowing that the Euskaltel squad would try to spring Zubeldia on the four laps of a hilly finishing circuit at Sallanches, where Bernard Hinault won the world's in 1980. But Armstrong again proved Hamilton's guardian angel. "Without Lance, I would have panicked. It was nice having him by my side," he said. "but I still couldn't relax until we crossed the finish line. I'd never been in that situation before."

In the end, Zubeldia crossed the line alongside Hamilton and Armstrong in a 23-strong group that finished 2:42 down on stage winner Jalabert—who soloed away from a six-man break on the second-to-last climb.

Hamilton is only the second American to win at the Dauphiné, 17 years after a 21-year-old Greg LeMond took the race when "winner" Pascal Simon was penalized 10 minutes for a positive drug test on the final day. That victory proved something of a breakthrough for LeMond, and it could do the same for Hamilton long term. In the short term, he would be going into the Tour more motivated than ever to serve team leader Armstrong. Yes, Hamilton would have his opportunity for payback ... probably on these same roads, sometime in July.

Preparing for the Tour

Four Americans, with four different objectives, talk about their preparations for the 2000 Tour de France ... and their ultimate ambitions in cycling.

TYLER HAMILTON: READY TO LAY IT ON THE LINE FOR ARMSTRONG

On a gray mid-April day, the U.S. Postal Service's Tyler Hamilton sat comfortably at a table, talking to a couple of reporters in the lobby of the Posthouse Hotel in Herstal, Belgium, a suburb to the north of Liège. It was the day after the Flèche Wallonne classic, and he spoke of his gradual build-up in the early season. It had been a slow progression, he said, and he had also been battling with allergies down in Spain. So aside from a couple of good time trials, he didn't have a whole lot to show in the way of results.

But all of this was part of the year-2000 plan for the New Englander, a plan which would have him peaking for the Tour de France in July. Spring is not his time of year. Wait until the summer. His time would come.

It is almost the story of Hamilton's career to this point: A slow, quiet build-up has led him to the brink of stardom. His time is coming. But not just yet.

The former ski racer's rise has closely followed the ascent of his Postal Service team. Hamilton didn't start serious racing until his sophomore year at the University of Colorado. A member of the CU ski team at the time, he broke his back and could no longer ski race. That's when he turned to cycling, and after starring on the CU collegiate squad, he spent a year on the national team before joining the then Bell-Montgomery team in 1995.

A promising young domestic pro in those early years, Hamilton was an Olympic-team alternate in 1996. But when the team took on the Postal Service as its main sponsor, switched to a full-time European focus and brought on seasoned veterans like Jean-Cyril Robin and Viatcheslav Ekimov, the less-experienced American had to fight his way back up the totem pole.

That wasn't a problem for the soft-spoken, understated Hamilton. Despite his quiet demeanor, his talent spoke for itself loud and clear, and now he's one of the top dogs in the Postal Service's kennel.

Hamilton has shown that he has the skills necessary to be a leader for the grand tours. He can climb with the best, and he has the ability to gain time—not just limit his losses—in the time trials. He demonstrated that in the 1998 Tour de France, when he placed second behind Jan Ullrich in the 58km stage 7 time trial, and again in 99, when he finished third in the Futuroscope time trial, on the second-to-last day of the Tour.

But for now, individual goals and a leadership role are secondary for the 29-year-old. Instead, he has totally embraced his job as Lance Armstrong's first lieutenant. Hamilton first took on that responsibility in last year's Tour stage to Alpe d'Huez. "I'll probably remember that the most, it's so special," he said. "It's a big part of the Tour de France. If there's any stage that somebody knows, it's Alpe d'Huez."

On that day, Hamilton was the last teammate by Armstrong's side, setting tempo for the eventual Tour winner until the serious attacks started near the top of the famous switchbacked climb.

"Kevin [Livingston] normally would have been in that position," Hamilton continued, "but because he wasn't feeling so good, we decided to use up his strength first, and save me. I was the last lieutenant there for Lance. Everybody else had done their work and was behind, so there was a lot of pressure on me there. I felt like I rose to the occasion and pretty much pushed my body to the limit."

The reward for his hard work on that stage and during the rest of the three-week Tour? Riding into Paris with Armstrong proudly wearing the coveted yellow leader's jersey. "It was a pretty incredible moment," Hamilton recalled. "I think we did 10 laps on the Champs-Elysées, and I had goosebumps the whole time. Really. The whole time. I was extremely tired, but I couldn't feel my legs."

Hamilton finished that Tour 13th overall, and if not for a couple of crashes, he would most likely have cracked the top 10. But, as Hamilton said, "It so happened last year that I ended up 13th, just because I was doing my job, and I guess I did it pretty well. It's not like I was riding for myself."

This year, the focus was just as narrow: "You have one goal, and that's to get Lance to Paris in the yellow jersey. You can't try to ice the cake, with a climber's jersey, or a green jersey for George [Hincapie]. You could, but that's just gonna take away from the chances of getting Lance to Paris in the yellow jersey. The more you focus on the smaller little things, the more you take away from that No. 1 goal."

That kind of selflessness is one of the unique aspects of the sport of cycling, and Hamilton was definitely prepared to sacrifice it all for Armstrong. "It's hard," he acknowledged back in April. "My whole focus is on the Tour de France, working for someone else. All of my training I feel right now is for my team and for Lance. Everything I'm doing right now is to get Lance to Paris in the yellow jersey."

But Hamilton also has his own personal ambitions to keep him driven. For 2000, it's the Sydney Olympics, where he felt that a time trial medal was within reach. "It's nice to know that there's something else down there," he admitted. "After [the Tour], the focus will change a little bit; hopefully, I'll get to ride for myself a little bit.

"My focus is definitely on the time trial. The road race is more of a crapshoot, more of a lottery," he said. "If I'm able to get selected and then focus on my training and go in there with good form, I think I definitely have a shot at a medal. And if Lance goes in there on form … maybe it's possible to have two medals in the time trial."

And after Sydney? "I don't like to look down the road too far, but I'd be disappointed if I never have the opportunity to ride as a team leader in the Tour," Hamilton said. "But right now, I'm happy in the position I'm in.

"Someday I think I could be team leader. For sure not this year.… But I think one day it will be possible."

His time is coming. But not just yet.

CHANN MCRAE: FINDING A NICHE WITH MAPEI

Just before the start of the final stage of the 1999 Vuelta a España, Chann McRae was relaxing in the hospitality village set up within the ancient Plaza de Mayor in the center of Madrid. As he waited for the whistle to signal the riders to assemble, the American sat down under one of the white sponsor tents in the shadows of the muraled plaza walls, recalling the last time he took part in the three-week Spanish tour.

"At the Vuelta in '96, I suffered big time," McRae said. That year, McRae was a 24-year-old neo-pro with the Spanish outfit, Santa Clara, which could be described as shaky at best. In his first year in Europe, McRae, along with fellow American Jonathan Vaughters, struggled through a full season with the insolvent team, living and racing in Spain, even when the bills weren't getting paid.

"The team didn't do anything at the Vuelta," McRae remembered. "They weren't paying us, and there was no morale."

Making matters worse, creditors were trying to collect on some of those past-due bills—right in the middle of the Vuelta. "They tried to repossess our truck on the 14th stage. And when you were riding for Santa Clara, all we had were two cars and the truck. Our mechanics didn't even work on our bikes, because all of the tools they owned were in that truck."

Some of the reasons behind this turmoil became apparent over the following winter. "I was still looking for a contract in January (1997), because the team folded. The owner went to prison for importing cocaine, supposedly," McRae revealed. "He's still in prison, and he deserves to be there."

But as shaky as that '96 season was, it set the groundwork for the steady progression that may now have McRae knocking on the door of a top-10 finish in a major tour. "Being a neo-pro, and showing up here and doing the Vuelta (in '96) was a good experience," he admitted, "and it helped me for later."

McRae's year with Santa Clara also helped him realize what he finds most important about his current situation with the high-powered Mapei-Quick Step team: stability.

In recent years, Mapei has been the New York Yankees of the cycling world, using its clout to assemble a squad full of all-stars. On this team packed with clean-up hitters, the lightly built, clean-cut American is still setting the table; but given the choice to be a team leader elsewhere, he planned to stick with Mapei's first-class organization.

"It's attractive to be a leader, but it's important to have stability," said McRae, who had been offered team leadership positions with Benfica of Portugal and Mercury of the U.S., but would end up re-signing with Mapei. "These decisions are based more on where I can find stability," he stressed.

A big reason behind this emphasis was McRae's wife of less than a year, Jen McRae, the former Timex team racer who moved to Italy during the summer of 1999 to be with Chann. At the time, she was leading the Saturn USPRO Tour, but the two of them decided that being together was a must. "She had to sacrifice all of that just to be with me. But I think if you want to have a real marriage, you have to spend time together. She's racing in America and I'm racing in Europe and we see each other three months out of the year? ... That's not a real marriage."

Now 28 years old and married, McRae has found a stability in his personal life that he's carrying over to his professional life. "For me, it made all the difference in the world because, basically, when you turn 28, 29 years old, you start to think more and more about your future, and one of the most important things is the person you're gonna be with the rest of your life," the sun-reddened McRae said in Madrid. "It's more serious now. Okay, you mess up when you're by yourself, you mess up for yourself, but if you mess up right now, you have other people to worry about."

So with the maturity that comes with marriage, and the security that McRae has found now that he's signed his new two-year deal with Mapei, what does the future hold for him? After finishing two major tours in 1999—the Vuelta and the Giro d'Italia—McRae felt that he was still progressing. His 19th-place overall finish in Spain showed that he was on the right track. That race saw him finish fifth in the first time trial and take ninth in the final mountain stage. But the main thing that impressed people was how well he rode in support of Pavel Tonkov in the mountains.

"My goal here was to bury myself for Tonkov," McRae said. And in doing so, he showed that he could climb consistently with the leaders, while doing a lot of work for Mapei's Russian leader. "I feel if I can prove myself in the team that I'm a good worker, some day I'll get my opportunity.... If you can move up the ranks on Mapei, you definitely deserve to be where you're going."

Where he's going, he hopes, is to a high placing in one of the three grand tours—the Vuelta, Giro or Tour de France. "I still need one more level to be with the guys in the top 10," he said. "I can see that next year. It's not that far off."

In the USA Cycling media guide, McRae is listed as a 5-foot 10-inch rider, but that's probably pushing it. And with his slight build, he has the ideal body type to be one of those top-10 guys. "I can do the time trials to where I'd be able to maintain my general classification. The weakness right now is the really steep climbs," he said, "but I should be able to do well on them, because of my power-to-weight ratio."

Admittedly, McRae still has a few other things to learn as well. That was evident in the final time trial, when he ate too soon before his start and paid the price. "We drove straight out of the hotel and descended a mountain pass and, I don't know, my food didn't settle at all before my warm-up," he related. The result? He threw up three times during the course of the 46.5km time trial, starting at the 10km mark.

But that was just a small bump in the road, and McRae seemed headed in the right direction—as proven by his stellar fifth-place finish in the road race at the world's in Verona, Italy. And with plans to work on his weak spots over the winter, with his Durango-based trainer Rick Crawford, McRae was confident that his progress in the grand tours will continue.

If so, look for the American to move up the organization chart on the Italian Mapei team, and maybe even make that top-10 cut on the general classification. Either way, keep an eye out for McRae at the end of the next three-week tour. And if you find him hanging around the team truck, you'll know that this time, the lease is fully paid.

———————————— ❄ ————————————

Almost nine months later, McRae was thinking about burritos. Right there in downtown Turin, surrounded by the classic Italian architecture of one of Italy's great cities, working his way through a mob of cycling fans eager to get a peek at their heroes, McRae had burritos on his mind. He was thinking about the ones at El Arroyo's ... and picnics in the Texas hill country and swimming at Barton Springs.

This was the last day of racing after three weeks in the Giro d'Italia, and anyone would be ready for a break. Tomorrow there would be a plane to catch, and McRae and his wife Jen would be on board, heading home to Austin for a bit of well-deserved R&R.

It had been the 28-year-old Texan's second Giro, but unlike 1999, McRae would have only a brief respite before turning around and heading back to the continent for another three-week tour. McRae was the only American taking on both the Giro d'Italia and Tour de France this year.

It hadn't been planned that way. Since late '99, the Tour had been McRae's goal for 2000. With that target in mind, he started his season later than usual and began to build fitness for July. But at some point, Mapei's Belgian team manager Patrick Lefévère figured that the Giro would serve as good preparation for the Tour.

"I think he felt that I was kind of floating," McRae reasoned. "I didn't really have an objective to work toward for the spring. It's a long time from February to July. So, they put me in the Giro as a helper for Tonkov. It keeps me on a good line for the Tour."

And despite the last-minute decision, McRae turned in a very respectable performance, riding in support of team leader Tonkov, and finishing 17th, about 25 minutes out of first. Respectable, but as McRae put it, "pretty meaningless when you're riding on the world's No. 1 team."

The team's status, strength and depth, noted McRae, probably meant that Mapei would be taking a different approach to the Tour de France than a team unified around a single leader, like, say, the U.S. Postal team.

"I think it's hard to say that we have a leader going into the Tour," McRae said. "This team is made up of all of these stars—Bettini, Bartoli, Steels, Nardello, Tafi—it's kind of like who ever has it, has it."

And talking to McRae makes it clear that he feels fully capable of being one of those Mapei riders who "has it" in July.

"I think for us, it'll be a lot like it was for [Giro winner Stefano] Garzelli here," McRae predicted. "You didn't even think of him as a favorite, and then all of a sudden the guy's in second place, right behind Casagrande—it just evolved that way. At the Tour de France, for Mapei, I figure it'll go down the same way and one of us will come through."

But even in late May, McRae got a scare when a list of the team's Tour squad—nine riders and three reserves—was posted on the Internet. An avid 'Net surfer, McRae spotted the list on a cycling site and saw that his name wasn't there.

"I saw that and called Patrick right away," McRae said. "He said I was on the team … that I was one of the 12 names on the list, but I could still get flicked."

Nonetheless, McRae remained confident that he would be in France in July for his first Tour, an event in which the defending champion is a fellow Austinite. Yet while Lance Armstrong's 1999 Tour win had brought some attention to other Americans racing in Europe, it certainly hadn't made things easier for those U.S. riders.

"No, no, the Euros still treat us like Yankees, basically," McRae laughed. "Lance's Tour win didn't gain any respect for the other Americans in the peloton. No way, it's hard-core."

Hard-core, yes, but so is McRae. And he has thrived in Europe, from his time on the bottom with the financially disastrous Santa Clara team, all the way up to Mapei. The last two years have shown him to be a serious contender in long stage races, coming on stronger in the final week, just as other riders are beginning to wane.

No, it wouldn't be a huge surprise to see McRae riding into Paris in strong position on July 23 ... and then, eating burritos in Austin on the 25th.

FRED RODRIGUEZ: HELPING SPRINTER TOM STEELS

It was the eve of the First Union USPRO Championship in Philadelphia, and in the Holiday Inn lobby, Fred Rodriguez was getting in a lot of face-to-face time. He and his girlfriend Annie Linderoth were sitting around a coffee table, when race announcer Jeff Roake stopped by to say hi and perhaps get a little insight into the next day's race. A few minutes later, Rodriguez was catching up with his former Saturn team director René Wenzel and former teammate Dede Demet Barry. Then, before the rising Mapei-Quick Step star sat down for a brief interview, Shimano's Andy Stone came over to talk a little shop with the outgoing young racer.

It seemed like an onslaught, but Rodriguez was having his usual great time in Philadelphia. "It's been kind of hectic," he said of the whole First Union week, after he finally settled down for a quick chat, "but it's nice. I only get home [to the U.S.] once a year to race, and only for one week."

Rodriguez was definitely a draw in Philly. With his short, dark hair slicked neatly back, and clad in a simple gray Mapei polo shirt, the Colombian-born rider had a friendly and approachable air about him, and he had no complaints about the attention he garnered. In fact, there are times back at his Italian base near Lake Maggiore, northwest of Milan, when he starts to crave that type of action.

"I'm from San Francisco, so I'm used to a lot of people," he revealed. "It's nice to go back to the apartment [in Italy] and relax, but after a week of sitting around and reading a book, I look around and say, 'Let's go.'"

And his team is quick to oblige. If there's anything that Mapei has done for him in his first year-and-a-half, it's been keeping him on the go. "I really like the travel and seeing new places," Rodriguez said. "The apartment is great, but I don't need to go home.... And for me, every race is new."

In addition to becoming acquainted with some new races, Rodriguez has also slowly learned the ways of the No. 1 professional team in the world.

"I had some growing pains," he admitted. "Your first year as an American over there, you don't know where you're gonna land. It took me a while to figure out how things work."

One of the biggest adjustments was to the high expectations. "Sometimes I'd get second and I'd be really happy with second. And they're telling me, 'You're capable of winning,'" Rodriguez said, recalling that the team wasn't satisfied with those second-place finishes, even from a first-year rider. "Sometimes you think, 'Are they just being mean to me?' But they know your potential, and want you to live up to it. It's different than in the U.S. On the [Euro] team rosters, they only list wins. In Europe, only first counts."

This year, Rodriguez has definitely made his races count. He has turned those seconds into firsts, including two stage wins and second overall at the Niedersachsen Rundfahrt, a win in stage 4 of the Four Days of Dunkirk and a stage win and third overall at the UNIQA Classic in Austria.

Then, after airline flight cancellations caused him to miss the U.S. Olympic trials [he was eventually selected as a coaches' choice], Rodriguez continued his streak of wins, this time on home soil at the First Union Classic in Trenton.

"I think I've stepped up a level," said the 27-year-old, who is also starting to have more of a say in his racing destiny. "I think finding my focus was one of the biggest things. Last year, I was telling the team, you tell me what to do, because I don't know," he said. "This year, I've had a lot more control."

His presence at the First Union series was a prime example. Originally, Mapei had scheduled Rodriguez to ride the Giro d'Italia, but the American spoke up with his own plans. "I turned [the Giro] down, because I knew I had a good shot to get results here. The team was kind of surprised," Rodriguez noted.

But the Californian showed his bosses that he had made the right decision, beating out U.S. Postal Service's George Hincapie for the coveted stars-and-stripes jersey in Philadelphia. It was a prize that Rodriguez would carry back to Europe with him, and proudly display in his first Tour de France.

That's right. After turning down the Giro, Rodriguez found out a few weeks later that he had been selected for Mapei's Tour squad, to support its sprinter Tom Steels.

"[The Giro] is actually probably a harder race for me, it's more mountainous," he said. "The Tour is more suited for me.... I'm going in as a workhorse for Tom Steels. This is the best team we've put together for Tom in a long time."

So when the spotlight of the world is on France in July, Rodriguez will be right where he likes to be: in the thick of things. "I always need to be in the circle of the team, included in what's going on," he explained.

And while he knows his role well on the Tour team, maybe, just maybe, the U.S. champion's jersey would inspire Rodriguez to unexpected heights in July.

"Once I get one win," he said, "it makes me that much more motivated for the next one."

JONATHAN VAUGHTERS: AIMING HIGH

'My mom was more than a little worried when I started talking about buying a house around here," recalled Jonathan Vaughters. "My parents really wanted me to think about some of the suburbs, but I couldn't imagine it. But I think she's come around ... especially now that the house has come along."

Actually, his mom had reason for concern. For much of the past 30 years, Vaughters's new 'hood—the so-called north side of Denver, around 32nd and Federal—was one of those places you avoided, especially after dark. Drugs, gangs, drive-by shootings, the works. And yet, there had always been something special about that area. You could see the past glory—and potential—in its turn-of-the-century homes, some meticulously maintained, others, perhaps converted to apartments, a bit worse for wear.

Vaughters saw the potential when he spotted a run-down, two-story brick Victorian that had been turned into a duplex. He noticed the tiled fireplaces, the ornately carved mantle piece and especially the sweeping open staircase leading to the top floor. "I think the staircase is the main reason I bought the place. You're not gonna see this at Highlands Ranch," he said, referring to one of Denver's newest bland-as-white-bread subdivisions.

And now, parked at the base of that staircase, there's a sign that someone else spotted some real potential in Vaughters himself. His new Look KG281 bike, with a Crédit Agricole jacket draped over the bars, serves as a reminder that there are a few changes in store for the 26-year-old former U.S. Postal Service rider.

By most standards, Vaughters had a remarkable season in 1999. There was his record-setting ride up Mont Ventoux during the Dauphiné Libéré, followed in rapid succession by overall victory at the three-day Route du Sud. But 1999 also handed him some disappointments: crashing out of the Tour de France on the perilous crossing of the Passage du Gois during the second stage, and being overlooked for the world's squad in October.

That final frustration came after Vaughters had already signed on with C.A. The team switch kept Vaughters off the Postal squad for the Vuelta a España, and that prompted USA Cycling coaches to overlook him for the world's—despite the fact that he had finished seventh in the time trial the year before.

"After the Tour, I had hoped to do well in the Vuelta, but you can't blame [Postal team director] Johan [Bruyneel] for that decision," Vaughters said. "What good does it do a team if a rider they already know is leaving racks up a bunch of UCI points for someone else?"

Still, despite missing out on the Vuelta and the world's, signing on with C.A. was a healthy and necessary move for the gangly (just 138 pounds at nearly 6 feet tall) Vaughters. The ride up Ventoux had put him in line as one of Lance Armstrong's chief lieutenants for the Tour. "I was expected to be a big help in the mountains," he said. But after Vaughters crashed out on stage 2, that role was more than filled by Kevin Livingston and Tyler Hamilton. He added, "And having three of us in that position is a bit of overkill—kinda superfluous."

And superfluous is not the role a rider with Vaughters's potential should expect to play.

Fortunately, the American's early-season performances had raised his stock in other places, particularly in France.

"Well, the races I did well in last year were big races on the international scene—big races, but not huge races," Vaughters said. "But in France, the Dauphiné, the Route du Sud, they are huge races. I mean, it makes sense that the place where I would be most valued as a rider and as a person would be on a French team."

A French team, yes, but one with a decidedly English-speaking twist to it. Crédit Agricole, the successor to gan, has been home to a host of British, Australian and American riders. It's been the base for Greg LeMond, Chris Boardman and Stuart O'Grady; last year, director Roger Legeay seemed ready to notch the team up to another level.

"There's always been a lot of talent there," Vaughters noted. "But certainly not the kind of dominating talent like an ONCE or a Mapei. To win races, they've often had to use some fairly bizarre—I should probably say creative—tactics. They would win their fair share of races, but they'd do it in exciting ways."

Around the time Legeay signed Vaughters, he also wooed Bobby Julich away from Cofidis. Julich is another American whose record is peppered with highs and lows. He made the podium in the 1998 Tour de France, but crashed out of the '99 Tour during the time trial at Metz. Then, after recovering from injuries sustained in that mishap, he crashed out of the Vuelta.

Given the records, it may be a bit of a risk, but Legeay was focusing on the extraordinary potential he saw in his two new acquisitions. And while both Americans were expected to take leadership roles at Crédit Agricole, Vaughters viewed their responsibilities as complementary.

"We're not in competition with each other," he said. "Now we have two strong G.C. riders, but riders that have shown talent in different kinds of racing. Clearly, he's the guy for the big tours. I think I can do a lot to help him. Conversely, I think I've proven myself in events where he hasn't always done well. I expect to be in a leadership position for those races like the Midi Libre, the Dauphiné.... Eventually, I'd like to prove myself as capable of doing well in a three-week tour, but for now, I'm happy to play a support role."

The team and Vaughters had set some pretty high goals for 2000: the Dauphiné, the Tour de France and, for several individual members, the Olympics.

"I could possibly medal in the time trial, but I figure my biggest obstacle right now is making the team," Vaughters said. "I think that says a lot for the state of American cycling. We have six guys who could medal in that event—Lance, Bobby, Tyler, myself, Christian [Vande Velde] and Dylan Casey—and only five spots."

For Vaughters, the fit with Crédit Agricole seems almost perfect, especially in an Olympic year. With his tendency toward methodical—almost fanatical—preparation, Vaughters's attention to the minute details of his training didn't always fit too well with his last team. So the young Coloradan was pleasantly surprised when he read the suggested training program offered to him by Crédit Agricole team manager Denis Roux. "It was awesome, almost exactly what I'd worked up for this year," Vaughters said.

Training is no hit-or-miss proposition for Vaughters. It has been a long process, dating back to his introduction to the sport as a teenager. He and best friend Colby Pearce used to talk for hours about, you know, the stuff most adolescent males like to talk about: power output, oxygen uptake, aerodynamics....

Vaughters made his first foray into Europe in a less-than-profitable tenure with the bankrupt Spanish squad, Santa Clara. But while Vaughters often didn't get his paycheck, he nonetheless left Santa Clara with something that could eventually prove to be far more valuable: "Data," Vaughters said. "Three years' worth of data. I rode almost the entire time with an srm Power Meter on my bike. I have training and racing data from all of '95, all of '96 and a big chunk of '97. I guess I was willing to ride around with that big computer and heavy crankset, 'cause I figured at my level back then, it didn't make much difference."

Now, Vaughters was back to acquiring data, probably using a much lighter Tune

Power Tap. "Thinking about this stuff makes bike racing more enjoyable," he said, "and opens up an intellectual side to the sport—a whole cerebral element to things. I mean, you gotta think about something when you're out on your bike for four, five, six hours."

And at home in Denver's north side, Vaughters pores over the data from his most recent blood test results submitted to the Union Cycliste Internationale. Vaughters is one of the few riders with a UCI certificate allowing him to ride with a hematocrit level above 50 percent.

"It took a long time to get the cert'," Vaughters explained. "They want data all the way back to my pediatrician. They want blood tests every three months and they want to confirm that the numbers they get from my doctor aren't being played with. But there are plenty of ways—more than just hematocrit level—to prove that this, my level, is naturally high, and they've looked at the numbers and acknowledged that."

In mid-January, Vaughters would leave his Denver home and head to Pau in southern France, for a training camp at the foot of the Pyrénées. Then, he'd join up with his old Postal team roomie Vande Velde, in Spain, where the two still share an apartment.

"For me, the first part of the season is going to be sort of like a two-month training camp," Vaughters predicted. "I'll be racing, but it's been a while."

From early April to mid-May, Vaughters would be back in Colorado "to let those racing miles settle in, do some strength training and then go back to Europe. We'll see how it all shakes out. It could be an interesting year."

Interesting? It could well be sensational.

Marco Pantani: 'Anger in My Heart'

One man more than any other has symbolized the drug-related problems that cycling has endured since the scandal-ridden Tour de France of 1998: Marco Pantani. This is his story—from Tour winner in July 1998, to Giro pariah in June 1999, and back to Tour contender in July 2000.

The symbolism was impossible to ignore. At the Vatican in Rome, after a tumultuous and scandal-filled year, Marco Pantani came back to competitive cycling where he had left it: at the Giro d'Italia.

It was far from certain that the Mercatone Uno team leader would even participate in Italy's national tour. He had made a few halting attempts at racing in the spring. So there were doubts if he, the winner of both the 1998 Tour de France and Giro, would even make it to the starting line. Indeed, for Pantani, May 2000 must have seemed a long, long way from the time two years earlier when he was universally hailed as the savior of cycling, one of the few men capable of guiding the Tour de France through its darkest hours.

Throughout the infamous Festina scandal of the 1998 Tour de France, Pantani remained focused on the race. As teams and riders were ejected, arrested or withdrew from the Tour in protest, Pantani remained a solid figure, concentrating on the challenges at hand and reminding those around him that the race itself was something that needed to be protected, respected and preserved. As prosecutors filed charges against the team directors of Festina and TVM, it was Pantani who helped steer the 1998 Tour toward its conclusion in Paris—something that had been in doubt soon after police stopped Willy Voet's Festina team car and discovered more than 400 vials of the blood-boosting drug EPO, human growth hormone and an assortment of other performance-enhancing substances. At least Pantani's performance, many suggested, could allay the fears and cynicism swirling around the sport. The little Italian climbing sensation was proof that the sport could be saved by someone who didn't need a sophisticated and organized doping program to succeed. It was an illusion that was placed in doubt less than a year later, just as Pantani was poised to win the 1999 Giro.

It was early in the morning of June 5, 1999, just a day before the end of the Giro and Pantani's likely triumphant ride into Milan, when medical officials from the UCI knocked on the doors of ten teams to conduct a now-standard blood test. A few hours later, before the start of the penultimate stage in Madonna di Campiglio, those same officials announced that one of the riders showed an excessive red-blood-cell count: Pantani. Pantani was ejected from the Giro and began a year that would eventually see him publicly shamed, investigated and ultimately indicted by prosecutors.

The sport and its governing body were shaken. UCI president Hein Verbruggen expressed disappointment that the rider upon whom many had staked their hopes was now at the center of his own controversy. "It's not only traumatic for the Giro, but also for cycling," he said, not mentioning the trauma the cyclist himself would—some would say deservedly—endure.

In his defense, Pantani strenuously denied any involvement with doping and then raised the possibility that the blood tested wasn't really his. It was an argument raised only once and dropped.

The test Pantani "failed" was not regarded as definitive proof that he had used EPO, the commercially produced recombinant form of the human hormone erythropoietin. At the time, no acceptable test to detect the drug existed. No, instead, the UCI did its best to guard against its abuse by testing for the effects of the drug. The hormone is naturally produced by the kidney in the event of hypoxia—the point at which the body signals that its muscles are not receiving enough oxygen. Increased levels of erythropoietin in the blood triggers receptors and prompts the bone marrow to produce more red blood cells. It is an elegant and beautifully subtle system, constantly monitored by a healthy human body.

For patients suffering from chronic anemia—either from kidney failure or some external cause like chemotherapy—EPO is a wonder drug. It can raise a dangerously low red-blood-cell count—lower than 28 or 29 percent—to a healthy level between 39 and 43 percent. Patients, once too exhausted to climb out of bed in the morning, can now lead close to normal lives.

Since its commercial release in the 1980s, unscrupulous doctors and athletes saw the performance potential of EPO in raising that healthy hematocrit of, say, 43 percent to 50, 55, 60 or even higher! That more-is-better philosophy is believed by some to be the cause of a spate of mysterious deaths among cyclists in the late 1980s. It is also what prompted the UCI to impose an upper hematocrit limit of 50 percent in 1996. With rare exception granted to those who could prove a naturally higher-than-normal red-blood-cell count, the UCI began imposing a mandatory two-week "rest period" on anyone found to exceed 50 percent. The short penalty and euphemistic language were intended to skirt the inevitable legal challenges resulting from efforts to control the use of a drug for which there was no effective test.

But in Pantani's case the penalty was significantly longer than the mandated "rest period" of two weeks. Theoretically, Pantani could have returned to the 1999 Tour to defend his title. He did not. Nor did he compete for the remainder of the year. Pantani variously explained his absence as having both emotional and physical causes. He did not directly address the allegations of drug use that surrounded him since his expulsion from the Giro.

By November, prosecutors in Turin, Florence and Forli decided it was time to raise the stakes and force Pantani to talk.

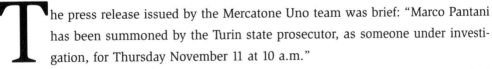

The press release issued by the Mercatone Uno team was brief: "Marco Pantani has been summoned by the Turin state prosecutor, as someone under investigation, for Thursday November 11 at 10 a.m."

It was to be his second appearance in as many weeks. A week earlier, Pantani had already been quizzed for three hours by anti-drug police in Florence, part of an inquiry by Ferrara prosecutor Guido Soprani into doping. Michele Leoni, the state prosecutor in the northern city of Forli, was also opening an investigation.

As for the meeting in Turin, team director Giuseppe Martinelli, said he didn't know what to expect. "At the moment, I just don't know what to say and I can't judge the actions of the magistrates who have summoned Marco. Pantani will go because he has been summoned."

State prosecutor Raffaele Guariniello was pursuing the matter under the provisions of a 1989 law that allowed anyone "tampering with the outcome of an sporting event" to be charged with a crime. Though intended as a means of prosecuting gamblers trying to "fix" an event, some interpreted the law as allowing the prosecution of athletes who derived some sort of competitive advantage by using a performance-enhancing drug. Logic and the appeals system upheld that interpretation. It was a charge that could carry a sentence ranging from three months to two years in prison and fines ranging from five million lira ($3000) to 50 million lira ($30,000).

That Thursday morning, Pantani did appear as ordered at the office of state prosecutor Guariniello. Accompanied by his manager, Manuela Ronchi, Pantani entered the office for what was expected to be a one- to two-hour session. But Pantani emerged minutes later announcing that he had exercised his right to silence.

"I reject the accusation and am exercising my right not to answer questions," he told Guariniello.

Pantani suggested that the test at the Giro and the subsequent investigations were merely an attempt to ruin his career and sully his reputation among die-hard Italian cycling fans, the tifosi.

"I feel that they are much closer to me than certain people would like," he said as he left Guariniello's office.

While the 1999 Giro was the event that triggered the investigation, Guariniello appeared to be most interested in an event that took place long before that. During the October 1995 Milan-Turin classic, Pantani was struck by an errant vehicle accidentally allowed onto the course after the main peloton had passed. The accident shattered his leg and promised to end his then-promising career. Indeed, the injury and Pantani's subsequent recovery and comeback were used as indicators of the feisty Italian's heroism. Now, Guariniello (along with Leoni in Forli) was examining the event as an indicator of Pantani's willingness to cheat.

An initial review of emergency room medical records showed that Pantani exhibited an astoundingly high red-blood-cell count when he was rushed to the hospital for treatment of his injuries in 1995. Blood tests at the time showed a hematocrit level between

59.3 and 61 percent. The level was well beyond natural and would be in keeping with what was assumed to be common among cheating cyclists a year before the UCI began regular hematocrit testing.

Guariniello was also interested in the mysterious disappearance of blood samples taken by doctors at a hospital near Salerno took after an accident involving Pantani during the 1997 Giro. The possible offense in that investigation, he said, would be "falsification by removal" of evidence.

Pantani and his attorneys seemed taken aback by the investigation's shift in focus. In his defense, Pantani argued that during competition, particularly after a 250km ride that ended in a car crash, "any athlete's blood count is subject to change." It was an argument Pantani also raised regarding the test taken at the 1999 Giro.

"After training at altitude, days spent racing in the mountains and dehydration, it is perfectly normal to see a rise in hematocrit," his doctor Roberto Rempi was quoted as saying.

A medical defense may not have been Pantani's best option. Nor would be the assertion that the samples taken during the Giro were from someone else. Prosecutors pulled out the stops.

The samples were all subjected to DNA tests. The results confirmed that the blood tested came from Pantani and that defense was dropped.

As for Pantani's assertion that the 1999 and 1995 results were within normal parameters, medical experts enlisted by the prosecutor's office in Forli disputed that.

Biologists examined the 1995 samples and concluded that "the exogenous assumption of erythropoietin, which has a half-life of around six hours, could explain virtually all of the biological parameters that appear to have changed in the blood sample provided by Marco Pantani."

As an example, the experts' report—issued in February 2000—cited iron levels in Pantani's blood that were nearly five times higher than the upper limit of what might be considered normal. Normal adult males usually have iron levels that vary between 25 and 225 nanograms per milliliter of blood. The samples pulled during the 1999 Giro showed Pantani's count was nearly 1200 ng/ml. Elevated iron levels are among a group of indicators used to suggest—though not prove—use of artificial erythropoietin.

That report concluded that there was a slight possibility that Pantani had not used the drug. The report cautiously—and somewhat comically—noted that it would require "physio-pathological mechanisms … hitherto unknown to the scientific world" to otherwise explain the results.

———————————❀———————————

Despite the embarrassment of the report and the likelihood of impending prosecution, Pantani tried to bring his focus back to racing. He marked his return to the professional peloton during February's Tour of Valencia in Spain. It was a difficult and halting beginning and a frustrated Pantani pulled out during the third stage.

He then set his sights on another Spanish race, the Tour of Murcia, but didn't show up. Meanwhile, Rempi, the Mercatone Uno team doctor at the 1999 Giro, was indicted in Trento on charges of "manipulating the results of sporting events," by providing his riders—Pantani in particular—with performance-enhancing drugs.

Pantani was shaken and announced that he was putting his cycling career on hold. Pantani shelved plans to compete in the Settimana Ciclistica Internationale and wrote an open letter to team director Martinelli explaining his reasons:

"I want to return to cycling with sincerity and enthusiasm. At the moment, even if from a physical point of view I am able to race, I am going through a difficult period involving much internal suffering. I need a rest and as things stand I can't say how long for."

Then, in April, Leoni, the state prosecutor in Forli, successfully sought to indict Pantani under the same 1989 law Rempi was charged with violating.

———————————❀———————————

As the 83rd edition of the Giro d'Italia approached, speculation was running rampant throughout Italy that Pantani would stage a dramatic return. He was rumored to be training. Reports filtered back that he had been seen climbing the very roads over which this Giro would be fought. Among the tifosi, the excitement was tangible.

On May 4, just nine days before the start of the Giro in Rome, Pantani's name appeared on the start list submitted by Mercatone Uno. "A sign of someone else's wishful thinking," said Pantani, denying reports that he would be at the race.

Pantani, who was in Ferrara to present evidence in yet another doping case, said he might return to racing in time to compete in the Tour de France in July.

"I don't know when I'll return to racing, but it'll be when I'm in just the right state of mind. I hope that won't be long. But I'm not making any promises because it would be sad if I couldn't keep them," Pantani said. "I'm doing what I can to get back my peace of mind and to make my comeback. I've always kept up my training, even though I haven't been able to do much because so many other things have interfered…. But I've never abandoned my profession."

The excitement tapered, but the tifosi remained hopeful. And this time, their hopes were fulfilled. The night before the start of the Giro, Mercatone Uno president Felice Gimondi confirmed that "the pirate is back" and would be competing the next day in Rome.

Gimondi made the announcement as participants, including Pantani, arrived at the Vatican for a private audience with Pope John Paul II. What better setting to start one's journey to redemption?

———————————— ❀ ————————————

Pantani immediately began to minimize expectations for his performance in the Giro. "I am here to ride in support of my team. I am here to regain my form."

Indeed, it was the Giro's eventual winner Stefano Garzelli—once known as the "little Pirate"—and not Pantani who was designated as Mercatone Uno's team leader. Pantani insisted he was racing to support his once-tireless lieutenant.

"But, ahh, when the mountains come…." seemed to be the mantra of the die-hard fans lining the roads. Italian television cameras focused much of their attention on Pantani. News from the road included status reports on the day's stage leader and his position relative to that of the group that contained the overall leader "Gruppo Maglia Rosa" and, a relatively new subject of interest, the "Gruppo Pantani."

Pantani's performance on the Giro's first climb above 1000 meters in stage 3 was thoroughly analyzed and dutifully reported to waiting Italian television audiences. But the real anticipation was focused on Stage 9's ascent of San Pellegrino in Alpe, a climb that averages almost 9 percent for 12.6km. This, said the tifosi, was where Il Pirata would make his move. No, it was where Francesco Casagrande made his move.

Casagrande took charge of the Giro right where he predicted he would: on the slopes of the San Pellegrino. The 1988 Giro winner, Andy Hampsten, had traveled to the climb from his home in Tuscany that day. The crowds, he noted, were full of anticipation of a stellar performance by their favorite rider.

"There must have been all of Tuscany and half of the of northern tribes there to watch Pantani sail away," Hampsten later wrote. "You could have heard a pin drop when he didn't."

Pantani crawled past some seven minutes after Casagrande. It was a pattern he would repeat as the Giro moved to the mountains, losing 17:32 on stage 13's brutal ride from Feltre to Selva Gardena, and losing still more time the next day as the Giro crossed the infamous Passo di Gavia.

The fans had come to the realization that Pantani would not be making a dramatic comeback. They could only hope for one significant performance—an indication, perhaps, of things to come. It finally came on Stage 19, through the Alps to Briançon, France, coincidentally the site of a scheduled stage finish for the 2000 Tour de France as well.

Nearly an hour behind in the overall standings, it was clear that Pantani could do little in this Giro except show that he still had the aggressive style and remarkable climbing form that once characterized his career. That day's stage—over the highest point in the Giro, the Colle dell Agnello, and then the famed Col d'Izoard—was perfect to show that the old Pantani was still there. The 15km Agnello, like the Gavia, is made up of a series of narrow switchbacks that reach grades of 13 percent.

Throughout the day, race leader Casagrande seemed content to shadow his main rivals Garzelli and a brash 28-year-old Italian, Gilberto Simoni. The Lampre rider, now lying in third, was not content to simply stay with the maglia rosa. He had been frustrated in his efforts to attack Casagrande in the previous day's stage to Pratonevoso—where he had confidently predicted he would take a minute out of the race leader.

On the Agnello, he charged off the front repeatedly, finally managing to get some distance, with only Mapei's Paolo Lanfranchi in his company. By the summit, Simoni and Lanfranchi were close to catching an earlier solo break by Jose "Chepe" Gonzales, the Colombian rider who had been aggressive throughout the Giro. Behind them in close pursuit were Casagrande, Garzelli and others. It was turning into a dramatic stage. But the Italian fans lining the Agnello were focusing their attention on the man in close pursuit of Casagrande. The fans were cheering wildly, not because of the drama at the front, but because their hero, Pantani, was finally making a show of it. There he was flashing that same style, that same panache he had displayed through most of the 1999 Giro.

All of the problems of the previous year, all of the disappointment of this Giro, all of the frustration, all of the embarrassment suddenly disappeared as Pantani crested the Agnello in hot pursuit of the leaders. The Pirate was back.

On the descent, Gonzales lost time and Pantani gained. Toward the top of the Izoard, Gonzales was gone, Simoni and Lanfranchi caught and—to the thrill of the tifosi— Pantani was with the leaders.

Presumably, Pantani was there to lend support to his teammate Garzelli. Indeed, Italian television replayed and replayed the moment when Pantani handed his teammate a water bottle. It was a role they were unaccustomed to seeing and one Pantani was apparently unaccustomed to playing.

Pantani attacked and attacked, occasionally leaving Garzelli behind and unwittingly towing Simoni along with him. Behind them, Lanfranchi had gone back to help his team leader Pavel Tonkov over the top of the Izoard. The pair chased and eventually bridged up to the leaders. Just as they rejoined, Lanfranchi charged ahead.

"It hadn't been my plan to attack," Lanfranchi later explained, "but with everyone else watching each other, it was time for me to try something."

Lanfranchi quickly built up a one-minute lead. He had a clear shot through the finishing straight up the narrow streets of Briançon.

Behind, Pantani charged off the front of the chase group, leaving his own teammate Garzelli behind. Lanfranchi realized he had the win and celebrated as he crossed the line. Pantani rode alone through an adoring mob as Simoni, Garzelli and Casagrande chased behind.

Pantani would later explain that day's performance as a response to year of frustration, disappointment and, above all, anger.

"I did not ride this way today because of the strength in my legs," he said in a post-race press conference. "I rode like this because of the anger in my heart. I wanted to make a statement."

Garzelli, who moved into the overall lead the next day, would later credit Pantani for "an inspiring performance" into Briançon. His teammate, he said, was instrumental in convincing him that he could win the Giro. Still, though Garzelli dedicated his win to his teammate, he knew that eventually he would be back in the role of lieutenant. By the fall of 2000, Garzelli would begin looking around at other teams.

Pantani, meanwhile, ignored the indictments, ignored the legal problems, forgot the troubled spring, and turned his attention toward the Tour de France....

Americans at the Tour

I f the Tour de France went back to being a race contested by national teams, the United States would be able to field an enormously strong squad. Not only would the U.S. have defending Tour champion Lance Armstrong as its leader, it would have other podium contenders like Bobby Julich and Tyler Hamilton, strong climbers like Kevin Livingston, Chann McRae and Jonathan Vaughters, and powerful team riders like Frankie Andreu, George Hincapie and Christian Vande Velde. All of these men have ridden multiple Grand Tours, and together they would be able to challenge any of the traditional European cycling countries. That's quite a stamp of approval for a country that didn't field its first Tour contestant until 1981 (Jonathan Boyer), and its first sponsored team until 1986 (7-Eleven).

Greg LeMond, of course, became the first American to win the Tour that same year—but LeMond was something of an anomaly, spending his entire pro career racing for French, Belgian and Dutch teams. If LeMond had had to rely on the support of a U.S.-only team, he would have had a hard time winning one, let alone three Tours.

That wouldn't be true today because U.S. professional cycling has made giant strides. In 2000, there would be nine Americans starting the Tour: five on the U.S. Postal Service team, two on Crédit Agricole of France and two on Mapei-Quick Step of Italy.

Frankie Andreu
Age: 33
Height: 6 ft. 2 in.   **Weight:** 180 lbs.
Hometown: Dearborn, Michigan
Team: U.S. Postal Service
Number of Tours: 8
Scouting report: Frankie Andreu is the cement that locks his Tour team together. First with Motorola in the early '90s, then with Cofidis for a year, and now with the Postal Service, the Michigander has finished all of his eight Tours. His reward for that long service finally came in 1999 when he rode onto the Champs-Elysées alongside his friend and teammate, race winner Lance Armstrong. That's a familiar place for Andreu, who was a constant confidence boost for Armstrong during the Texan's fight back from cancer. So nothing would please Andreu more than to see his buddy win again.

In return, nothing would please Armstrong more than to see Andreu finally win a Tour stage—assuming that the circumstances made that possible. One way, for sure, would be winning the team time trial. They came close to doing this with Motorola, in 1994, at Armstrong's second Tour, when they finished second in the TTT, only six seconds behind stage winner GB-MG (the predecessor of the Mapei squad).

If the TTT didn't bring Andreu a stage win, then look for him to go with a breakaway later in the Tour—perhaps on the long stage to Troyes, the day before the finish. If such a breakaway succeeded in staying clear of the peloton, then Andreu would be a very hard man to beat.

Lance Armstrong
Age: 28
Height: 5 ft. 11 in.   **Weight:** 158 lbs.
Hometown: Austin, Texas
Team: U.S. Postal Service
Number of Tours: 5
Scouting report: When Lance Armstrong says he is on schedule to have top form in July, then you believe him. He even said, following two good race performances in late April, that he was on better form than a year earlier. In other words, you had to believe that the U.S. Postal Service team leader would again be challenging for the Tour de France yellow jersey.

Things were different, of course, than a year before. Since winning the 1999 Tour, the Texan had become an icon for the cancer community, a media celebrity in the U.S. and a corporate marketer's dream. He also became a dad. Combined, the many new demands—along with collaborating on a best-selling book about his life—left Armstrong little time for off-season training.

Since returning in February to his European home in Nice, his focus returned to the bike: long training rides in the Alpes-Maritimes, a gradual stepping up of his efforts in Spanish stage races using a power meter, regular physical check-ups and a return to the climbing work-outs that proved so successful in 1999. Despite starting his preparation later, Armstrong indeed seemed to have good form in late April—a crash put him behind the eight ball at the Amstel Gold Race in the Netherlands, but three days later he took second in the hilly French Cup race Paris-Camembert and at the end of the same week, in Switzerland's top-rated GP Kanton Aargau, he was again strong enough to make the winning break— although last-minute cramps saw him finish fourth in the four-up finishing sprint.

In his build-up to the Tour, Armstrong repeated the specific training camps he did last year to reconnoiter the Tour's mountain stages, which resulted in a scary high-speed crash on May 5 in the Pyrénées. Then, in the Dauphiné Libéré June 4-11, he finished an impressive third after assisting teammate Tyler Hamilton to the overall victory.

One Tour stage that would get special attention was the team time trial between Nantes and St. Nazaire. Like Motorola, Armstrong's team when the Tour last had a TTT, his troops would ride that course and experiment with different line-ups in the week before the Tour.

Knowing Armstrong, he would dearly like to make a statement in the two early time trials—the opening, 16.5km individual test at Futuroscope, and the TTT three days later. If he did, then, as he showed in 1999, he would be a hard man to stop.

Tyler Hamilton
Age: 27
Height: 5 ft. 8 in.   **Weight:** 140 lbs.
Hometown: Marblehead, Massachusetts
Team: U.S. Postal Service
Number of Tours: 3
Scouting report: On any other team, Tyler Hamilton would be regarded as the leader, the one rider who had all the qualities to win the Tour de France. He is among the top time

trialists in the world, he's also one of the fastest climbers, and—perhaps most important of all—he never gives up.

At the 1998 Tour, the day after he took a shocking second place in the stage 7 time trial behind Jan Ullrich, Hamilton was ill with a stomach virus that would have knocked out most riders. But even though he was voluntarily abandoned by his team, Hamilton managed to finish the stage within the time limit, and then showed tremendous courage to get through the next two days, both of them in the mountains.

In 1999, he crashed heavily on stage 2, and rode hard for team leader Lance Armstrong for the rest of the opening week in great pain—and still came through with a strong ride in the Metz time trial. Then, in a rainstorm on the vital alpine stage to Sestriere, he crashed again, opening up some of the same wounds and acquiring new ones. Despite that, Hamilton came through the very next day to lead Armstrong up the torturous climb to L'Alpe d'Huez.

What's most remarkable is that Hamilton ended that Tour strongly, took third place (behind Armstrong and Alex Zülle) in the closing time trial, and managed to place 13th overall.

Now he was ready to do it all again....

George Hincapie
Age: 27
Height: 6 ft. 3 in. **Weight:** 175 lbs.
Hometown: Greenville, South Carolina
Team: U.S. Postal Service
Number of Tours: 5
Scouting report: He didn't get a lot of publicity during the 1999 Tour, but George Hincapie was Lance Armstrong's guardian angel on the race's flatter stages—and even made huge contributions to the Postal team's efforts in the mountains. It was Hincapie who set the pace for Armstrong on the critical approach to the Passage du Gois causeway on stage 2— making sure that his team leader was in the front group, while others (including eventual Tour runner-up Zülle) languished at the back and lost six minutes by the stage finish.

Hincapie is tall, fast and powerful. These are qualities that have helped him develop into one of the best classics riders in the world. And the more he has progressed in single-day racing, the more indispensable he has become for his Tour team. A big part of Armstrong's '99 Tour victory was due to his team riding a steady tempo at the head of the peloton day after day—either to stop breaks developing on stages before the mountains, or to limit a breakaway's gains later in the race. And there is no better tempo rider than Hincapie.

Besides his heavy team duties, this native New Yorker has the finishing speed to shoot for stage wins. In 1998, Hincapie almost took the yellow jersey after featuring in a long breakaway on stage 3, and in '99 he had several top-10 finishes in mass-sprints. If he did win a stage, it would be a pure bonus, not a top-priority goal.

Bobby Julich

Age: 28

Height: 6 ft. **Weight:** 150 lbs.

Hometown: Haverford, Pennsylvania

Team: Crédit Agricole

Number of Tours: 3

Scouting report: In his eight years as a pro cyclist, Bobby Julich has known more downs than ups; but all of his experiences—good and bad—have helped mold him into a top Tour contender. The Colorado native didn't start racing in Europe until 1995, but two confidence-building seasons with Motorola followed by three years with Cofidis have seen him reach maturity.

Julich has all the assets of a potential Tour winner—attentive in his preparation, strong in time trialing and climbing, good recovery between stages, and a fervent ambition. All those qualities crystallized after he took 17th in his race debut at the 1997 Tour, a race in which he got stronger and more confident as the race went on. So it was not a great surprise in '98, when he held second place for much of the Tour, before ending up in third behind Marco Pantani and Jan Ullrich.

The scene was set for Julich to make a real challenge for victory in 1999. But springtime sicknesses and injuries left him behind in his training, and he struggled through the Tour's first week—before crashing out of the race in the stage 8 time trial.

Later in the year, at the Vuelta a España, Julich had a second serious fall, which ended his season. On a more positive note, he signed a good contract with another French team, Crédit Agricole, and he started the 2000 season with a confidence-building second place in February's Mediterranean Tour.

So, with his health intact and his form slowly building through the early season, Julich could again be expected to be a top contender. He is comfortable with his new team, which has LeMond's former directeur sportif Roger Legeay at the helm, fellow Coloradan Jonathan Vaughters as its climbing specialist, Germany's Jens Voigt as the all-around strongman and Aussie Stuart O'Grady as team captain on the flats.

Kevin Livingston

Age: 27

Height: 6 ft.   **Weight:** 155 lbs.

Hometown: Austin, Texas

Team: U.S. Postal Service

Number of Tours: 3

Scouting report: In 1999, Kevin Livingston continued the steady progression he has followed since entering his first Tour de France in 1997. That year, as well as the following one, he was on the Cofidis team, riding alongside fellow American Julich. Livingston's strong climbing played a big role in helping Julich finish on the Paris podium in the '98 Tour. Then, Livingston moved to the Postal Service team, to be back with his Texas training partner, Lance Armstrong. And it's now part of Tour de France lore how Livingston was Armstrong's guiding light on the two longest climbs of the '99 Tour: the Col du Galibier in the Alps and the Col du Tourmalet in the Pyrénées.

His role in 2000 would again be to ride hard for Armstrong on the Tour's major climbs. And that meant following a similar preparation to his team leader. Livingston's early season went according to plan until the last day of Spain's Tour of the Basque Country in early April. Then, after showing good form in bridging up to a break on a climb, he was involved in a pileup on slick roads and broke his collarbone in two places. That set him back a little, but he was back racing by mid-May, giving him adequate time to be at his best by July.

Livingston is probably the most up-beat guy on the American team, so we could expect his high spirits to keep his training partner on track to win that yellow jersey again.

Chann McRae

Age: 28

Height: 5 ft. 9 in.   **Weight:** 136 lbs.

Hometown: Austin, Texas

Team: Mapei-Quick Step

Number of Tours: 0

Scouting report: Although he is the same age as Lance Armstrong, grew up in the same

Texas town (Plano, near Dallas) and was considered his equal in junior cycling, Chann McRae has had a vastly different racing career. McRae didn't turn pro until 1996—with a low-budget (no budget?) Spanish team sponsored by a porcelain manufacturer, Santa Clara. The team folded that same year and McRae began 1997 with another low-budget squad, Die Continentale of Germany. Some good early-season results there earned him a place on the U.S. team, Saturn, with whom he began to show his true ability—especially in contending for the overall win at eastern Europe's two-week Peace Race in both '97 and '98.

McRae's good results attracted Italy's world-leading Mapei-Quick Step formation, which signed him in 1999. He didn't disappoint. The quiet Texan rode strong races for the team at both the Giro d'Italia (48th overall) and Vuelta a España (19th), and ended the year with an excellent fifth place in the world road race championship.

Starting 2000, Mapei scheduled McRae for its Tour de France team—until he was told in mid-April that he was also wanted for the Giro. With an earlier focus (the Giro started on May 13), McRae had to step up his training, and showed he was on target by taking second place on the final stage of the Tour of Trentino on April 27. At the Giro, he rode for his Russian teammate Pavel Tonkov and came in 17th overall. At the Tour, his team leader would be Michele Bartoli, assuming the Italian was fully recovered from the knee problems that wrecked his spring classics season.

It would be McRae's first Tour. But with the confidence he had garnered from his first 18 months with the world's No. 1 team, he was expected to show his all-around strength—particularly his climbing skills.

Fred Rodriguez

Age: 26

Height: 5 ft. 10 in.   **Weight:** 150 lbs.

Hometown: San Francisco

Team: Mapei-Quick Step

Number of Tours: 0

Scouting report: Since turning pro with Saturn in 1996, Fred Rodriguez—the son of a former Colombian racer—has built a strong reputation as a fast finisher. Ironically, many of his more notable victories have come in Asia: a stage of the Tour of China in 1996, two stages of Malaysia's Tour de Langkawi in '98 and another Langkawi stage in '99. In 2000, his second season with Mapei, Rodriguez had continued his progression with a string of wins—including the stars-and-stripes jersey at the USPRO Championship in Philadelphia and a stage of the Tour of Switzerland.

His role at the Tour was clear: Help his senior teammate Tom Steels win as many stages as possible. Rodriguez's chance of glory could come later in the race.

Jonathan Vaughters
Age: 27
Height: 5 ft. 11 in.   **Weight:** 135 lbs.
Hometown: Denver, Colorado
Team: Crédit Agricole
Number of Tours: 1

Scouting report: The bean-thin Jonathan Vaughters is one of the fastest climbers in the world: He proved that in 1999 by breaking the time-trial record for ascending Mont Ventoux (which has a 5000-foot elevation gain in 20km), to win stage 3 of the Dauphiné Libéré. That performance helped Vaughters place second overall at the Dauphiné, before he went on the win (with Lance Armstrong's help) the Route du Sud.

Those two performances marked Vaughters as one of the key men to aid Armstrong's Tour de France bid. But the Tour and Vaughters don't seem to click. In 1998, he was scheduled to ride his first Tour with the Postal Service team—until a freak crash in a warm-up race left him on the sidelines. Vaughters did get to the Tour start line in '99, but he was a victim of the big stage 2 pileup on the Passage du Gois causeway, and was forced to quit.

In 2000, as a member of French squad Crédit Agricole, Vaughters hoped to get a little farther—hopefully all the way to Paris. His job would include riding strongly in the team time trial, being team leader Bobby Julich's right-hand man in the mountains, and maybe going for a stage win. And it just so happens that stage 12 of the Tour would finish atop Mont Ventoux.

Lance's Ultimate Test

What a difference a year makes. In 1999, injuries prevented previous Tour de France winners Jan Ullrich and Bjarne Riis from starting the race, and defending champion Marco Pantani temporarily quit the sport after a humiliating above-the-limit blood test when on his way to winning the Giro d'Italia. In their absence, Lance Armstrong dominated the Tour, winning all the time trials and the key mountain stage, and only needing to keep his eye on distant challengers Alex Zülle and Fernando Escartin to remain wearing the yellow jersey all the way to Paris.

It was a remarkable story: the comeback from cancer; the turnaround from one-day *wunderkind* to unbeatable grand tour champion; and the magnificent effort by the previously unheralded U.S. Postal Service squad.

In 2000, Armstrong and the Posties looked even stronger-and so did the opposition. Ullrich and Pantani were back; Zülle and Escartin were more ambitious than ever; and a host of would-be challengers like Laurent Jalabert, Bobby Julich, Abraham Olano and Laurent Dufaux had targeted the Tour as their season goal.

It looked like being the best, most aggressive and exciting Tour in a decade. But the Tiger Woods of cycling, a certain Texan from Austin, looked set for a second victory.

Here's how the top 20 contenders were rated:

LEAGUE OF HIS OWN

Lance Armstrong (USA)

Pedigree: Since his comeback from cancer, Armstrong, 28, had ridden two three-week stages races, finishing 4th at the 1998 Vuelta and 1st at the 1999 Tour. He can win time trials and mountain stages, and has incredible determination.

Team: The U.S. Postal Service squad proved unbeatable in '99 under the direction of Johan Bruyneel. Armstrong's lieutenant Tyler Hamilton was even stronger than a year earlier, while Kevin Livingston had come back strongly from a broken collarbone.

Form: Following the same program as last year, Armstrong looked even stronger, winning the time trial at June's Dauphiné, and helping Hamilton win the eight-day race on his way to third overall.

BEEN THERE

Marco Pantani (Italy)

Pedigree: Pantani, 30, won the Giro and Tour in '98, and was dominating the '99 Giro when he tested above the 50-percent hematocrit limit and was automatically suspended. He is the fastest climber in the world, but not a natural time trialist.

Team: The all-Italian Mercatone Uno-Albacom squad has plenty of experience defending leads for its stars Pantani and Stefano Garzelli (who wasn't riding the Tour), but would its younger riders have the strength to give Pantani a shot at the lead?

Form: The recent Giro was Pantani's comeback to top competition, and by the last mountain stage he showed signs of his best form returning.

Jan Ullrich (Germany)

Pedigree: In his three Tour starts (1996, '97 and '98), Ullrich, 26, had finished 2nd, 1st and 2nd. An injured knee kept him from starting in 1999. Ullrich is the world time trial champion, and at his best is a powerful climber.

Team: Tekelom is one of the strongest teams and won the team time trial at the Tour of Switzerland on June 13. Ullrich's support for the mountains were veterans Udo Bölts, 33, and Alberto Elli, 36, and the experienced Giuseppe Guerini.

Form: Ullrich had no notable performances in 2000, his race schedule having been restricted by viruses, back problems and overweight. He showed signs in the early stages of the Tour of Switzerland that he would be ready for the Tour-but probably not at his best.

Alex Zülle (Switzerland)

Pedigree: Zülle, 32, twice finished second at the Tour (1995 and 99), and twice won the Vuelta (1996 and 97). He can match Armstrong and Ullrich in time trials, and also has the ability to win mountain stages. His propensity to crash or miss key moves are negatives.

Team: Banesto was built more for the mountains than the flat stages, and could have problems in the team time trial. José Maria Jiménez was the team's best climber and could prove an invaluable lieutenant for Zülle.

Form: Zülle had raced less than usual, but he showed signs of approaching his best form at the Dauphiné Libéré, where he came in fourth overall.

IN THE WINGS
Joseba Beloki (Spain)

Pedigree: Beloki, 26, was making his debut at the Tour. He showed his all-around promise by taking fourth at the 1999 Dauphiné and then being signed by French squad Festina after his first two pro seasons with the low-budget Euskaltel-Euskadi team

Team: Festina has been completely rebuilt since its 1998 exclusion from the Tour, the one remaining member being strong time trialist Christophe Moreau, whose experience could help Beloki.

Form: Beloki placed only 24th overall at the Dauphiné, but fourth place in the time trial (just behind Tyler Hamilton) and fifth place on the marathon stage through the Alps, showed that he would be ready for his first Tour.

Laurent Dufaux (Switzerland)

Pedigree: Dufaux, 31, twice finished fourth at the Tour (1996 and '99), and at the Vuelta placed 2nd (1996) and 3rd (1997).

Team: The Saeco-Valli & Valli team is normally built to help sprinter Mario Cipollini win stages at the Tour; but a June 10 training crash that saw Cipollini crack two ribs and have 30 stitches in facial wounds would prevent him from starting.

Form: Dufaux won a hilly stage of the Tour de Romandie in May, and was using the Tour of Switzerland (June 13-22) as his final build-up to the Tour.

Fernando Escartin (Spain)

Pedigree: Escartin, 32, has improved with age. He had yet to win a three-week tour, but his third place at the '99 Tour, following second and third at the Vuelta, meant the top step of the podium was still a possibility.

Team: Kelme-Costa Blanca is a team built for the mountains, with Colombian Santiago Botero and Spaniard Roberto Heras being Escartin's first lieutenants.

Form: A slow build-up, ending with the Tour of Catalonia, looked like bringing Escartin to the same good form as 1999.

Laurent Jalabert (France)

Pedigree: Jalabert, 31, had been ranked No. 1 in the world for most of the past six seasons, mainly thanks to his expertise in week-long stage races. He did win the Vuelta in 1995, but fourth was his best performance at the Tour (1995) and Giro (1999). He is a good time trialist, but shows weakness in climbs topping 2000 meters (6500 feet).

Team: ONCE-Deutsche Bank is a well-balanced team, with a wealth of team workers and climbers. They would do well in the team time trial. The presence of co-leader Abraham Olano could allow Jalabert to show his attacking strength in the hilly stages.

Form: Jalabert had a strong spring, and then took a break to make the Tour his focus. Winning the last stage of the Dauphiné (12th overall) showed that his form was starting to peak at the right time.

Bobby Julich (USA)

Pedigree: Since finishing ninth at the 1996 Vuelta. Julich, 28, has focused on the Tour. In his 1997 debut, he started as a team rider for Tony Rominger, and became the leader after Rominger crashed out. Julich then matched the best climbers to finish 17th overall. In '98, he did well in the time trials and mountain stages to finish third overall. In 1999, he had health problems, then crashed out of the Tour before the mountains.

Team: Although Crédit Agricole is a Division II team, it has the strength to ride a good team time trial, while Jens Voigt and Jonathan Vaughters should provide invaluable support for Julich in the mountain stages.

Form: Julich started the season strongly, and after a break began a slow build-up toward the Tour. Although he finished only 25th in June's Dauphiné, a sixth place in the time trial and some aggressive riding in the mountain stages showed that his form was heading in the right direction.

Abraham Olano (Spain)

Pedigree: The record of Olano, 30, in the grand tours is quite impressive: 1st (1998) and 2nd ('95) at the Vuelta; 3rd ('96) at the Giro; and 4th ('97) at the Tour. His strength is time trialing, while his climbing ability has always been erratic.

Team: With the ONCE team's collective strength, it's possible that Olano could be in the yellow jersey after the team time trial. If so, the team could be inspired to defend the lead—as happened when Olano was with Banesto at the '98 Vuelta.

Form: Three stage race wins in February and March showed that Olano's decision to lose weight in the winter paid off. In his build-up to the Tour, he showed improving form at the Dauphiné (18th overall, seventh in the time trial)

THE PRINCIPAL ABSENTEES

Injured: Mario Cipollini, Christophe Rinero.

Not invited: Laurent Brochard, Oskar Camenzind, Igor Gonzalez de Galdeano, Haimar Zubeldia.

Not on their schedule: Francesco Casagrande, Stefano Garzelli, Ivan Gotti, Gilberto Simoni, Pavel Tonkov.

The 20 Teams

U.S. Postal Service (USA)

1. Lance Armstrong (USA), 2. Frankie Andreu (USA), 3. Viatcheslav Ekimov (Rus), 4. Tyler Hamilton (USA), 5. George Hincapie (USA), 6. Benoit Joachim (Lux), 7. Steffen Kjaergaard (Nl), 8. Kevin Livingston (USA), 9. Cédric Vasseur (F). Directeurs Sportifs: Johan Bruyneel, Dirk Demol.

Banesto (Spain)

11. Alex Zülle (Swi), 12. José Luis Arrieta (Sp), 13. Dariusz Baranowski (Pl), 14. Vicente Garcia Acosta (Sp), 15. José Maria Jimenez (Sp), 16. Francisco Mancebo (Sp), 17. Jon Odriozola (Sp), 18. Leonardo Piepoli (I), 19. Orlando Rodrigues (P). Directeurs Sportifs: Eusebio Unzue, José-Lius Jaimerena.

Kelme–Costa Blanca (Spain)

21. Fernando Escartin (Sp), 22. Santiago Botero (Col), 23. Carlos Contreras (Col), 24. Roberto Heras (Sp), 25. Francisco Leon (Sp), 26. Javier Otxoa (Sp), 27. Javier Pascual Llorente (Sp), 28. Antonio Tauler (Sp), 29. José Angel Vidal (Sp). Directeurs Sportifs: Vicente Belda, José-Ignacio Labarta.

Mapei–Quick Step (Italy)

31. Michele Bartoli (I), 32. Manuel Beltran (Sp), 33. Paolo Bettini (I), 34. Chann McRae (USA), 35. Daniele Nardello (I), 36. Fred Rodriguez (USA), 37. Tom Steels (B), 38. Max Van Heeswijk (Nl), 39. Stefano Zanini (I). Directeurs Sportifs: Serge Parsani, Marc Sergeant.

Rabobank (Netherlands)

41. Michael Boogerd (Nl), 42. Jan Boven (Nl), 43. Erik Dekker (Nl), 44. Maarten Den Bakker (Nl), 45. Marc Lotz (Nl), 46. Grischa Niermann (G), 47. Leon Van Bon (Nl), 48. Marc Wauters (B), 49. Markus Zberg (Swi). Directeurs Sportifs: Theo De Rooy, Adri Van Houwelingen.

ONCE–Deutsche Bank (Spain)

51. Laurent Jalabert (F), 52. David Cañada (Sp), 53. David Etxebarria (Sp), 54. Ivan Gutierrez (Sp), 55. Nicolas Jalabert (F), 56. Peter Luttenberger (A), 57. Abraham Olano (Sp), 58. Miguel Angel Peña (Sp), 59. Marcos Serrano (Sp). Directeurs Sportifs: Manuel Saiz, Sebastian Pozo.

Telekom (Germany)

61. Jan Ullrich (G), 62. Udo Bölts (G), 63. Alberto Elli (I), 64. Gian Matteo Fagnini (I), 65. Giuseppe Guerini (I), 66. Jens Heppner (G), 67. Alex Vinokourov (Kaz), 68. Steffen Wesemann (G), 69. Erik Zabel (G). Directeurs Sportifs: Walter Godefroot, Rudy Pevenage.

Mercatone Uno–Albacom (Italy)

71. Marco Pantani (I), 72. Simone Borgheresi (I), 73. Ermanno Brignoli (I), 74. Fabiano Fontanelli (I), 75. Riccardo Forconi (I), 76. Massimo Podenzana (I), 77. Marcello Siboni (I), 78. Marco Velo (I), 79. Enrico Zaina (I). Directeurs Sportifs: Giuseppe, Alessandro Giannelli.

AG2R Prévoyance (France)

81. Jaan Kirsipuu (Est), 82. Christophe Agnolutto (F), 83. Lauri Aus (Est), 84. Pascal Chanteur (F), 85. David Delrieu (F), 86. Arturas Kasputis (Lit), 87. Andrei Kivilev (Kaz), 88. Gilles Maignan (F), 89. Benoit Salmon (F). Directeurs Sportifs: Vincent Lavenu, Laurent Biondi.

Saeco–Valli & Valli (Italy)

91. Laurent Dufaux (Swi), 92. Daniel Atienza (Sp), 93. Salvatore Commesso (I), 94. Armin Meier (Swi), 95. Massimiliano Mori (I), 96. Pavel Padrnos (Cz), 97. Dario Pieri (I), 98. Paolo Savoldelli (I), 99. Mario Scirea (I). Directeurs Sportifs: Antonio Salutini, Guido Bontempi.

Festina (France)

101. Christophe Moreau (F), 102. Joseba Beloki (Sp), 103. Angel Casero (Sp), 104. Felix

Garcia Casas (Sp), 105. Jaime Hernandez (Sp), 106. Pascal Lino (F), 107. Laurent Madouas (F), 108. David Plaza (Sp), 109. Marcel Wüst (G). Directeurs Sportifs: Juan Fernandez, Roberto Torres.

Farm Frites (Netherlands)

111. Sergei Ivanov (Rus), 112. Andreas Klier (G), 113. Servais Knaven (Nl), 114. Jans Koerts (Nl), 115. Michel Lafis (S), 116. Glenn Magnusson (S), 117. Robbie McEwen (Aus), 118. Koos Moerenhout (Nl), 119. Geert Van Bondt (B). Directeurs Sportifs: Hendrik Redant, Johan Capiot.

Cofidis (France)

121. Frank Vandenbroucke (B), 122. Laurent Desbiens (F), 123. Laurent Lefèvre (F), 124. Massimiliano Lelli (I), 125. Nico Mattan (B), 126. Roland Meier (Swi), 127. David Millar (GB), 128. David Moncoutié (F), 129. Chris Peers (B). Directeurs Sportifs: Bernard Quilfen, Alain Deloeuil.

Lotto–Adecco (Belgium)

131. Rik Verbrugghe (B), 132. Mario Aerts (B), 133. Serge Baguet (B), 134. Sebastien Demarbaix (B), 135. Jacky Durand (F), 136. Thierry Marichal (B), 137. Kurt Van de Wouwer (B), 138. Paul Van Hyfte (B), 139. Geert Verheyen (B). Directeurs Sportifs: Jos Braeckevelt, Claudy Criquielion.

La Française des Jeux (France)

141. Stéphane Heulot (F), 142. Frédéric Guesdon (F), 143. Gregory Gwiazdowski (Pl), 144. Frank Hoj (Dk), 145. Xavier Jan (F), 146. Emmanuel Magnien (F), 147. Christophe Mengin (F), 148. Sven Montgomery (Swi), 149. Jean-Patrick Nazon (F). Directeurs Sportifs: Marc Madiot, Yvon Madiot.

Polti (Italy)

151. Richard Virenque (F), 152. Jeroen Blijlevens (Nl), 153. Rossano Brasi (F), 154. Enrico Cassani (F), 155. Mirco Crepaldi (F), 156. Pascal Hervé (F), 157. Rafael Mateos (Sp), 158. Fabio Sacchi (F), 159. Bart Voskamp (Nl). Directeurs Sportifs: Gianluigi Stanga, Giovanni Fidanza.

MemoryCard–Jack & Jones (Denmark)

161. Bo Hamburger (Dk), 162. Michael Blaudzun (Dk), 163. Tristan Hoffman (Nl), 164. Allan Johansen (Dk), 165. Nicolay Bo Larsen (Dk), 166. Arvis Piziks (Lat), 167. Martin Rittsel (S), 168. Michael Sandstod (Dk), 169. Jesper Skibby (Dk). Directeurs Sportifs: Alex Pedersen, Johnny Weltz.

Crédit Agricole (France)

171. Bobby Julich (USA), 172. Magnus Bäckstedt (S), 173. Fabrice Gougot (F), 174. Sebastien Hinault (F), 175. Anthony Langella (F), 176. Anthony Morin (F), 177. Stuart O'Grady (Aus), 178. Jonathan Vaughters (USA), 179. Jens Voigt (G). Directeurs Sportifs: Roger Legeay, Serge Beucherie.

Vini Caldirola–Sidermec (Italy)

181. Romans Vainsteins (Lat), 182. Massimo Apollonio (I), 183. Gianluca Bortolami (I), 184. Filippo Casagrande (I), 185. Roberto Conti (I), 186. Andrej Hauptman (Slo), 187. Zoran Klemencic (Slo), 188. Mauro Radaelli (I), 189. Guido Trentin (I). Directeurs Sportifs: Giosué Zenoni, Fabrizio Bontempi.

Bonjour (France)

191. Jean-Cyril Robin (F), 192. Walter Beneteau (F), 193. Franck Bouyer (F), 194. Pascal Deramé (F), 195. Christophe Faudot (F), 196. Damien Nazon (F), 197. Olivier Perraudeau (F), 198. Didier Rous (F), 199. François Simon (F). Directeurs Sportifs: Jean-Renè Bernaudeau, Thierry Bricaud.

Part Two

The 87ᵀᴴ Tour de France

Tales of the Unexpected

I f anything is guaranteed at the Tour de France—as at every edition since the race was first run in 1903—it's the unexpected. That's what keeps the crowds flocking back to the roadsides of France and, in the modern era, to their TV sets. Every year, the fans are shocked by dramatic crashes, stunned by personal dramas, elated by inspiring attacks in the mountains, and astonished by the athletes who emerge as challengers for the coveted yellow jersey. It was impossible to predict what would happen at the Tour, but we could certainly speculate....

This 87th edition promised a match-up between the Tour's last three winners: defending champion Lance Armstrong, 1998 winner Marco Pantani and '97 victor Jan Ullrich. Each of them brought different talents and strategies to the start line in Futuroscope on July 1, 2000.

Armstrong was totally focused on the Tour and, despite a bad training crash on May 5, was on target to come into the race on top form. That was vitally important, as the Tour didn't open with a short (less than 8km) prologue, but a full-fledged time trial of 16.5km (just over 10 miles). In such a distance, strong time trialists like Armstrong, Ullrich, Alex Zülle, Abraham Olano and Laurent Jalabert could gain as much as two minutes on other race contenders like Pantani and Fernando Escartin—whose specialty is climbing.

Futuroscope is a theme park near Poitiers, in the plains of west France. To avoid reaching the mountains too early, the organizers decided to open the race with a big clockwise loop, so that by the end of stage 7, the Tour would be at Limoges—only a two-hour drive from Poitiers! This meant that all the stages of this opening week would be affected by winds from the nearby Atlantic Ocean.

After the Futuroscope time trial came two flat stages for the sprinters: to Loudun and Nantes. The expected battle between fast finishers Mario Cipollini and Tom Steels would not take place as Cipollini had withdrawn from the Tour—due to a head-first crash in training a couple of weeks before the start.

The most difficult challenge of the opening week came on day 4: a 70km team time trial along the windswept roads beside the Loire Estuary, from Nantes to St. Nazaire. There were unlikely to be big time gaps between the top teams on this stage. Both Armstrong's U.S. Postal Service squad and Ullrich's Telekom team looked like being among the fastest in the TTT, as did Olano's and Jalabert's ONCE-Deutsche Bank formation. But Pantani's Mercatone Uno-Albacom, Zülle's Banesto and Escartin's Kelme-Costa Blanca teams would likely struggle. Each team's stage time (based on its fifth rider across the line) would be added to riders' individual time overall, so Pantani and Escartin could have overall time deficits as big as five or six minutes after just four days of racing.

After this intense opening came five stages, all of around 200km, and all favoring the sprinters: at Vitré, Tours (that annually hosts the Paris-Tours classic), Limoges (where Lance Armstrong won a stage in 1995), Villeneuve-sur-Lot and Dax. There was no finish at Bordeaux, which is usually the sprinters' favorite stage.

The climbers wouldn't get a chance to regain any time until the race reached the Pyrénées, starting with the stage 10 finish at Hautacam.

It looked like being just the sort of opening week that the crowds would be looking for: two time trials, a few spectacular sprints, and probably a host of long breakaways—depending on which way the wind was blowing. It would also, most likely, see the emergence of some unexpected new names....

STAGE 1

Futuroscope TT • July 1

Millar Time

HE'S A STRAPPING SIX-FOOT-THREE, WITH BRITISH GOOD LOOKS, AN ENGLISH PREP-SCHOOL ACCENT, tan face, thick black eyebrows and perfect white teeth that often flash a mischievous smile. He doesn't act like a potential superstar cyclist, but David Millar started this, his first Tour de France, like someone who's going somewhere—fast—in the new millennium. Only 23, his speed in the opening day time trial was such that even an impressive Lance Armstrong could get no closer than two seconds to the Brit's time of 19:03 for the 16.5km.

Millar's near-52 kph effort created a sensation when his time was announced, as his huge finishing effort took him hurtling through the throng of cameramen, reporters and team soigneurs beyond the line.

The athletic Cofidis rider came to a halt at the end of the barriers, in a post-effort daze. He let his red aluminum MBK time-trial bike drop to the street, and flopped down in a corner. TV cameras focused on him from all angles; there was even one directly above his head, pointing vertically down.

Millar propped himself up against the metal barrier, screwing up his eyes as they filled with salty perspiration. His mouth wide open, gasping for air, the Scottish rider slowly regained his composure. A team soigneur wiped his face and put a red Coca-Cola print towel around his neck. That's as much comfort as he would get for the next 10 minutes.

For a young man suddenly thrust into a media maelstrom, Millar handled himself with typical British phlegm. When asked if he thought his time was good enough to take the yellow jersey, he calmly replied, "I don't know about that." He knew there were still 31 riders to come, including Armstrong and all the other Tour favorites.

The reporters persisted: Think your time will stick?

"No ... I just know that it's a good start for the white jersey," Millar understated, referring to the separate competition for riders 25 and under. "If something else happens, then that's a pleasant surprise."

He would know within half an hour....

That wasn't long to wait at the end of a day that had begun before breakfast with blood tests for all 180 riders. Three of those men tested above the 50-percent hematocrit limit, giving the Tour the sullied start it was seeking to avoid. Fortunately, that morning story would be replaced with evening glory for a young man called David. But could he defeat the Goliaths?

Already his sensational time had cut 13 seconds from the stage-leading 19:16 of ONCE-Deutsche Bank's Laurent Jalabert—who had displaced U.S. Postal's Viatcheslav Ekimov from the early lead. Now, the Tour's big guns would be firing: Jan Ullrich (starting at 7:08 p.m.), Abraham Olano (7:09), Michele Bartoli (7:11), Alex Zülle (7:13) and Armstrong (7:14).

Fred's diary
June 27
Varese, Italy

Seeing as this is my first Tour and my first journal entry, I will introduce myself. This is my fifth year riding as a professional. I currently ride for the Italian Mapei team—ranked No. 1 in the world for three years running.

This year has been a turning point in my career. In the past few months I have won seven races: five in Europe, and two in the United States, including the USPRO Championship in Philadelphia, on June 4. The lead-up to the championship race was quite unusual, as I was scheduled to ride the Giro d'Italia—which runs 23 days, the last day being the day of the race in Philadelphia. In the weeks preceding the Giro, my form began to improve tremendously; I won four races in just a few weeks.

But while I was excited to have been selected for the Giro team, my thoughts kept returning to the USPRO Championship race. I figured I was on a roll, and perhaps this was the year I was going to pull off the big win. After consulting with my team, the decision was made that I would race for the stars-and-stripes jersey in Philly.

The USPRO Championship race is the last of four races sponsored by First Union. I placed third in Lancaster, the first race of the series—and the same race I had won as an amateur, back in 1996, becoming the first American to win this event. I placed eighth in the second race of the series, but was feeling better and better each day.

The third race in Trenton, New Jersey, was a hot one—over 90 degrees! The race was aggressive and fast, a true sprinters' race. I was able to get

into the winning break, albeit without any teammates. I would have to fend for myself at the finish line. With several Mercury and U.S. Postal riders represented in the break, I was able to play off these teams' efforts in setting up their sprinters for the win. Mercury took the lead coming into the last mile. I knew if I wanted to win the race, I had to position myself within the Mercury lead-out. With 500 meters to go, I got into position. It all came down to a final surge for the line—a surge that would earn me a victory. I was now ready for the big one.

The way the championship race in Philly works is that the first American to cross the line, whether he is the winner of the race or not, is deemed the U.S. professional champion. The day of the race, I was fairly relaxed. I was feeling confident and knew my team was strong. We were ready.

My team rode a great race. They were able to keep me out of trouble for most of the day, allowing me to be fresh for the finish. By the last lap, there was a break of seven riders. I decided to attack up the last climb (known as the Manayunk Wall), hoping to get away from the other Americans. I made it across to the break. As I guessed would happen, U.S. Postal's George Hincapie joined the break shortly thereafter. George won this event two years ago, and was more than capable of winning it again. At this point, I knew the race for the jersey was between George and myself.

I was focused on winning the championship, and not necessarily the race. The non-American riders often play off the dueling Americans by constantly attacking at the end of the race. Such was the tactic of Henk Vogels, who after two other attempts, launched his third and final attack to take the victory, leaving the race for the jersey to

(to page 80)

A first indication of their relative strengths came on a Cat. 4 hill that climbed a modest 122 feet in a kilometer. By the top, 3.7km into the time trial, Armstrong was fastest in 4:19, four seconds ahead of Jalabert, Millar and Ullrich, with Bartoli a further second back.

The course then headed out into the Poitou plain, a mixture of small vineyards and fields of wheat, sunflowers and barley. The first part was into a gusting westerly wind, and Armstrong later said that he found this stretch much harder than he expected. The Texan probably experienced slightly stronger head winds than Millar, because by the halfway check, 8km from the finish, Millar was fastest—three seconds ahead of Armstrong, six ahead of Jalabert and seven ahead of Ullrich.

Armstrong wasn't spent though, and after turning left, he looked as strong as he did a year ago, when winning the much longer Futuroscope TT: spinning his 55x11 at a phenomenal cadence (up to 120 rpm), his upper body slightly rocking, his eyes focused on the smooth road unwinding before him.

The effort seemed to be working and with about 4km left, Armstrong had pulled ahead of Millar by one second. That gap remained when Armstrong made the final turn, exactly a kilometer from the line.

Waiting in the stands with his mother Avril, Millar could now only hope and pray. He was looking at a TV monitor, showing Armstrong heading for the line, a read-out of his time against Millar's on the screen.

When time ran out for the defending champion and Armstrong was still 30 meters from the line, Millar put his head in his hands and cried. British reserve be damned! His emotions had finally caught up with him. The stage was his ... and the yellow jersey.

For Armstrong, second place was an initial disappointment, but a longer-term plus. Instead of having to see his troops defending the yellow jersey from the get-go, it would be Cofidis that would have that responsibility, while the Postal riders would be able to

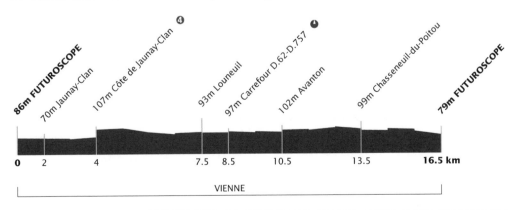

be battled from behind. At the line, I was able to outsprint George for the U.S. pro title.

This win had been a personal goal of mine for several years, as I had placed second in national championship races five different times—including two times at the pro championships. Now my jersey finally bears the stars and stripes.... Ten days after winning the championship, I showed off my new jersey with a win in the second stage of the Tour of Switzerland. Oh, how sweet it is!

I am proud to wear this jersey in the Tour de France, which will be the hardest racing weeks of my cycling career to date.

# # #

Tyler's Diary
June 30
Poitiers

It's odd being back at Futuroscope. A huge wave of memories and emotions fell over me as we drove through the entrance of this space-age theme park on Wednesday. It was a case of visual déjà-vu, that kind of feeling that makes you ask: Were we here a year ago or yesterday? To add to that feeling, we're even staying in the same hotel as last year. And when we looked over the start and finish areas—you guessed it—they're carbon copies of '99. So to keep in sync with our familiar surroundings, we've even kept our goal the same: Keep Lance in yellow. And we know this will only be possible if we apply the same kind of teamwork as the last time around.... All in all, my teammates and I are on the eve of the opportunity to relive a dream—the same dream we've replayed in our heads a million times since July 1999.

This will be the fourth consecutive Tour de France contested by the U.S. Postal team. I've been lucky enough to be named to all four teams and can tell you that a ton has changed since 1997. In a very short period, this team has gone from feeling just happy to be here … to defending the title of the Tour de France champion. And it's been an epic journey. We started out with a couple of rented campers and a small handful of supporters. Now we're traveling in style with a full-scale fleet that includes trucks, buses, sponsors and press. I don't want to use the Cinderella analogy here, but it has been quite a transformation.

Yesterday, we were invited to see an IMAX movie at the Futuroscope theater. The park wanted to film us watching one of their movies. I hope no one I know sees this video of us, because I was probably looking kind of sick for half of it. It was the first time I had ever been asked to wear a seat belt in a movie theater. And to make matters worse, each of us had to wear a pair of 3-D goggles. When the film finally began, they proceeded to take us on a journey to the underwater world of Atlantis. The seats were programmed to physically move with every jerk and turn of the visuals on screen. All I could think of was my last ride on a roller coaster, which was not all that pleasant. It was the toughest four-and-a-half minutes of my entire day.

Our team suffered a bit of a setback yesterday, as it was decided that Christian Vande Velde will not ride the Tour. He is suffering from an infection, which the doctors think started with a spider bite. He had worked hard all year toward the Tour, and he fought back like a madman from a broken collarbone he suffered in May to make the team. We're going to miss him, for sure. Steffan Kjaergaard will be his replacement. It will be his first Tour.

ride themselves in before stage 4's team time trial.

Furthermore, Armstrong had defeated Ullrich by 12 seconds, Zülle by 18, Olano by 37 and Bartoli by 53. As for the other expected contenders, Bobby Julich was 1:15 back (in 55th), Michael Boogerd at 1:23, Richard Virenque at 1:29, Fernando Escartin at 1:30 … and Marco Pantani at 2:14. In this mountainous Tour, those gaps may not mean much; but, for now, Armstrong was just where he wanted to be.

Vande Velde: Along Came a Spider

It was just a spider bite, but it was enough to keep Christian Vande Velde out of the Tour de France.

Asleep in his apartment in Spain, the 24-year-old U.S. Postal Service rider woke up in the middle of the night, a few days before the start of the Tour, and felt what was probably an insect bite. At first, it wasn't a problem, even though it was in a bad location.

"Right where I sit on the bike, right under the tailbone," Vande Velde said on the eve of the Tour. "Still, I went ahead and rode for about five hours the next day. Maybe if I hadn't done that, I'd be all right, but it got infected, I got sick and now I'm on antibiotics."

Vande Velde, team director Johann Bruyneel and general manager Mark Gorski consulted with a doctor and decided that the bite wasn't healing quickly. Vande Velde was out.

Steffen Kjaergaard was named to take Vande Velde's place on the team. The easy-going 27-year-old Norwegian, in his fifth year as a professional, is a former national time trial champion who has proven himself in shorter stage races, and was gearing up for the Tour for most of the early season. He was called up on Thursday, arrived in France on Friday, and rode the time trial on Saturday, finishing about a minute down on winner David Millar.

The decision was especially tough for Vande Velde since he had just struggled back from breaking his collarbone in late May.

"I didn't fool around from the time I broke my collarbone, straight to here, I was totally dedicated to coming back," Vande Velde said. "I was lifting, riding the Computrainer and everything I could to get me ready for it and I was going good in Catalonia—obviously, since they put me on the [Tour] team right away."

Sitting in front of the team bus a few hours before the team presentation at Futuroscope, Vande Velde said he was coming to terms with "a really tough decision."

"It would be hard to leave if I was all bright-eyed and bushy tailed and ready to ride, but still it really hit home when Steffen showed up," he said. "With everyone going to the team presentation and all; I just remember what it was like last year and how excited I was and how, this year, I don't feel like I'm even part of the show. It's weird."

A few hours later Vande Velde grabbed a flight home to Boulder, Colorado, to start getting ready for the rest of the season.

"I mean, the Olympics are still going on," he said.

Tyler's diary
July 1
Poitiers

I'll humbly admit that I was nervous prior to the start today. We've been cooped up in our little hotel rooms for almost a week, thinking and talking about nothing else except the job at hand. Too much discussion can get your mind racing all over the place, so I'm glad to be finished with the pre-race speculation and on with the show.

I have a mixed history with the Tour de France opener-prologues, and short, flat time trials aren't always an opportunity for me. My strengths are more suited to technical courses and longer distances.

Today, I left the start house at 5:54 p.m., a little more than halfway through the start list. It had been raining on and off from about noon, but fortunately, nothing torrential. My biggest concern was the wind. Johan [Bruyneel] later informed me that I looked like I was being blown all over the place. I guess I was being pushed around, perhaps even weaving a bit. I finished ninth, and while it wasn't the most spectacular ride of my life, I thought it was a fine showing, under the circumstances…. Although we were a little disappointed to see Lance edged out for the win, it was great to see a guy like David Millar do so well. Not bad for the first day of his first Tour. Britain has a new hero tonight, for sure.

I was able to get fitted for my new Trek TT bike on Thursday. Our team's mechanic, Geoff Brown, met me out by the truck bright and early that morning so we could get my position right. Geoff and I have been working together for a long time, and I owe him a great deal for taking such good care of my machines. The new frame felt great, right from the get-go. I was looking forward to testing it out during the stage today—it's the lightest bike I've ever ridden. Which, come to think of it, may have worked against me. Maybe I'll request a lead frame for the next windy TT— just kidding.

From the Rumor Mill: Word around the dinner tables last night was that Crédit Agricole's New Zealander, Chris Jenner, was called up to replace Anthony Langella on their Tour team. Turns out Jenner thought he was on hiatus after being left off the initial Tour roster. Story has it, he went home after the Route du Sud, put his bike in the closet, hit the pool and indulged in a few non-regime dinners. Needless to say, he wasn't on the line this afternoon. If this is a true story, then I do feel bad for the guy. I know he was looking forward to riding the Tour.

Before the start of the race, we visited the Tour de France medical staff for our physicals. For some reason, the Tour organizers like to mix the medical checkup with a little race promotion. Each rider is given a cardiogram, weighed, and has his height taken. Next, they ask us a few questions, like: How many Tours have you started and how many have you finished? Then every rider has to face a French television camera and state the findings of this inquiry and give a few anecdotes, perhaps describing their favorite hobby. In addition, they ask the riders to announce which stage they would like to win. I just laughed and said, "Win? I've gotta take care of this guy," while pointing at Lance.

So was Millar…. Making the most of his moment in the spotlight, the happy-go-lucky Scotsman told the British TV reporter: "My friends and sister will be at a party watching this tonight—they'll all be drunk!"

It may have been Millar time, but for once, his partying would have to wait. He had a jersey to defend.

David Millar: Six Countries and Counting

This Tour has drawn riders from 25 countries around the world. Sometimes it seems as though David Millar has lived in all of them.

He was born on the Mediterranean island of Malta in January 1977, the first son of a Scottish fighter plot in the Royal Air Force and his English wife. The family soon moved to northeast Scotland, where Millar senior was based at the Kinloss airfield, and young David attended the local Forres Primary School. After his parents split in the late-1980s, David at first chose to live with his mother and sister in the countryside north of London. Then he decided to move to Hong Kong, where his father became a commercial pilot for Cathay Pacific.

Millar thinks of Hong Kong as his home and the place he will eventually return to live for good. It was there, in a city now part of mainland China, that Millar learned to race a bike—first BMX, then mountain bikes. Then, after graduating from an English high school in Hong Kong, he lived for a while in Ireland, where another Scottish native, Alisdair MacLellan—who went to the same Forres Primary School as Millar ("but a generation earlier")—was the cycling coach for the Irish national squad.

MacLellan was in Futuroscope July 1 to see his one-time charge take the opening time trial. He stood with a group of friends and Millar's mother Avril, all clad in black David Millar Supporters Club T-shirts. MacLellan didn't take any credit, though, for their man's success. He explained how Millar went to northern France in 1995 to race as an 18-year-old as the first beneficiary of a scholarship from the David Rayner fund—set up in memory of the British pro racer killed in a fight outside an English barroom in late 1994.

In France, Millar's racing talents were recognized by Martial Gayant, a former teammate of coaching guru Cyrille Guimard. With Guimard starting the Cofidis team in 1997, Millar received Gayant's recommendation—and the nascent French team landed a gem.

"Cofidis is due all the credit," said MacLellan. "They've looked after him, and not over-

Tyler' diary
July 2
Loudun

The last thing my wife said to me this morning was, "Stay up front and stay out of trouble." Easier said than done, I guess.

I can't explain my track record at the Tour, in regard to crashing. Today was just another one of those times when I was in the wrong place at the wrong time. The guys up front locked it up for some reason, which triggered a domino effect. By the time the wave of breaking reached the area around me, guys were coming to a full stop. Needless to say, when you go from 60 kph to a complete stop, there's going to be some carnage. Luckily, it wasn't a major deal. My elbow and knee are a little scraped up, but other than that I'm fine. This kind of thing is to be expected early on in the Tour. In fact, these can be the most difficult—and the most decisive—stages of the race. Remember stage 2 last year?

Thankfully, I didn't lose any time today. Frankie [Andreu] waited for me to get back on my bike and helped me regain contact with the peloton. I guess I was a little shaken up, because it took me almost the rest of the race to get back in a groove. Or maybe it was the head wind....

Our team was in first place overall this morning, due to a decent collective showing during stage 1. Before each stage, they bring the highest-ranked team onto a podium in the start area and present them with miniature stuffed lions and medals. We achieved this honor during a few stages last year, and more than once, a couple of us started the race with Tour medals in the back pockets of our jerseys. It doesn't take long to figure out they're there—because they weigh a ton.

Hamilton had his "usual" early crash.

Johan had quite a collection of these things in the team car last year.

TV station France 3 had a funny clip of David Millar running today. They taped him going to bed in his yellow jersey last night. He's a pretty funny guy, and evidently a good sport as well. There aren't many other riders who would poke fun at themselves on national television.

Speaking of France 3, we got into a bit of skirmish with some folks from this network the other day. [They provide live coverage of the Tour de France for the entire country of France.] While out training together on Friday, a France 3 car came really close to taking our whole group down. We went chasing after it to let the driver know that brushing up to us wasn't a cool thing to do. A short but heated exchange followed. And that night, during their sports update, the anchorman reported that all the teams looked fit and ready for the Tour—except for the U.S. Postal team which looked "strange." It turns out one of the network's head honchos was in the car that we "expressed our feelings" to. I wonder what people thought when they heard the report....

raced him. And now he has Tony Rominger as his mentor. Cofidis knows his potential, and that's why they've signed him to a long-term contract [through the end of 2003]."

Millar has a reputation for being a partygoer, and celebrating each New Year's in a different country. But after a disappointing 1999 season, the 23-year-old rider decided he needed to get serious. He stayed in England for the millennium, and went training. And he has since kept up a strict regime that has seen him lose weight.

"He's the lightest he's ever been," said MacLellan. Which means the six-foot-three Millar is less than the 158 pounds quoted in his team manual. Combine that with the speed and strength he showed in the Tour's opening time trial and Millar should someday be a force in the mountains.

He's still learning, of course, but there is confidence in the growing predictions that this Millar—who's unrelated to the Scottish climber of the 1980s, Robert Millar—will one day become the first Brit (or whatever other nationality he can claim) to win the Tour.

In the meantime, he has a relaxed, wait-and-see attitude. Or, as former coach MacLellan put it: "David's so laid-back, he's almost horizontal."

STAGE 2
Futuroscope–Loudun • July 2

Return to Go

ANYONE WHO HAS EVER PLAYED A BOARD NAME LIKE CHUTES AND LADDERS KNOWS THE FRUSTRATION of landing on a square that orders you to "Return to Go." Well, the opening road stage of this Tour was just like that. One of those Yogi Berra déjà-vu-all-over-again times. Another Groundhog Day—the sort of day you want to get over with and move on....

This second stage started in the colorless confines of Futuroscope, where the teams had now been holed up for days, staying in hotels with names like Campanile, Frantour, Ibis, Mercure and Météor. This was getting old, already. The theme park's motley collection of futuristic buildings was also the last major halt of the 1999 Tour, which made this year's sojourn seem even longer.

So it was great to get on the road again, and be out in the beautiful French countryside, to see shoals of French families waiting for the race in prime picnic spots, on the looping 194km course around the Vienne region. The riders seemed relieved, too, because they began the stage at a very friendly 29.6 kph (18.5 mph), as if on a pleasant spin in the country.

Fred's diary
July 2
Loudun

My first Tour de France hasn't started like I wanted it to, but we ended up with a win anyway. I wanted to be there leading out Tom Steels for his stage win today, but when you're not feeling great, it's hard to focus on the race. I asked my soigneur what it could have been, and he said you should never drink a glucose drink if it's hot. The drink was in my back cage and it was all I had left—I'd been drinking fresh bottles all day from my front cage. It tasted strange, but I figured it was like that because it was warm.

This happened just before the big rollers with about 60km to go; and all the pain made everything hard to do. I was trying to move up, but I just seemed to be going backwards. I went up to Lance and said, "For the last 100 kilometers we've been flying like it's the final sprint." Lance just said, "It's normally like this from the start." Luckily, we started off *piano*—I was pleased about that.

Near the end, I tried to move up in the peloton. But there was a head wind and nowhere to go: It was like hitting a brick wall of riders. Finally, in the last 4 or 5 kilometers, I was getting near to the front again. Then there were some near-crashes. At one point there was nowhere to go but into a field. After that, there was no chance of me getting back to the front.

I was a little disappointed that I wasn't able to support like I wanted to do. But Tom [Steels] thanked me anyway, for helping him earlier—

when I was riding in front of him protecting him from the wind and making sure he was okay. "We still have plenty of days," he said. But I wanted to be in the middle of the whole thing.

We were all a bit surprised that Tom won. Three days before, he had a fever of 104 degrees. He didn't train for two days before the start. But now that he's got the confidence, he'll be hard to beat.

At the team meeting this morning, we discussed everyone's role for the whole race, everything from the G.C. riders to the sprint part of the team. It was decided that Chann, Beltran and Nardello would be holding back, keeping them for the second two weeks. Bartoli and Bettini would be more like freelancers, to see how they were going in the next couple of days. For today, the plan was to give Tom a full-team leadout, with even Bartoli, Bettini and Chann in the line. We only got it going about 50 percent, though.

At dinner tonight we celebrated like we always do. We do this shout, starting real quiet and then getting louder and louder. And we had champagne. Patrick [Léfeverè], our manager, said we need to get a champagne sponsor, we have so many wins…. It was hard to celebrate because of the soccer: the European championship final between Italy and France. The Italians kept on getting up to check on the score.

I hope I'm feeling better tomorrow.

That benign pace changed very quickly when, after 36km, Rabobank's Erik Dekker—10th in the stage 1 time trial, 36 seconds down on Millar—made a sudden attack. He was chased and joined by the familiar figure of Lotto-Adecco's Jacky Durand, and the race was on!

After only 13km together, this duo had gained four minutes, and they continued at a remarkable 46-kph pace for the next two hours. That forced Millar's Cofidis team to pull the peloton out of its collective stupor and ride a debilitating team time trial on a course that became progressively more difficult—long rolling hills and a strong head wind awaited them in the last 55km.

Dekker's plan was to collect as many bonus seconds as he could at the three intermediate sprints—which he did, taking the maximum 18 seconds. But the effort cost him a much bigger payment. The 29-year-old Dutchman cramped up when the field caught him, and by the finish he had lost almost 15 minutes.

Durand hung out front for a little longer, until he too was swept up, with 46km remaining. It was now clear that the stage would end in a sprint. But what sort of sprint?

Without Saeco's Mario Cipollini and his famous red guard, the sprints in this opening week were sure to be a lot different than they had been in recent years. That was proven on this second stage, when no one team took control of the finale into Loudun, and the sprint became a much more even *mano-a-mano* contest.

In fact, the Cofidis team was still setting tempo with only 6km to go. That's in sharp contrast to the tactics adopted by Cipollini's men, who would have taken charge of the pace with 20km or even 30km remaining.

It took an attack from Crédit Agricole's Jens Voigt and Saeco's Salvatore Commesso to finally derail the Cofidis train. And that derailment goaded Erik Zabel's Telekom squad into action, to chase down the two aggressors. That done, only 4km of the stage remained—but Telekom didn't continue its effort. Instead, sprinters like Zabel, Tom

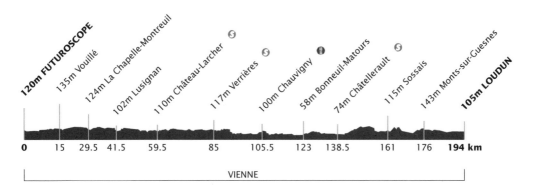

VIENNE

Steels of Mapei-Quick Step, Robbie McEwen of Farm Frites and Marcel Wüst of Festina each had one or two teammates leading them into the final kilometer. It was a situation that allowed opportunists such as Stuart O'Grady of Crédit Agricole, Romans Vainsteins of Vini Caldirola and Dario Pieri of Saeco to be competitive up the final straightaway.

Steels—recovering from the high fever he suffered three days before the Tour—was the favorite for the win, but he almost didn't make it. Just as he began his final kick for the line in the with-the-wind sprint, Telekom lead-out man Gian Matteo Fagnini swung far left, forcing Steels to stop pedaling for a moment and swerve left, before picking up his effort 100 meters out. The big Belgian then had to dig deep to catch the speeding Zabel, and even when he passed the German and raised his arms in victory, it seemed as if he may have celebrated too soon.

On his right, beyond Zabel, Aussie fastmen O'Grady and McEwen had been diving for the gap by the barriers. McEwen missed out when he was hit by a spectator's out-stretched hand, and O'Grady got the slot. The Adelaide rider came hurtling though, to throw his bike at the line in a typical trackman's tactic. The effort took him past Zabel, but O'Grady's front wheel was still a rim-width behind Steels's at the line.

Exciting stuff. Too bad that after dusting themselves down, donning their sweats and climbing into their team buses, all the riders had to go back to their hotels in Futuroscope.

Now, that's what they mean when they say "Return to Go." At least it's better than that Monopoly square called "Go to Jail." Or is it?

STAGE 3
Loudun–Nantes • July 3

Steels Wheels in Again

AT THE RATE HE IS STEAMROLLERING THE WORLD'S BEST SPRINTERS, TOM STEELS, ONLY 28, HAS A chance of becoming one of the top stage winners in Tour de France history. At Nantes, one day before the long-awaited team time trial, Steels collected his ninth Tour stage win: two so far this year; three in 1999; and four in '98. And that total would probably have been bigger if Steels hadn't been thrown out of the race during his Tour debut in 1997: At the height of the sprint into Marennes on stage 6, Steels threw a water bottle at French sprinter Frédéric Moncassin. The act was one of frustration rather than intimidation, when Steels felt that Moncassin had moved across the road into the Belgian's sprinting line. The judges disagreed with Steels and disqualified him.

Steels is now much more mature. Winning—especially surrounded by riders from his No. 1 team Mapei-Quick Step—breeds confidence. As he said before this Tour started: "When you win a stage, the hardest part is over. The other wins generally follow much easier."

Such was the case on this second stage from Loudun to Nantes, where the team's strategy worked to perfection. Through the final kilometer, American champion Fred Rodriguez started the Mapei leadout, followed by Dutchman Max Van Heeswijk—Steels's roommate—with Italian Stefano Zanini providing the last kick before the sprint.

The stage ended in a field sprint because Millar's Cofidis team again set a perfect tempo—fast enough to catch two breakaway riders (German Jens Voigt of Crédit Agricole and Dane Michael Blaudzun of MemoryCard-Jack & Jones), who had a maximum lead of 6:10 halfway through the 161.5km stage; and just fast enough to prevent any surprise breakaways in the technical run-in.

Some riders claimed that the finale was not just technical, but dangerous. The last 20km took the 177-strong pack along some winding country roads, and then down narrow suburban streets, replete with frequent traffic islands and awkward turns. It was on a section that narrowed suddenly that two riders touched wheels and fell near the head of the pack. Others went down and several riders were held up, including Polti's Dutch sprinter Jeroen Blijlevens.

Race leader Millar was also headed toward the pileup, and had a choice: fall on the riders or hit the hay bales. He chose the softer alternative. "I panicked a little," Millar said, "and I took a while to put my chain back on." But the Cofidis rider soon joined the awaiting Massimiliano Lelli—his friend and roommate—and they chased back to the end of the

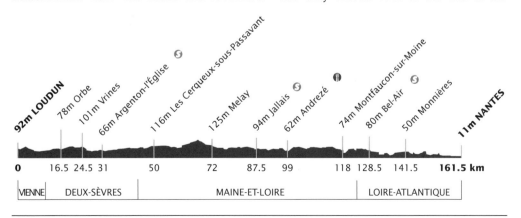

Chann's diary
July 3
Nantes

Today went exactly according to plan. All our team had to do was repeat yesterday's victory. Easier said than done, but it worked. Steels came through again. Freddy, Max [Van Heeswijk] and ZaZa [Stefano Zanini] did the last 2km at 65-70 kph, and none of the big-boy sprinters could even mess with them. If we keep this up, our team bonus pool is going to have to be refilled by the time this Tour is over....

I'm just taking it day by day, right now, considering that this is my first Tour. Everything seems pretty much like the rest of the three-week races that I have done—except that the Tour has much better media coverage, and seems to be more exciting for everyone.

Tomorrow is our team time trial, and Mapei has offered us a bonus of $100,000 if we win. We'll have to wait and see if the team has the power; if we do, maybe we can be the dark-horse team that pulls it off.

Speaking of horses, did you see Freddy doing the leadout? He was going from 800 meters out to 450 at maximum speed, but it looked like he was riding a horse. He did the whole leadout on his tops, which is quite unusual in the last kilometer of a race. We were all making fun of him, calling him "The Cowboy."

It's time for some shut-eye now, so take care, ya'll.

strung-out peloton in less than a kilometer.

The yellow jersey had been saved—at least for another day—although the finish-line judges almost took it away.

Why? Well, after Rodriguez stopped his lead-out effort and pulled off to the side, a gap was left between the first 25 riders and the rest of the peloton. According to the rules, when the gap between the last rider in a group and the first rider of the next group is more than one second, the groups are given separate times. In this case, the sprint between Steels, Wüst and Zabel was so intense that the time difference between stage winner Steels and 27th-placed Rodriguez was nine seconds. When applied to overall times, that deficit left Millar still four seconds ahead of Armstrong (who was also in the main pack); but Jalabert and Ullrich (both in the first group) moved to within six and seven seconds respectively of the yellow jersey.

As for the sprinters' green-jersey competition, Steels's second win put him in a 16-point lead over O'Grady, with Zabel and Wüst another couple of points adrift.

It's not just power that brings Steels his successes. He is a former track racer—the one-kilometer time trial was his specialty—and he says, "I like to feel the pedals moving fast." That's why he has only a 52-tooth big chainring, a tooth less than most of his rivals.

Using a smaller gear for his finishing efforts should mean that Steels's wheels will still be spinning as fast in four or five years' time. On the all-time Tour de France stage-win list, he is already level with that famed sprinter of the 1990s, Djamolidin Abdujaparov, and only three behind Cipollini. Beyond them, Freddy Maertens in the 1970s and '80s had 15 wins, while the sprinter with the highest number of victories remains Frenchman André Darrigade—who took 22 bouquets in 11 Tour starts. That could be a goal for Steels. Certainly not the all-time stage-win haul of 34 held by Eddy Merckx.

TTT Time Tomorrow

Ever since the 2000 Tour de France route was announced last October, the buzz had been that the team time trial would be the key stage of this opening week. We were about to find out if that was going to be true, as on Tuesday afternoon the 20 teams in the Tour would race separately over an almost flat 70km course between Nantes and St. Nazaire.

Each team's time would count toward the individual G.C. times of all the riders on that squad. So should, say, Marco Pantani's Mercatone Uno squad set a time three minutes slower than that of Lance Armstrong's U.S. Postal Service team, then Pantani would concede three minutes on overall time to Armstrong. And as the Italian climber had already dropped 2:14 to the American in the stage 1 time trial, he would be down by more than five minutes before even reaching the first mountain climb. That's why the TTT was so important.

The teams would start the TTT at five-minute intervals, in reverse order of the current team general classification, which meant that those with the strongest time trialists (based on the stage 1 results) were stacked at the end of the field. The last team to start would be U.S. Postal, giving Armstrong's men a distinct advantage—they would know what times had been set by all the others at the intermediate check points. Which meant they could base their tempo on that of the previous fastest squad.

Starting immediately ahead of Postal would be the ONCE-Deutsche Bank team of Laurent Jalabert and Abraham Olano, while Jan Ullrich's Telekom team would start three ahead of Postal. These three squads were the stage favorites, while strong performances were also expected from Mapei-Quick Step (with Italian Michele Bartoli and the Americans Chann McRae and Fred Rodriguez), and Crédit Agricole (also with two

Tyler's diary
July 3
Nantes

We can officially check off mission No. 1, as it has been sufficiently accomplished. Our primary goal was to get through stages 1 through 3 unscathed. We're heading into the team time trial the way we had hoped, with no one on the team having lost time due to crashes. Lets just hope things continue to go as planned.

The last 20km of today's stage was like a slalom course due to a succession of mini-islands, known as "road turtles," dividing the streets. To make matters worse, some of these islands weren't marked. Now I'm generally not one to get riled up and start complaining about stuff—but this is one instance where I think it's worth making a serious point. The Tour de France Society likes to lecture the riders again and again about being responsible. Yet, on days like today, they fail to hold up their end of the bargain. It was no surprise to anyone that today's stage would culminate with a sprint finish. Under these circumstances, I don't think it's unreasonable to expect a clear path to the line. The sport is dangerous enough. We don't need to navigate an obstacle course after 160km in the saddle. Marking an island is as simple as asking a cop to stand in the road and wave a flag. And I've even seen some finish towns go to the extreme measure of digging islands up and re-paving the road for safety's sake. Of all the things considered in preparation for a Tour finish, safety should be priority one. *Compris?*

On a lighter note, France won the Euro 2000 soccer tournament last night against Italy. I can't tell you how important a championship like this is for the Europeans. It's as if national pride is on line with every game. France kicked in a tying goal with 12 seconds to go, and then managed to wrap up the win in overtime. We missed out on much of the hoopla, as we returned to our hotel rooms at Futuroscope for one more night. We're pretty isolated here—but we could see on the television that the Champs-Elysées was jampacked with screaming fans. My wife even said that our somewhat comatose town of Villefranche was whooping it up with fireworks, horn honking and lots of cheering.

To give you an idea how seriously the French take their favorite sports: One of the main stories being covered in the cycling press is an argument that the Tour de France organizers are not loyal enough to their own countrymen. Only one in five riders at this year's Tour is French. And it's the strong opinion of the locals here that there were not enough French teams selected during the "wild card" phase of the qualification process. We'll see how this effects things next year.

Americans, Bobby Julich and Jonathan Vaughters).

Vaughters said Monday that he didn't think that the time differences between the top teams would be huge, and that the hype over the stage was a little out of whack with the truth. However, he did concede that some of the weaker teams could lose big-time. At greatest risk, perhaps, was 1999's third-place Tour finisher Fernando Escartin, whose Kelme-Costa Blanca team was packed with lightly built climbers—a combination that could see them losing maybe five minutes to the top team.

Postal was one of the few teams that had reconnoitered the course. Talking Monday, one of the American team's strongest men for the TTT, George Hincapie, said, "The course is mostly long straights, except at the end, when it gets technical coming into the finish. The bridge is going to be the hardest (part)." Hincapie was referring to the Pont de St. Nazaire, which climbs almost 300 feet in less than 2km, crossing the Loire River estuary 11km from the finish. If there was a wind blowing from the nearby Atlantic Ocean—and one was forecast—then the exposed bridge crossing would cause even more problems than just its climb.

None of the teams had contested a TTT this long since the 1995 Tour, although much shorter TTTs in the recent Tour of Switzerland and Tour of Catalonia gave some of the squads a dress rehearsal.

Of all the likely outcomes, the one that seemed most certain was that the current race leader David Millar would lose the yellow jersey. His Cofidis team had ridden the equivalent of two TTTs in the previous two stages, and its members would have a hard time staying within two minutes of the winner.

These were the start times (all times French):

2:25 PM	Polti (Virenque)
2:30 PM	La Française des Jeux
2:35 PM	Bonjour
2:40 PM	MemoryCard-Jack & Jones
2:45 PM	Saeco-Valli & Valli (Dufaux)
2:50 PM	Lotto-Adecco
2:55 PM	Farm Frites
3:00 PM	Kelme-Costa Blanca (Escartin, Heras)
3:05 PM	Vini Caldirola-Sidermec
3:10 PM	Rabobank (Boogerd)
3:15 PM	Credit Agricole (Julich, Vaughters)

3:20 PM	AG2R
3:25 PM	Mercatone Uno-Albacom (Pantani)
3:30 PM	Banesto (Zülle, Mancebo)
3:35 PM	Mapei-Quick Step (Bartoli, McRae)
3:40 PM	Cofidis (Millar, Vandenbroucke)
3:45 PM	Telekom (Ullrich)
3:50 PM	Festina (Beloki, Moreau)
3:55 PM	ONCE-Deutsche Bank (Jalabert, Olano)
4:00 PM	U.S. Postal Service (Armstrong, Hamilton)

STAGE 4

Nantes–St. Nazaire • July 4

Bridge that Gap

ANYBODY WHO HAS RACED A BIKE KNOWS THE DESPERATE PANIC THAT GRIPS YOU WHEN YOU'VE BEEN gapped by a paceline and are frantically trying to close two bike-lengths … that suddenly seem like two miles. Now put yourself in the place of first Frankie Andreu, and then Tyler Hamilton, at around 5:14 p.m. on July 4, in this stage 4 team time trial, knowing that the fate of your team leader Armstrong depends on your survival.

First, Andreu.

Moments before his crisis, three U.S. Postal Service colleagues—Cédric Vasseur, Benoît Joachim and Steffen Kjaergaard—were dropped as the team, led by Armstrong, climbed the wide, open highway that led up the giant St. Nazaire Bridge. Armstrong later said the team might have made an error in using three-spoke front wheels, because several of his teammates were actually scared to get out of the saddle, unable to control the bike on the bridge in the vicious crosswinds.

At the top of the exposed bridge, 280 feet above the muddy waters of the mile-wide estuary of the Loire river, a sidewind was blowing from the left, gusting at 50 kph.

Suddenly, Andreu was two lengths adrift, desperately trying to close. He knew that the team's time—and consequently Armstrong's time—would be that of its fifth rider across the finish line. If Andreu didn't make it across, only five would be left—and if one of them had a problem in the remaining 11km, the team could lose a substantial margin, perhaps even enough to threaten Armstrong's defense of his Tour title.

A half-hour or so earlier, the mighty Mapei squad also had faced a crisis here. The team's Fred Rodriguez explained, "It was hard, because no one could hear the others (as) the wind was so loud. I dropped back off Nardello's wheel when I saw that we had a gap, but he didn't hear me. Other guys didn't hear each other, and we were all over the place."

Andreu, riding his ninth Tour, was having the same problem. He said he was shouting, "Slow down!" But the others didn't appear to hear Postal's most experienced man—who was on the 1995 Motorola team with Armstrong that finished second in that year's TTT. Now, he summoned up all the strength he had gleaned from previous brushes with extinction … and hitched back on the train just before it started rumbling down the north side of the bridge.

Crisis over? No.

"The descent was crazy," Andreu said. "The wind was so strong we couldn't control the bikes."

This was when Hamilton began to struggle. As he dropped to the back of the line after making a pull, he couldn't hold the wheel of the last rider. He later said, "A small gap, and it gets a little bigger…. I'd been doing a lot of hard efforts. To be honest, I don't have a whole lot of experience with team time trials."

He has a little more now.

After twice, three times digging deep to try to close, Hamilton got a little respite when teammate Ekimov, dropping from the front, slotted into the gap … and the American had just enough remaining power to pull himself back from the brink.

Before the bridge, Postal was 26 seconds down on the leading team, Jalabert's ONCE-Deutsche Bank, and 51 seconds ahead of Ullrich's Telekom. By the finish, after the six Posties regrouped, their lead over Telekom was only 0:40, while the deficit on ONCE grew to 0:46.

It could have been a whole lot worse, and the verdict was somewhat sweetened when

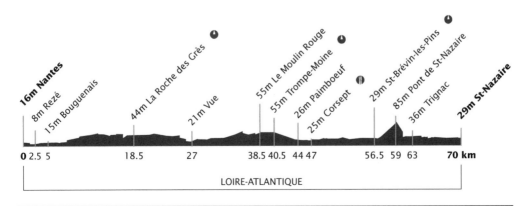

Tyler's diary
July 4
St. Nazaire

On June 27, we made a pre-Tour trip to Nantes to practice for the team time trial. Clearly, we weren't the only ones with this idea, as we saw a number of other teams doing the same thing that day. We were even a little amazed to see that the press was on hand to capture everyone's dress rehearsal…. It was difficult to find time to practice for an event like this when the team had two simultaneous schedules going throughout the spring season. Believe it or not, I hadn't seen some of my Tour teammates for months until that day. It was good for all of us to arrive a little early and get reacquainted.

By now, it seems like we've all been together for weeks. Tour time does not move at the same pace as reality. In fact, coming off the time clock of a grand tour is one of the toughest transitions of the season.

Today was pretty challenging. We faced a brutal head wind during this point-to-point 70km event. The team time trial is always a tricky thing. We were going pretty well, though, until we hit the long bridge—where the wind was whipping and we almost came unglued. Luckily, we kept it together and wound up with a second-place finish.

Some people may not understand the positives of our finish today, but personally, I'm thankful for two things: 1) No wheels touched during a wind gust as we crossed the bridge (i.e. no one crashed); 2) We aren't facing the daunting task of protecting the yellow jersey in week No. 1. All in all, the day worked out well, but I have to say, it took a lot of effort.

It's 6 p.m., I'm in the team car and I'm starving. Speaking of food, the French sports newspaper, *L'Equipe*, ran a feature the other day on our team's chef, Willie Balmat. He's been working the Tour for a number of years. Jim Ochowicz discovered him, so his initial travels were with the Motorola squad. Willie is 65 years old, but he acts like he's 35. He's a big-time jokester who loves to yuck it up with the riders. He worked for Swiss Air for 30 years, and his short stints with us are like freelance trips from his retirement. It's great having him around. His personality helps to keep morale high—but his cooking is what really keeps us going.

He makes the best pasta and risotto I've ever had. And if he can make those two dishes taste good to a cyclist, that's saying something. Most of the time, we are so sick of the stuff we can't even face it, let alone enjoy it. But Willie's dinners are always something to look forward to. One of his secrets is that he brings his own olive oil from Italy, and he makes it himself from olive tress on his vacation property in Tuscany. The other teams are definitely missing out.

Happy 4th to my American friends.

the judges penalized ONCE 20 seconds—because its directeur sportif Manolo Saiz drove closer than 10 meters to protect Marcos Serrano from the wind, when he almost dropped off the line at the start of the bridge crossing. Despite that penalty, Jalabert easily took the yellow jersey, as Cofidis was defeated by almost three minutes and Millar dropped to 24th overall.

The day's biggest gains were made by ONCE, Postal and Telekom—and Crédit Agricole, fourth on the stage, only six seconds behind Telekom. The French squad finished faster than even ONCE (see "Stage Analysis"), thanks to a masterly ride by Julich, who described the team's successful strategy over the bridge: "We just really stayed calm and easy, and I felt good.... We tried to do it with just one guy on the front—which was me—and we had to make sure that we didn't go too fast (going) up there. We had to make sure we didn't explode the whole team. We finished with seven, so it went perfect."

It was not so perfect for 1999 Tour runner-up Zülle, who seems to be jinxed by St. Nazaire. Almost a year ago to the day, the Swiss arrived in this port city six minutes behind the leaders after he had crashed on the Passage du Gois causeway, and lost the subsequent "team pursuit" that was led by ONCE and Postal. This year was no better for Zülle: His Banesto team could place only 12th in the TTT, four minutes down. So it seemed, once again, that his challenge was over before the Tour had barely gotten underway.

And if it hadn't have been for those tremendous fight-backs by Andreu and Hamilton, who knows where Armstrong's chances may have ended up....

The Tour, as always, was living up to its brutal reputation.

Zülle, Escartin the Big Losers

While the battle for the 2000 Tour de France had barely begun—less than a minute separated the top 10 after Tuesday's crucial team time trial—the race had already been lost it seemed by 1999 runner-up Alex Zülle and third-place finisher Fernando Escartin. With the race still five days away from the mountains, Zülle had a four-minute deficit on defending champion Lance Armstrong, while Escartin was a further two minutes behind.

Zülle and Escartin were the biggest victims of the TTT, due to the respective 11th and 13th places of their teams: Banesto and Kelme-Costa Blanca. As for Marco Pantani, his Mercatone Uno-Albacom squad did much better than expected, taking ninth on the stage—only one place and 16 seconds slower than the mighty Mapei! Even so, Pantani had so far accumulated a 5:26 deficit on new race leader Laurent Jalabert; and 5:02 and 4:19 respectively on the other race favorites, Armstrong and Jan Ullrich.

But given Pantani's explosive climbing ability and the abundance of long, steep climbs in the Tour's second week, those time gaps might not be an insurmountable barrier.

Between the TTT and the first mountain stage came five stages that would give the opportunists a chance to shine. None of the so-called sprinters' teams had shown enormous strength to date, while more than 100 riders were already more than five minutes down on overall time—which meant that Jalabert's ONCE team had a wider cushion than Cofidis had on the first road stages.

Stage Analysis

This chart shows exactly where the top teams gained or lost time on each of the five timed sections of the team time trial. Jalabert's ONCE squad averaged 49.074 kph for the 70km, its fastest stretch being the 22km second section, when it did 51.6 kph against a strong head-crosswind. Its slowest stretch was the 7km section that included the bridge crossing, at 43.8 kph.

The chart also shows how Armstrong's U.S. Postal Service squad remained a close second to ONCE on each of the first three sections, and then was the slowest of the top five on the remaining 13.5km to the finish. Other interesting points: Julich's Crédit Agricole team matched ONCE on the last part, and was actually the fastest on the final 6.4km on the technical loop in St. Nazaire.

| kilometers | 0-18.5 | 18.5-40.5 | 40.5-56.5 | 56.5-63.6 | 63.6-70 |
conditions	city	sidewind	head wind	bridge	city
ONCE	23:37	25:35	18:44	9:43	7:56
USPS	23:40	25:53	18:49	9:55	8:04
Telekom	23:44	26:14	19:15	9:48	8:00
C.A.	23:55	26:14	19:19	9:46	7:53
Rabobank	24:01	26:31	19:23	9:53	7:59
Mapei	24:27	26:49	19:24	10:02	8:10
M. Uno	24:12	27:01	19:36	10:20	8:00
Banesto	24:40	27:10	19:46	10:09	8:13
Kelme	24:46	27:25	19:59	10:13	8:20

STAGE 5

Vannes–Vitré • July 5

Over the Brown

MOST ROAD MAPS IN EUROPE USE SHADING TO INDICATE VARYING TOPOGRAPHY: VALLEYS AND PLAINS are in green, mountains in white, and hills are brown. So at the former Tour of Britain Milk Race, riders coined the expression "going over the brown," to describe those stages that spent most of their time in the hills—an apt description for this 200km-plus fifth stage of the Tour de France. It offered no hill higher than 545 feet above sea level, but the constant changes in elevation—on narrow back roads that never ceased to twist and turn, dip and climb through the hilly Brittany countryside—gave the feeling of one of those early-1960s stages in the rolling hills of England.

The big difference was the speed.

Whether in the Milk Race of the Tour de France, such a stage would have been raced at perhaps 40 or 41 kph. There would have been plenty of attacks and long breakaways, and the race would have been split into several groups by the finish.

But things have changed. Many of the back roads have had the kinks taken out of them; the erratic grades have been eased; and the roughest surfaces repaved. Combined with the advances in bike technology and training sophistication, the improvements have raised racing speeds by 5 kph or more—and made it much more difficult for breaks to succeed.

This stage of the Tour was a classic example, and the manner in which it was raced would greatly affect the strategies adopted for the following few stages....

It was a perfect day for racing: Heavy rain in the night had cleared the air, while high white clouds drifted in a blue sky over the start in Vannes. Down by the ancient town's port, where sleek yachts were lined up in the marina, tall masts swayed from a strengthening southwest wind as the stage began.

The favorable wind encouraged attacks from the start, despite most of the riders feeling the effects of the previous day's team time trial in their legs. The first seven attacks all failed, though. That was due to: (a) teams not wanting to miss the key break; and (b) the Polti and Mapei-Quick Step teams wanting to keep things together so their respective climbers, Richard Virenque and Paolo Bettini, could contest two KoM sprints in the first 35km.

The first climb was the hardest of the stage: the infamous Cadoudal hill at Plumelec, which, with its steep grade and switchback turn, was a mini-preview of the mountains

Tyler's diary
July 5
Vitré

We rode through about 100km-worth of steady rain today. This can make things kind of tricky because the roads can slick over when water mixes with oil left behind by cars and trucks. Luckily, it wasn't too bad. Even so, we didn't want to take any chances. The whole team rode around Lance up at the front, right behind the ONCE train, just in case.

I wasn't feeling so hot at the beginning of the race. I was definitely suffering the effects of yesterday's effort. My legs didn't loosen up until about a quarter of the way through the stage. Another reason why not having the yellow jersey this early was a blessing in disguise. ONCE spent the day at the front. A couple of those guys had to feel just as tight and fatigued as the rest of us after the effort they put in yesterday. I remember that feeling from last year—and I wasn't envious of them today.

It seems that there has been a senseless crash at the end of every stage so far—and today was no exception. A group of guys went down 200 meters before the 1km-to-go sign—which split the field. Jalabert (and the rest of the peloton) got caught behind it, and wound up losing 10 seconds to Lance. After the hard day in the saddle, that was probably a tough pill for Jalabert's teammates to swallow.

Every night we receive massages; a man named Ryszard Kieplinski works on me. He's from Zakopane, Poland. Eddie B found him in '95, so he's been with the team as long as I have. We've built up a pretty good friendship over the years.

Ryszard is the guy who gets to put me back together every night. If I've crashed, he cleans and bandages the wounds. If I need extra work in a specific area due to a cramp, he'll take care of it. If my back is hurting, he'll give me a good crack and additional massage if needed. And if there's a saddle sore giving me trouble—you guessed it, he's my second set of eyes.

It's funny that soigneurs are only really known for rubbing legs, because that's only about 10 percent of their day. It's pretty amazing how much these guys do for us, especially considering what they face from the crack of dawn until late into the evening. They monitor everything from our meals, to the feed zones, to hotel room preparation. By the time they get around to massages, they've already put in a full day. At this year's Tour, there are roughly two riders per soigneur. Anything beyond that would be an overload, given the stress and the amount of work they face.

Check out George Hincapie's Web site at www.hincapie.com—he's partnered with a company called General Bean to sell Tour de Café coffees during the Tour de France. There are four different blends to choose from and 20 percent of the proceeds benefit the Lance Armstrong Foundation. If you're reading this, you must be a cyclist—and I haven't met a cyclist yet who didn't need a good cup of joe to get rolling in the morning. So, if you buy beans anyway, you might as well buy some of these and support a good man and a great cause.

awaiting in four days' time. It was here that Erik Zabel won a 1997 Tour stage at the summit, ahead of Frank Vandenbroucke. And it was here that Tour debutant Bettini now took the prime, ahead of Rabobank's Markus Zberg and Virenque. Displaying the form that won him this spring's Liège-Bastogne-Liège, Bettini also won the sprint at the Cat. 4 Coët-Bugat summit—eight seconds behind solo attacker Jacky Durand of Lotto-Adecco.

The constant attacks resulted in 47.3km being covered in the first hour—despite the hills. Something had to give soon. And it did.

As the pack headed toward the day's first points sprint at 51km, Crédit Agricole's German all-arounder Jens Voigt saw that his Aussie teammate Stuart O'Grady was not well-placed; so Voigt decided to go for the sprint himself, to prevent the points going to O'Grady's rivals for the green jersey. Voigt's attack with Sebastien Demarbaix of Lotto was so successful that they were 15 seconds ahead at the sprint line in Mohon.

It was the sort of impromptu attack that has always been successful in cycling—and this one was, too. Voigt and Demarbaix kept going hard, and within 6km had created a one-minute margin before being joined by three chasers: Farm Frites' Koos Moerenhout, Polti's Spanish rookie Rafael Mateos and Rabobank's Erik Dekker—who had already made an earlier solo attack of 10km.

The break was now racing through a part of Brittany that's a hotbed of cycling, and every town bore marks of recent races: posters pasted on stone houses; direction arrows painted on the roads; and photos of local racers hanging in bike-shop windows. This is the area where five-time Tour winner Bernard Hinault learned his craft. And today, citizens of his current hometown of Calorguen—where he has a 150-acre dairy farm—were celebrating Hinault's cycling career. There was a reception attended by 2000 people in the village hall and a photo exhibition organized by his wife Martine.

By the time the five leaders reached Calorguen's steep Cat. 4 hill, after being together

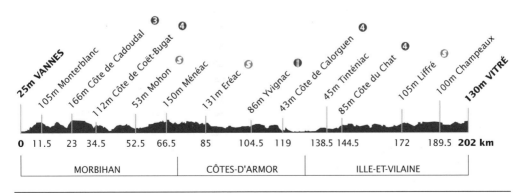

Fred's diary
July 5
Vitré

The wake-up call felt like it came at 6 a.m., when it was actually 9:30 a.m. Getting out of bed, the first things I felt were my legs—yesterday's grueling team time trail did a number on them. I wondered how long it was going to take to get them feeling all right again.

The hotel was in a beautiful setting, right along the coast. The view from my room was amazing, looking directly over the ocean. And the room itself wasn't half-bad, either. It had a loft, and the bathroom was as big as the bedroom. I kept thinking how nice it would be to be on vacation here—right now. Wishful thinking.

At breakfast, I could tell that my teammates were also feeling their legs. When [Sergio] Parsani, our director, told us that our job today was to follow the early breaks, I don't think he made anyone too happy. It's impossible to grasp how hard a team time trail is just by looking at it on paper. I was having a good day, and still, I was suffering as bad as the next guy.

After ONCE's winning performance yesterday, it was clear that they where out to control the stage. The early parts of the race were lightning fast, as the first mountain-point climbs were not too far into the stage. This meant that there would be no early break for me—it was simply too fast. No problem, I was content just to follow the pace.

Bettini had a great day, winning the first Category 3 climb and taking second in the next Cat. 4 climb. A break formed shortly after that second climb, ensuring that Bettini would be wearing the climber's polka-dot jersey tomorrow.

This morning, Bartoli promised Bettini that if he won the jersey he would paint his hair to match the red and white of the jersey. We'll see tomorrow morning if Bartoli stays true to his word.

Through the first half of the race, we encountered rain that didn't make me too happy, as I had to put on my rain jacket and cover up my stars-and-stripes. Luckily for all of us, the rain was temporary and we had a dry second half.

When you put your body through so much pain, it sometimes takes more pain before it feels better. That was the case today. I actually started to feel good around 150km, which I was happy to see. Then I started to get motivated for the finale, knowing that we would most likely be setting Tom Steels up for another sprint. About 25km from the finish, when the break had two minutes, Festina decided to take on the chase to ensure a sprint finish for its sprinter Marcel Wüst. We decided to play off that and wait and see if their work would pay off.

It did, and that left us to do our thing. This time, Chann and Bartoli helped keep us at the front; and we shared the job of bringing the sprinters in with Telekom. At this point we were 2km out, when Van Heeswijk took control and brought us closer. At less then a kilometer, I gave it my best and brought the break back at the 500-meter mark, leaving the rest up to Zanini and Tom. Once again, we had done our job perfectly, and now left Tom to do his. Unfortunately, Tom was still feeling his legs from yesterday. We came out with Zanini third and Tom fourth. Not bad, as we kept the green jersey on Tom's shoulders.

After today, I feel like things are coming along and my fitness is getting better. Tomorrow we will have a similar day, so look for me again in the stage's finale....

for 60km and racing through heavy rain showers, they had a 3:40 gap. That was as much as they would be allowed. Jalabert's ONCE team didn't want Voigt—only 1:36 back on G.C.—to steal the yellow jersey, so the squad was riding a strong tempo in the chase.

To say "strong tempo" gives little indication of the once riders' effort, only 24 hours after an excruciatingly hard team time trial. Riding at 47 kph on difficult roads was making this another hard day for everyone. And it still wasn't over....

With 30km to go, Marcel Wüst's Festina team took over the chase and chopped a minute from the gap in 8km. Seeing the time splits falling so quickly, Voigt and Dekker, the strongest of the leaders, realized they had to do something fast. They increased their tempo, dropped the other three, and then just flew over the remaining rollers. Even so, their lead dropped to a minute 12km out, and 30 seconds with 6km to go.

Neither man held anything back as they made the short climb past Vitré's 15th century castle—and they still had another 3km before reaching the finish on the far side of town, On the final turn, with 1400 meters remaining, the gap was just 10 seconds.

Would it be enough?

No. With Mapei setting up the sprint for Tom Steels, a super-fast pull by Rodriguez took the sprinters' train past Voigt and Dekker, 400 meters from the line. After leading the race for more than 150km, the two men's despair at seeing the stage win vanish can only be imagined.

There was no such frustration for Wüst, though. He followed Steels's wheel up the straightaway, and then, 100 meters from the line, he switched to Zabel's and sped past his fellow German for a huge victory. "The best of my career," Wüst said. And for a rider who has won a total of 13 stages at the Vuelta and Giro, that was quite an endorsement.

This was the colorful German's first stage win at the Tour. It probably won't be his last. If he can take a stage "over the brown," then who could bet against Wüst fulfilling the dream he revealed at his post-race press conference: a victory on the Champs-Elysées?

A Look at the Sprinters

History has a habit of repeating itself at the Tour de France. It happened at Vitré, when for the third time the race has visited this medieval town a sprinter won the stage. In 1985 it was Belgium's Rudy Matthys, in 1995 Italy's Mario Cipollini, and this year Germany's Marcel Wüst. Matthys won three stages in the '85 Tour, and Cipollini won two in '95. So the chances of Wüst taking at least one more stage this year seemed quite good.

Remarkably, Wednesday saw the 32-year-old Wüst, now in his 13th season as a professional cyclist, win a Tour stage for the first time. It's surprising because the multi-lingual German has won 12 stages of the Vuelta a España, including 10 in the past three years (three in 1997, three in '98 and four in '99) and one stage of the Giro d'Italia (in 1997). But he had ridden only one previous Tour de France, in 1992, when he crashed out on the first stage in San Sebastian, Spain.

Wüst looked likely to get his first chance to add to his victory score the following day: Stage 6 from Vitré to Tours was similar to 1999's stage 4 from Laval to Blois (which is 60km from Tours). Cipollini won that stage at a record Tour road stage average speed of 50.355 kph, with the Italian beating out (in order) Erik Zabel, Stuart O'Grady and Tom Steels.

Cipollini did not start the 87th Tour because of injuries sustained in a training accident a couple of weeks before the July 1 start, but there were plenty of other sprinters ready to take his place, including Wüst, Robbie McEwen of Farm Frites and Romans Vainsteins of Vini Caldirola. But another record speed wasn't expected. Although the 198.5km leg was just as flat as 1999's Laval-Blois stage, that one had a very strong tail wind, encouraging attacks right from the gun.

The forecast for stage 6 included temperatures in the mid-70s, along with a 20-kph wind blowing from the northeast. That meant the riders would have a crosswind, not a tail wind, probably meaning an average speed in the mid-40s.

Looking at history, only four road stages have finished in Tours: French sprinter André Darrigade won in 1957 and 1961; Italian sprinter Marino Basso in 1970; while Frenchman Thierry Marie took the sprinters by surprise with a last-kilometer attack in 1992. There aren't any explosive finishers like Marie in the current peloton, and on a final straightaway that is almost 2km long, completely flat and dead straight, a power sprinter like Steels would have the advantage.

STAGE 6

Vitré–Tours • July 6

Battle Lines

CONTENDING AT THE TOUR DE FRANCE IS NOT AN EASY TASK. AFTER ASSEMBLING A STRONG TEAM, making a season-long commitment and undergoing intense preparation comes the 21-day task of leadership responsibilities. That started to become clear on this sixth stage between Vitré and Tours, when the relative roles of Mercatone Uno (Pantani), ONCE (Jalabert and Olano), Telekom (Ullrich) and U.S. Postal (Armstrong) began to take shape.

The initial battle lines had been drawn in the stage 4 team time trial, and now the big teams had to decide what tactics to adopt as the race made its northern turn, and began heading south in four giant steps: via Tours, Limoges, Villeneuve-sur-Lot and Dax.

Already, there had been hints of tension mounting after the finish of stage 5. Manolo Saiz, ONCE's directeur sportif, complained that the day's main breakaway had started when his leader, Jalabert, was off the bike taking a pee—and attacking in those conditions goes against race protocol. Saiz also claimed that after a crash on the final corner in Vitré, 1400 meters from the line, Postal's Ekimov had deliberately let a gap open behind Armstrong, knowing that Jalabert was behind him. [The incident caused a split in the peloton, similar to the one on stage 3 at Nantes; this time it allowed Armstrong, Ullrich, Julich and 27 others to gain 10 seconds on Jalabert, Zülle, Escartin and the rest of the field.]

Saiz continued his accusations on this sixth stage, after a 12-strong break developed in the early kilometers and went on to gain eight minutes—resulting in Jalabert losing the yellow jersey to Telekom's Alberto Elli. Again, Saiz's tirade centered on Jalabert being attacked when he had stopped for a pee (after only 10km of the stage). [Strangely, no one asked why the race leader stopped that soon after the start, especially when there was a favorable wind and early moves were expected.]

Saiz said that Jalabert, paced by four teammates, was still chasing back through the line of team cars when local man Durand—racing past fans holding "Allez Jacky" and "Allez Doudou" banners—fired off an attack 13km out of Vitré. He was quickly joined by 11 others, including Elli and headed by Rabobank's Leon Van Bon, Marc Wauters and

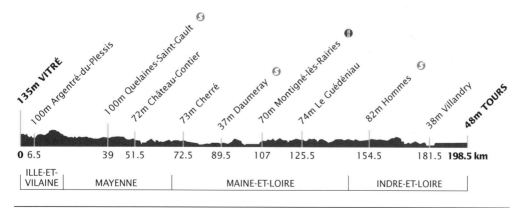

Tyler's diary
July 6
Tours

Last night, Manolo Saiz, the director of the ONCE team, called our director, Johan Bruyneel, to express his dissatisfaction with our performance at the finish of stage 5. The crash with 1.2km to go had split the field. Luckily, Lance was on his toes. He reacted immediately and sprinted across the gap. Eki wasn't able to match Lance's power and lost contact with his wheel—ultimately creating the 10-second gap recorded at the finish.

ONCE interpreted the move to be a little more strategic than it was. Eki was straight out, plain and simple. But ONCE thought Eki knew Jalabert was behind him and sat up on purpose to slow him down—and give precious seconds back to Lance. While this may have looked like sabotage in hindsight, it was anything but. ONCE thought differently, though, and vowed not to pull for an inch in the next day's stage. Due to this misunderstanding, we half expected the shake-up that occurred today.

The first major event of the day happened around 10km into the race, when Laurent Jalabert pulled off the front of the peloton to water the flowers. There's kind of an unwritten rule that protects the leader of a race in this situation, which is basically that no one should attack while the fertilizer is flowing. Magnus Bäckstedt attacked anyway, and the peloton went nuts. He was immediately chased down. But once he was caught, Jacky Durand went for it. This was the beginning of the successful break that gained over seven minutes on the field.

The breakaway was gaining minutes by the kilometer. The gap could have easily grown to 30 minutes, if the peloton didn't respond when it did. So even though the time gap makes it look like we had an easy day lagging behind, that was hardly the case. The pace was fast enough that guys were getting dropped—which is something you don't always see during week one.

Another nasty crash at the feed zone left Stuart O'Grady out of the running with a broken collarbone. Amazingly, he finished the stage! It was one of those manic days when anything was possible. I'm glad the Postal Service made it through unscathed.

Leon Van Bon put in an impressive win, especially since he was giving Markus Zberg a leadout. He did such a good job that Zberg couldn't come around him. Van Bon had set himself up for the win. Not bad.

Although the changes to the overall standings look catastrophic … don't panic just yet. We're as happy to see Telekom inherit the yellow jersey as we were to see ONCE do so. Now they will be faced with the difficult choice of pleasing their sponsors by defending the lead, or saving themselves for Jan Ullrich in the mountains. We won't exactly be sitting back and relaxing while they work this internal dilemma out, but we will be watching and taking careful inventory of any strain this causes them in the next day or so. Believe it or not, we are exactly where we want to be.

Markus Zberg. With representatives from 10 of the Tour's 20 teams, and all of them with something to gain, the break was soon working as a perfect 12-man paceline.

The daring dozen gained 25 seconds before once organized its forces and began the chase. And although the lead was quickly cut to 18 seconds—a gap of about 250 meters on the smooth, straight road heading southeast past fields of corn, wheat and poppies—that was the last time the pack saw the 12 leaders, because ONCE suddenly decided that another long team time trial wasn't to its liking.

The gap quickly opened to a minute, before the race took a left turn into a 6km section of one-lane back road, between hedgerows of tall green ferns and multi-hued wildflowers. Emerging from the farm road, the smooth-working break had more than four minutes on the slow-moving pack; and by the day's first sprint, at Quelaines-St. Gault, another 8km down the road, the gap was an enormous 12:37!

With once having conceded the yellow jersey, it would be instructive to see which teams would respond to the break's challenge, because none of the favorites could allow Elli—a top-10 finisher at the 1994 Tour de France—to race away unchecked.

"It's a poker game between Manolo Saiz and Johan Bruyneel," claimed Crédit Agricole's Vaughters, referring to the mind games being used by the ONCE and Postal team directors. In this case, it was Postal's Bruyneel who decided to take the situation in hand: He delegated Vasseur and Kjaergaard to ride tempo at the head of the pack, where they were joined by riders from the Polti team of Virenque (confirming the Frenchman's ambitions at this Tour) and Bonjour (whose Jean-Cyril Robin was also hoping for a good Tour).

This combination was enough to cut the lead to a more reasonable 8:15 by the feed zone; but just after, a crash in the front third of the peloton broke the chase's rhythm, and the gap remained around eight minutes for the rest of the stage.

The crash happened where local fans were greeting the Tour with pounding drums and clashing cymbals. Some riders "got a little nervous, because they thought the sounds of the drums were the sounds of a crash," Vaughters later explained, "so they slammed on their brakes. People went piling into each other...."

The pileup split the pack into three groups, spread over a minute. Interestingly, and confirming his ambitions for the Tour, Pantani was in the front group, along with the other top favorites: Armstrong, Ullrich and Jalabert. Riding near the front is not something that Pantani would have done a couple of years ago, when few people considered that he had a chance of winning the Tour. Times have changed.

What can I say? In Europe, we call it *dormi sul bici*—sleeping on the bike. That's what we were doing today when the semi-crucial break went up the road and got 13 minutes. The ONCE guys decided that it wasn't their job to chase … mmm. After their previous day's work, they opted for a rest day. I think we learned a pretty big lesson from what happened today, and we will start having to play our cards a.s.a.p.

One of the things I've noticed that's unique to the Tour is that it is always fast. During my first week of my first Tour, it seems every time I've looked down at my computer, it reads 50 kph. It's like every rider who shows up to ride the Tour is here to race. As for me, when the second week comes, my eyes will be open and looking for opportunities.

One of the motivating factors for all of us is that our team has won two stages and has two jerseys. With the mountain jersey, sprint jersey, Italian and U.S. national championship jersey, our staff has a hard time finding us in the feed zones. On that note, look for our maze of colors as we continue our forward momentum.

One favorite who had the bad luck to be involved in the crash was Julich, who had to chase with the back group for about 15 minutes to close a 57-second gap. Extra efforts like that can add up over the course of three weeks.

Worse off was Julich's Australian teammate Stuart O'Grady. Screaming with pain when he was picked up off of the road, the Aussie had a red bruise on his forehead and an apparent broken right collarbone. Not knowing whether it was fractured or just a bad bruise, O'Grady doggedly continued with nine others to the finish 87km away. An x-ray later confirmed the worst, and O'Grady remained in the hospital at Tours for a few days after the complicated fracture was pinned.

By the time O'Grady's group arrived in Tours, 22 minutes down, Elli was already having a press conference. The Italian started his career in 1987, and was now in his 11th Tour, having raced for Ariostea, MG-Technogym, Casino and, for the past two years, Telekom. After this stage, Elli, at 36 years and four months, became the oldest leader of the Tour in 60 years.

Hired as a worker for Ullrich. Elli seemed almost embarrassed that he had taken the yellow jersey. "It's a special thing," he conceded. "It would be good to keep it until the mountains, where I'll be happy to hand it over to Ullrich."

As for the stage's finale, the three Rabobank riders didn't mess up: Wauters set a ferocious pace up the famed 1800-meter-long Avenue de Grammont (where he won the Paris-Tours classic last year), before passing the baton to Van Bon, who led out the sprint—and took the stage from teammate Zberg.

Rewards for the Workers

No one expects Alberto Elli to win the Tour de France. And he won't. But the veteran Italian could celebrate the fact that in the twilight of his 14-year pro career he would wear the Tour's yellow jersey for at least a day. Elli was the best-placed of the 12-rider break, but he never expected to end the day in the race lead. "I had some luck," he said.

One part of that luck is that he is a teammate of Ullrich on Telekom, which hired him a couple of years ago to ride as a team worker in the mountains. Elli has always been something of a climber—good enough to earn him victories in races like the six-day Midi Libre in southern France and the four-day Tour of Luxembourg (which he won for the second time a month before the Tour). His best performance in the Tour de France was in 1994, when he placed seventh overall, riding for the MG team.

The other part of Elli's luck was the reluctance of Jalabert's ONCE-Deutsche Bank team to conduct another long, fast chase. The reasoning of ONCE team director Saiz was that none of the 12 men out front was a real danger for the final victory, and that they would be better off letting others bear the weight of controlling the race.

It seemed unlikely that Telekom would make a huge effort to keep Elli in the yellow jersey in the upcoming stages. A more likely scenario was for Rabobank or Crédit Agricole to shoot at the lead. Rabobank had three men in the break: Van Bon won the stage from teammate Zberg, while Wauters moved into third place overall 1:17 behind Elli.

As for Crédit Agricole, its Fabrice Gougot was only 12 seconds behind Elli—a margin that could be made up in three intermediate sprints, which each provide time bonuses of six, four and two seconds. More important, Gougot is French and rides for a French team. Crédit Agricole would love to have the publicity associated with the yellow jersey. Like Elli, Gougot, 28, is a faithful team worker, He has had only one win in five years as a professional.

Yes, it was a day for the workers.

Tyler's diary
July 7
Limoges

Our biggest challenges of the day were wind and rain. At one point, it was raining so hard I couldn't see. Water was pouring through the space between my forehead and glasses, and I was literally riding blind at certain times during the stage. It was plenty scary—especially being wheel-to-wheel in the middle of the peloton. In fact, it was the perfect opportunity for disaster to strike. Luckily, we made it through. Check off another day.

Magnus Bäckstedt was the big topic of discussion today: Did he know Jalabert was taking a leak when he attacked yesterday? He says he didn't. Okay, Magnus, we'll give you the benefit of the doubt.

How about Alberto Elli—36 years old, in his 11th Tour and in the yellow jersey. Pretty amazing. I'm in my fourth Tour, and I asked my wife if she thought she could put up with me through seven more. Her response was quick: Absolutely not. We'll see about that … she was laughing when she said it.

You may have noticed a familiar face among the U.S. Postal Service staff: Dave Lettieri. He's taking a little time off from running his Fast Track shop in Santa Barbara to make a special guest appearance with the team during the Tour. Lettieri is working specifically for Lance—maintaining his three primary machines (road, time-trial and climbing bikes) along with his spares. He's also driving one of our campers from the starts to the finishes. For those of you who don't know who Dave is, he was the director of the Chevy-L.A. Sheriff team a few years back.

Traditionally, there are two mechanics for every rider. I work with Geoff Brown, who joined us after his five-year stint with the Motorola squad. He originally started out with the Canadian national team, and has been "wrenching" for 12 years. This is his seventh Tour. Geoff is one of those unbelievably patient guys who puts up with a lot of last-minute requests. We work well together, because he understands how I get before big races—especially time trials. I like to think I'm concentrating on the task at hand; he likes to say that I go "brain dead."

I guess a good example of this happened prior to the start at Futuroscope last year. I was approaching the start house and thought Geoff was right behind me to transport my bike up the stairs. So I let go of it and continued walking. Geoff was about one step off my pace and my TT bike crashed to the ground. I didn't even look back because I didn't want to stress out—and I knew Geoff would take care of the situation. With less than two minutes to go before my start, he calmly picked up my bike, checked it for damage, proceeded up the stairs and handed it off to the starter. You could say that he puts up with a lot. And if I drive him nuts, he doesn't show it. Talk about a nice guy.

STAGE 7

Tours–Limoges • July 7

On the Alert

A SWIRLING CROSSWIND, SOME TORRENTIAL RAIN SHOWERS AND ANOTHER 200KM-PLUS STAGE OF CONSTANT attacks added to the mounting stress of this opening week. In the end, Christophe Agnolutto of AG2R Prévoyance rode into Limoges alone to score the first stage win by a Frenchman since 1998—when Durand took a four-up sprint on a baking hot day into Montauban.

Although Agnolutto did not pose any sort of threat on G.C., the top teams still could not relax, as this wide-open Tour was again on the verge of breaking apart. Postal's Andreu summed up the situation when he explained why his team chased a sudden 10-man break that developed 15km before Limoges. "We ride when we're not sure who's in a split," Andreu explained. "We knew there were 10 guys...."

One of the 10 was Mapei's U.S. champion Rodriguez, who said, "I jumped across to the split ... saw that Elli and Commesso were up there and realized this wasn't going anywhere." Also in the attack was Rodriguez's teammate Manuel Beltran—a former climbing domestique for Banesto, who came to this Tour with a lot of personal ambitions.

In a race this open, even riders like Beltran cannot be given any leeway. That's why the Postal team is smart to chase down breaks like this one, before they have a chance to develop into something more serious.

Earlier in the day, between kilometers 38 and 75, Telekom had taken charge of the race for its race leader Elli, when a whole battery of attacks threatened to produce another

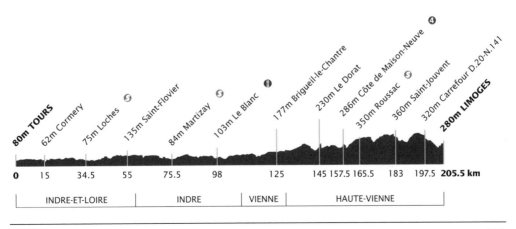

Tours-type breakaway. Eight of those attacks gained enough time to be announced on Radio Tour. And the last of these was the springboard for Agnolutto's solo move.

Again, Rodriguez was involved. "I was in a group of four (during one of the downpours). We had like 10 seconds on Telekom for about a minute," he said. "We weren't getting anywhere. So (the pack) knows there's a break, sees three guys sit up … and lets the other guy go." The "other guy" was Agnolutto, a brave, but not particularly talented rider, who has put together a respectable career with these kinds of efforts. At the 1997 Tour of Switzerland, he joined a breakaway group of non-favorites on the second stage, then split from them to win the stage solo by several minutes. Amazingly, he managed to defend his yellow jersey for the remaining week of the race that included several mountain stages. Then, also in Switzerland, he won the final stage of the 1998 Tour de Romandie.

This is the 30-year-old Agnolutto's fifth pro season, and he knew that this break would perhaps be his one and only chance of winning a stage at the Tour. Battling the sidewind for 80km, he built up a lead of eight minutes, with 48km still to go. It was not a forgone conclusion that he would win, and his bid finally hinged on there being a lull between the Telekom team ending its tempo riding (when Agnolutto was 4:30 ahead with 20km to go) and Wüst's Festina team taking up the chase. Agnolutto hung on to win by just over a minute, with Wüst easily taking the sprint for second.

In the last, uphill kilometer, Crédit Agricole's Fabrice Gougot tried to make it a double French triumph. Part of the 12-man break the day before, Gougot was lying in second place, just 12 seconds behind Elli. The time bonus for finishing second on a stage is 12 seconds, and if Gougot could get to the line with at least a second's gap over the field, he would take over the yellow jersey. It was not an impossible goal for Gougot, who had won a stage of June's Dauphiné Libéré with a late solo attack. Here at Limoges, he managed to take a 50-meter lead, but no more, and was swallowed up by the sprinters with about 100 meters still remaining....

In the Tour, you never know when your time will come. It was Agnolutto's today. Who would claim his moment tomorrow?

Difficult Stage Coming Up

With the Tour's first mountain stage only a weekend away, the race favorites would get a good chance to loosen their climbing muscles on stage 8 from Limoges to

Villeneuve-sur-Lot. The 203.5km stage was on winding departmental roads—a reverse of the stage that Lance Armstrong won into Limoges to honor his deceased teammate Fabio Casartelli five years ago.

The stage had four classified climbs (one Cat. 3, three Cat. 4s), and dozens of other hills that would test everyone's fitness. Luckily for the peloton—down to 174 riders after Dane Jesper Skibby of MemoryCard pulled out Friday with tendinitis and Aussie Stuart O'Grady didn't start because of his broken collarbone—the weather wouldn't be hot, as it usually is in July. A cool northwest wind was forecast to keep temperatures in the 70s.

All those climbs would make it hard for the Telekom team to have as easy a day as it had Friday in defense of Alberto Elli's yellow jersey, and a small group was expected to get away and stay away. The only other time a Tour stage has finished at Villeneuve-sur-Lot was in 1996, when the solo winner was Italian veteran Massimo Podenzana of Mercatone Uno.

Podenzana wasn't expecting to win again. Besides being the oldest man in the race—he would be 39 a week after the Tour—his task was to protect team leader Pantani from the wind on hilly stages such as this, so that the 1998 Tour winner would be ready for the big climbs looming on the horizon.

STAGE 8

Limoges-Villeneuve-sur-Lot • July 8

The Real Tour de France

SUN SHINING FROM A SKY FILLED WITH FAST-MOVING WHITE CLOUDS. A NARROW BACK ROAD WINDING through a neat village of sandy-hued stone cottages and gardens of climbing roses and purple hydrangea. Spectators standing in doorways and sitting on picnic chairs. A brass band playing in the square adding to the festive mood. And then the cries of "les voilà"—there they are!

A bright red car comes racing into town, followed by a platoon of 17 racers in their multicolored uniforms, bikes glinting in the mid-afternoon sunlight as they whoosh past, followed by 14 white team cars carrying their racks of spare bikes and spinning wheels, and a multitude of press vehicles sparring for the best views of the race. This is Les Eyzies, deep in the remote Dordogne region of southwest France. And this is Le Tour. Just like it has always been. Quelle spectacle!

Fred's diary
July 8
Villeneuve-sur-Lot

Boy, where do I start? I'll start by telling you straight out that I am one tired rider. It just amazes me how the Tour is so aggressive, day after day. I don't think I've had a moment to relax in the whole of this first week.

At the 0-kilometer marker today, we had our first attack—a dangerous one at that. Luckily, we had Nardello and Bettini to cover it. This move put the Postals on the defensive and they had to put their whole team at the front to chase. We were flying as the Postal boys brought the break back, and as I expected, we didn't slow down once they were done. It was a constant series of attacks from every team, and we were maintaining speeds of up to 75 kph. I couldn't believe guys were even able to go any faster, but there were always fresh bodies to give it a shot.

Finally, a group went away, and unluckily, we had no one up there. That left us with the one option suggested by our team director: chasing. But I had a feeling that we would not bring them back, as the break was 14-guys strong. So I decided to attack and see if I could motivate the field to keep on the attack. To my disbelief, I was let go to ride by myself after the group. I decided to soft pedal and hope that a group would form and come across to me.

Two guys finally had the courage to join me [Maignan from AG2R and Sandstod from MemoryCard], but even then I felt it was hopeless. One of the guys asked me if we had a chance of getting across. I really didn't know what to say, as we were almost two minutes behind the break at this point, but I said, "Let's

see what time tells." So, about 12km before the feed zone, we made a plan: to go as hard as we could to the feed zone and hope that we would catch. If that didn't work, we said we would quit and wait for the field; but to my amazement, we made it. I still can't believe we did it.

Then we were 17 guys in a group that had around 10 minutes on the field, so it looked good on making it to the finish. At that point, I needed time to recover from my effort on coming across, and luckily, it looked like the group was also looking for an easier tempo.

The first attack of our group came around 35km out from the finish, which I couldn't believe. This immediately split the group into pieces, but I was able to remain in the first part. At that point, my plan was to roll through the group and make sure that we came to the finish, knowing I was one of the fastest and it would suit me better. I kept rolling through, trying not to miss a pull, when I noticed that most of the guys were opting to sit on.

So I decided to take a break myself. That's when Dekker rolled away. It wasn't an attack, but none of us reacted; we just let him ride away. We were not able to organize and bring him back. Instead, everyone wanted to try and jump across, but it made for a non-cohesive group that would not commit to a chase. That gave Dekker the advantage, as he was rolling at a steady pace, while we kept on attacking each other and then slowing. Finally, I realized that he wasn't coming back and the race was for second place. But again, attacks in the last kilometer let two guys ride off, leaving me to win the group sprint for fourth.

I came up a bit short. Still, I'm happy that I have had the power to be a player in my first Tour.... Wish me better luck next time, as I am still going for it. I'll sleep well tonight.

After the leaders have passed through, 10 minutes before the pack, conversations turn to speculating: Who will win today's stage when they reach Villeneuve-sur-Lot, still 85km and countless more hills away? Will it be a sprint, or will one of those 17 riders break away alone? All the fans know for sure is that it will be a great battle.

Like the riders, they are keenly aware that a stage win at the Tour de France is an immense milestone in a cyclist's career—equal to winning a one-day classic, or better. They understand that a victory at the Tour will bring worldwide publicity, due to the gigantic media presence that's perhaps 10 times the size of that at an average World Cup race.

Take the case of Mario Cipollini, He isn't present at this Tour because of injury, but it has been his 12 career stage wins in the Tour that have created his fame. In fact, Cipollini has never even won a World Cup classic, despite being the most consistently fast sprint finisher over the past decade.

Although he's absent, Cipollini still has had an influence on this Tour. The Italian sprinter and his red guard gave everyone the mind-set that Tour stages in the opening week always end in field sprints. That idea reached its climax at last year's Tour, when the first seven stages all had mass finishes, four of them taken by Cipolini. So "Here we go again," was the feeling when sprinters took the first three road stages of this year's Tour. But that inevitability eased even more when a solo Agnolotto survived to win stage 7.

Now, the lid was off the toy box, and the boys were ready to play.

Such was their eagerness to make the day's first attack that maneuvering began even before race director Jean-Marie Leblanc had dropped the flag to start stage 8.

The roll-out from Limoges ended with a long downhill to the actual start, just beyond a roundabout, from which the race route immediately climbed a not inconsiderable hill. The downhill sped things up, and the fight for places at the front resulted in the riders

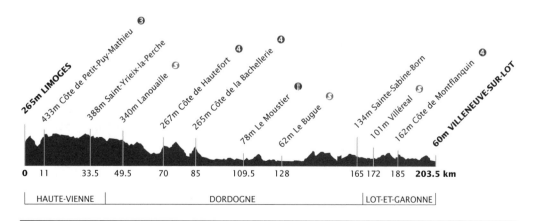

Tyler's diary
July 8
Villeneuve-sur-Lot

It was another difficult day, right from the gun. There was literally an attack at kilometer zero. Kevin, George, Eki and I were told to cover all the early breaks. But we didn't expect so much action right off the bat, and we weren't in position to respond to the early charge. Needless to say, the four of us were immediately in the doghouse with our director.

After being caught off guard, the only thing left to do was bring the break back. So we chased. And chased. The wind was howling again, making things even rougher. But we managed to catch the early escapees—just in time for another attack to launch. By this time we were all close to spent, but Frankie managed to go with them for a bit. Mercatone Uno took over the chase and we hammered away in the wind for the rest of the day. For a little added challenge, I flatted with 6km to go. Steffen gave me his wheel and waited for the team car. I definitely owe him one.

Tonight we're staying in an isolated hotel all by ourselves. It's kind of nice being the only team here. It's a lot calmer than the usual night's stay, which generally consists of five teams crammed in a Novotel. Last night we bunked down with Mercatone Uno, Crédit Agricole, Saeco and AG2R. It was a mad house. You couldn't make your way through the lobby without being approached by a slew of race fans—many more than turn out to see just one team. But tonight, we're all enjoying the peace and quiet: a rarity at the Tour.

Life on the road is fairly regimented. And even though there is hardly ever a variation to our routine, our daily schedule is distributed by our director every evening at dinner. The list of daily milestones goes something like this:

✢ It begins by telling us what time to wake up—which for me means five minutes before breakfast. Next, it tells us what time to be at breakfast, which is always three hours before the start. We're then told when to have our suitcases ready to be picked up by the soigneurs to be taken to the next hotel.

✢ After breakfast we all attend a pre-race meeting, which is usually held 20 minutes before our departure for the start. Departure times can vary, depending on whether we are traveling by car or bike.

✢ Most importantly, our schedule reminds us of the start time and lets us know the approximate finish time. We're also told how we will travel on to our next hotel—which, like traveling to the start, is either by bike or bus, depending on the distance.

✢ When we arrive at our hotel, everyone showers, grabs a quick snack (i.e. a protein shake) and gets a 45-minute massage. We also meet with the chiropractor and then it's off to dinner. Sometime during the evening we find time to call home, write our journal entries and do a reading up on the next day's stage. And then it's lights out.

being at race speed as they hurtled around the traffic circle.

Frenchman Frédéric Guesdon went too fast and fell, skidding on his backside and ripping his shorts. By the time Guesdon picked himself up, the first attack had been started by the insatiable Dekker, already the author of long breakaways on stage 2 (with Durand) and stage 5 (with Voigt). At the hilltop, he had been joined by 17 others—including a number of potentially dangerous outsiders: Mapei's Daniele Nardello, Telekom's Alex Vinokourov, Saeco's Laurent Dufaux and Bonjour's Robin.

It was the sort of move that Armstrong's team had to shut down before it developed. But by the time the Postals became organized, the gap was already half-a-minute. The resulting chase was incredibly fast, hilly roads be damned. Already, two riders had been dropped from the break—Voigt and Festina's Jaime Hernandez—and the speed set by the Postal riders saw a dozen or so fall back from the peloton. The first man to go, Jans Koerts of Farm Frites, would never get back. And despite riding the rest of the day as hard as he could, he reached Villeneuve-sur-Lot 44 minutes down, well outside the time limit. His Tour was over.

The Postal team's Tour was very much on; and the American team's initial chase—which Pantani's Mercatone Uno men joined—lasted 22km. But the pack didn't stay together for long. As the roads became more tortuous and narrow, heading across the limestone ridges and wooded valleys of the Dordogne, the attacks became harder to contain. Eventually, four riders got more than 10 seconds; seven others (including Dekker and Andreu) chased; and three more came across—to produce a 14-man break. And since Postal had a rider up there, the team had no need to chase. But when another big group tried to bridge, Postal quickly closed that one down. After that, the 14 in front soon gained ground.

With almost 80km of hilly terrain covered at an "insane" average of 49.3 kph, everyone was tired. So there was no reaction when Rodriguez—seeing that his Mapei team didn't have anyone in the break—charged off the front. Nor did the pack worry when the U.S. champion was joined on a long downhill by Frenchman Gilles Maignan of AG2R and Dane Michael Sandstod of MemoryCard. "Let them die out there in no-man's-land," was the general opinion.

And that looked likely when a time check at kilometer 96 saw the trio seven minutes ahead of the main field ... and still a yawning 1:52 behind the leaders. But the three, on passing the sign announcing "feed zone at 12km," made a pact and, according to Rodriguez, "decided to put our heads down." In unison, they raced a perfect paceline along the twisting roads of the Vézère valley, and bridged within 15km.

"That took a lot out of me," Rodriguez later said, still a bit startled that he'd made it into the day's winning break—that now had a 10-minute lead and was heading though Les Eyzies.

One of the riders in the group was a danger for the overall race: Giuseppe Guerini of Telekom. The Italian was in front to police the break for race leader Elli, but Guerini is also capable of being a leader himself. He is a climber who won the Alpe d'Huez stage of the Tour last year, and has twice finished third in the Giro d'Italia (1997 and 1998). His break was on a pace to gain 27 minutes by Villeneuve-sur-Lot. And a rider of Guerini's caliber can't be given that sort of advantage before the big climbs even begin.

Knowing this, Pantani ordered his Mercatone Uno to start chasing again, later aided by Escartin's Kelme team. Another factor that came into play was that many of the riders in the break stopped working, realizing that their teams didn't want them to help Guerini (and his Telekom team), The two factors prevented the gap from expanding, and with the Guerini danger under control, speculation again turned to who would win the stage.

Rodriguez was the fastest sprinter in the break, but as another sprinter, McEwen, noted: "They're not going to let a sprinter win. They'll keep on attacking, and won't let a sprinter stay with them to the finish."

And that's exactly what happened. After Polti's Bart Voskamp began the attacking with 40km to go, and took the stage's last time-bonus sprint just after, his fellow Dutchman Dekker counterattacked … and no one chased. He was 12 seconds clear before anyone reacted, and by this point Dekker was in his biggest gear, taking advantage of a straight, smooth road and a tail wind. Ten riders took up the chase, but not in unison, and the gap opened to 37 seconds.

On the last little climb, just inside 20km to go, six of the 10 began to close. At the summit, the gap was down to 22 seconds, and it seemed that Rodriguez, Voskamp, Xavier Jan of La Française des Jeux, Didier Rous of Festina, Pieri of Saeco and Vicente Garcia-Acosta of Banesto would catch the solo Dekker. But Frenchmen Rous and Jan started attacking each other, the others chased, and then all six sat up.

This stop-go played into the steady hands of Dekker, who rode away to a victory that, like all stage victories at the Tour, meant instant fame. His attack in the first kilometer of this 203.5km stage was not quite as suicidal as it seemed....

Back in Les Eyzies, the villagers were probably talking about what a great battle there'd been, just as they expected.

Strategies

In what was the most exciting day of racing yet in this Tour de France, the teams of all the leading contenders had to be alert and strong. They would also have to answer a number of questions through the day: When to attack? When to chase? When to ride tempo? Who's a potential contender? Who is not?

As it happened, the strategic danger posed by Guerini was fairly easily thwarted. And by the stage finish, the Italian was only 15th, 2:03 behind solo winner Dekker, and 3:39 ahead of the pack. Guerini moved up to 12th place on G.C., a handful of seconds ahead of the best-placed favorites, Jalabert (in 14th) and Armstrong (in 16th).

Another day was over. The Tour was another day closer to the mountains. And then pure strength would take over ... not just strategy.

STAGE 9

Villeneuve-sur-Lot–Dax • July 9

À la Darrigade

THIS STAGE WOULD END IN DAX, THE HOMETOWN OF ANDRÉ DARRIGADE, WHO MORE THAN 30 years after he retired from racing remains the most famous sprinter in French cycling history. Back in the days when the Tour was contested by national teams, and sprints were a tactical battle on 51x14 gears, Darrigade was a national hero. Many stage finishes were on velodromes where the packed crowds looked for Dédé's blue-red-and-white French

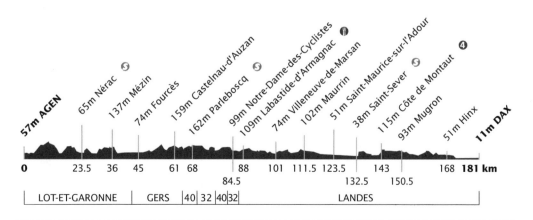

Chann's diary
July 9
Dax

My Mapei teammate Paolo Bettini never ceases to amaze me. Today he was going like a beast again. I think he found his L-B-L legs with 40km remaining to the stage finish here in Dax; and from then on, he was going ballistic, totally annihilating his breakaway partners on every hill.

And what made his victory even more impressive is that he was suffering so much in the first half of the race, he told our team director that he was going to drop out. Never give up is another lesson I am slowly learning in the Tour de France.

After the first nine days, I can confirm that this race is harder than the Giro or Vuelta—but it's a different kind of hard. My director told me before we started the Tour that it is just that one notch higher of suffering every day that makes the difference. He was right, because there is no one in this race who does not have motivation.

Tomorrow is the first day of the Tour for me: The mountains have arrived, and we will see who is good, and who has been faking it. To tell you the truth, I have no idea how I am going to do. If I have the legs that I had in the Giro, then I will be up there; but if those legs are missing, then I will have to re-analyze everything that I have decided to do in this past month. I decided to put this pressure upon myself, and now is the time to see if I can deliver the goods.

The entire American contingent is looking good, and I am sure that Postal is going to do some damage on tomorrow's stage. They've been keeping Lance out of trouble, and they know every part of the road tomorrow. Mercatone Uno,

ONCE and Kelme are also going to make things difficult. Everybody is nervous, but for a good reason: The finish up to Hautacam will tell all.

To make it even more pleasant, the forecast calls for rain all day. Have fun watching; I have to go prepare my rain bag.

# # #

Tyler's diary
July 9
Dax

How many times can I say "today was pretty difficult"? Surely, by now, you know the Tour de France is no piece of cake. Today was fast—and again my main objective was to cover any early breaks. After yesterday I didn't want to be caught off guard, so I was ready from the gun. As expected, things got going fairly quickly and I found myself in the first break of the day. We were working pretty hard and all the teams were represented. I thought for sure it was going to stick. But Mercatone Uno had other ideas and chased us down.

There were a couple of other break attempts throughout the day—but it was fairly clear that the business of gaining minutes per stage had come to an end. None of the teams wanted to hit the mountains with additional deficits. With about 60km to go, Festina took control of the race. They rode a hard tempo at the front for their sprinter Marcel Wüst.

The highlight of my day came with about 15km to go. A massive pileup. I still don't know what caused it. I landed on bodies and bikes. Eki was right in front of me and went down as well. He's pretty beat up, with a black eye, road rash and a fat lip. I have three pretty good bruises—one on my chest from landing on someone's stem and two on my left leg from landing on I don't know what. As I write this, I am lying under a blanket of ice bags. Johan thinks my crashing for a second time is a good sign, since I crashed three times last year and seemed to do okay. My wife thinks his logic is a little whacked.

Speaking of my wife—she has found a new hobby since meeting me: keeping a log of stupid questions people ask her when she mentions her husband is a professional cyclist. Here's a sample of some of her favorites:

1. "But what does he do for a living?"
2. "Does he get paid for that?"
3. "Does he live off a trust fund?"
4. "Are you riding the Tour of France with him?"
5. "How many thousands of cyclists sign up for the Tour de France?"
6. "What cause does the Tour de France raise money for?"
7. "Do you really think cycling is a team sport?"
8. "How much longer is he going to ride his bike around Europe before getting a job?"
9. "Does he do a lot of sight seeing in Europe?"
10. "Are there port-a-potties along the race routes?"
11. "What is that thing on his head?" (Our time trial helmets)
12. "If he burns 5000 calories a day riding, can he eat a whole pizza for dinner?"
13. "If he travels all the time, why hasn't he taken you on a honeymoon yet?"
14. "Do you train with him?"
15. "Does he know that Lance Armstrong guy?"
16. "If the Tour de France is only three weeks long, what does he do for the rest of the year?"
17. "Do his legs get tired doing that?"
18. "Does he have to ride his bike every day?"

team jersey and his wispy blond hair. They would then look for his sudden, darting acceleration—which took him to 22 stage wins between 1953 and 1964.

Besides those successes in the Tour, Darrigade was a brilliant single-day racer: He won the world road championship at Zandvoort in the Netherlands in 1959; and he outsprinted Fausto Coppi to win the 1956 Tour of Lombardy, when the Italian classic finished on Milan's Vigorelli velodrome.

That's the sort of palmarès that a rider like Paolo Bettini would like to have one day. The 26-year-old Italian has already started to build his record: This spring, he took the Liège-Bastogne-Liège classic in a three-man sprint ... and here at Dax, he took a stage win in this, his first Tour de France.

If you read only the result of stage 9, you'd assume that the stage ended in a mass sprint, since 157 riders were all given the same time as Bettini. But the five-foot-six, 128-pound Bettini is not a field sprinter ... and he needed much more than speed to win a 181km stage in strong head and crosswinds. But as the stage reached its final hour, and Bettini knowing that no break has been able to gain more than 40 seconds all day, he would have to act fast if he wanted to avoid a mass sprint. So maybe McEwen, Wüst or Zabel would take this last stage before the mountains.

With that in mind, Bettini suddenly took charge. With 40km to go, the Mapei man sprinted for the KoM points on the Cat. 4 hill at Montaut, ahead of Frenchman Rous of Bonjour and Belgian Geert Verheyen of Lotto-Adecco ... while Spaniard José Vidal of Kelme joined them on the swerving downhill.

The four took an initial lead of 250 meters, and then, very slowly, began to pull away. Bettini was the driving force, pushing the pace on every little climb and swooping down fast descents through the villages of Mugron and Montfort-en-Chalosse. Within a dozen kilometers, they had eked out a one-minute margin—despite the strong tempo being set behind by Wüst's Festina and McEwen's Farm Frites men.

When the chasers reached the flat roads on the edge of the Landes pine forest, the four leaders were in sight up the long, straight road. The gap started creeping down. It was 55 seconds when a pileup in the field (which included Postal's Hamilton and Ekimov) momentarily disrupted the chase. The gap went back up to 1:10 at the 15km-to-go marker. Maybe they would make it....

Now Telekom joined Festina and Farm Frites in the chase, and the pack got closer: 1:05 at 10km to go ... 0:32 with 5km left. Clearly, it would be touch-and-go.

Then, with the lead down to 20 seconds and 3km remaining—mostly in the narrow streets of Dax, past low, whitewashed houses—Bettini accelerated, both to assess the strength of his three companions and to increase their chances of staying away. His tactic worked: The gap was still 18 seconds at the 2km mark, and was 14 seconds with 1.5km remaining, when Bettini got out of the saddle and looked back toward the peloton.

He liked what he saw, and there was time to do a little finessing in the 740-meter-long finishing straight before Bettini first followed the leadouts of Rous then Verheyen, before sprinting impressively to the win.

The local man with the balding head and still-glinting eyes watching from the stands must have approved. Bettini had won the sprint just like he used to—à la Darrigade.

Mountains Ahead

With the flat stages over, Lance Armstrong was the best placed of the overall contenders. Other than the enigmatic Laurent Jalabert—who had yet to prove that his bid for the podium would survive the high mountains—the American had an advantage on all the other favorites. He was 0:19 ahead of Abraham Olano; 0:43 ahead of Jan Ullrich; 2:05 ahead of Bobby Julich; 2:33 ahead of Angel Casero; 2:49 ahead of Michael Boogerd; 4:05 ahead of Alex Zülle; 5:12 ahead of Marco Pantani; 5:32 ahead of Richard Virenque; and 6:02 ahead of Fernando Escartin.

With nine days, 1432km and 33 hours of racing behind them, the 171 riders still in this 87th Tour de France were finally going to face their toughest task: the first mountain stage. Stage 10 would take them into the heart of the Pyrenees—where forecasters said they would face thick mists, high winds, heavy rain and temperatures in the mid-40s. It was a daunting prospect for a day that featured five ascents: one cat. 3, one Cat. 2, one Cat. 1 and two hors-categorie climbs—the Col d'Aubisque and the one to the finish at Hautacam.

It looked like being one of the toughest stages of the Tour, and defending champion Armstrong knew that this is where he would need to show his climbing strength, and his strength of mind. The Texan would recall (he'll never forget it!)that on the fourth of the day's peaks, the Col du Soulor—or rather on its descent—he crashed heavily when scouting out this stage on May 5. It was sunny and warm back then, while in the race Monday it would be cool and misty.

If the stage ran according to form, that descent would probably see a dozen or more riders come together. Armstrong was hoping that his teammates Tyler Hamilton and Kevin Livingston would be alongside him, both to help contain any attacks and to be with him on the first slopes of the 8-percent, 13.5km climb to the finish at Hautacam.

As for the current race leader, Alberto Elli had a 5:54 margin over Armstrong; but Elli was in the Tour to ride for Telekom leader Ullrich, and the veteran Italian will not be racing to defend his lead. If he did lose the yellow jersey, the likely race leader at Hautacam was more likely to be Armstrong than Ullrich.

The mountains were waiting. That horrible weather, too. It looked like being a day of high drama.

TOUR DE FRANCE, July 1–9.

STAGE 1
Futuroscope Time Trial. July 1.

1. David Millar (GB), Cofidis, 16.5km in 19:03 (51.968 kph); **2. Lance Armstrong (USA), U.S. Postal Service, 19:05;** 3. Laurent Jalabert, 19:06; 4. Jan Ullrich (G), Telekom, 19:07; 5. David Cañada (Sp), ONCE-Deutsche Bank, 19:19; 6. Alex Zülle (Swi), 19:23; 7. Viatcheslav Ekimov (Rus), U.S. Postal Service, 19:24; 8 Simone Borgheresi (I), Mercatone Uno; **9. Tyler Hamilton (USA), U.S. Postal Service, 19:36;** 10. Erik Dekker (Nl), Rabobank, 19:39; 11. Abraham Olano (Sp), ONCE-Deutsche Bank, 19:42; 12. Joseba Beloki (Sp), Festina, 19:43; 13. Jens Voigt (G), Crédit Agricole, 19:47; 14. David Plaza (Sp), Festina, s.t.; 15. Gilles Maignan (F), Ag2R Prévoyance, 19:52; 16. Nicolas Jalabert (F), ONCE-Deutsche Bank, 19:56; 17. Ivan Gutierrez, ONCE-Rabobank, s.t.; 18. Marc Wauters (B), Rabobank, 19:57; 19. Daniele Nardello (I), Mapei-Quick Step; 20. Félix Garcia Casas (Sp), Festina, both s.t.

OTHERS: 24. Kevin Livingston (USA), U.S. Postal Service, 19:59; 27. Fred Rodriguez (USA), Mapei-Quick Step, 20:01; 31. Chann McRae (USA), Mapei-Quick Step, 20:06; 33. Jonathan Vaughters (USA), Crédit Agricole, 20:07; 34. Benoît Joachim (Lux), U.S. Postal Service, 20:08; 39. Frank Vandenbroucke (B), Cofidis, 20:10; **45. George Hincapie (USA), U.S. Postal Service, 20:14; 55. Bobby Julich (USA), Crédit Agricole, 20:20;** 62. Michael Boogerd (Nl), Rabobank, 20:28; 72. Richard Virenque (F), Polti, 20:34; 75. Fernando Escartin (Sp), Kelme, 20:35; 136. Marco Pantani (I), Mercatone Uno-Albacom, 21:19; **153. Frankie Andreu (USA), U.S. Postal Service, 21:30.**

STAGE 2
Futuroscope–Loudun. July 2.

1. Tom Steels (B), Mapei-Quick Step, 194km in 4:46:08 (40.680 kph); 2. Stuart O'Grady (Aus), Crédit Agricole; 3. Erik Zabel (G), Telekom; 4. Romans Vainsteins (Lat), Vini Caldirola; 5. Marcel Wüst (G), Festina; 6. Dario Pieri (I), Saeco-Valli & Valli; 7. Robbie McEwen (Aus), Farm Frites; 8. Zoran Klemencic (Slo), Vini Caldirola; 9. François Simon (F), Bonjour; 10. Jans Koerts (Nl), Farm Frites; 11. Markus Zberg (Swi), Rabobank; 12. Christophe Mengin (F), La Française des Jeux; 13. Jaan Kirsipuu (Est), Ag2R Prévoyance; 14. Fabio Fontanelli (I), Mercatone Uno-Albacom; 15. Tristan Hoffman (Nl), MemoryCard-Jack & Jones; 16. Jean-Patrick Nazon (F), La Française des Jeux; 17. Millar; 18. Massimiliano Mori (I), Saeco-Valli & Valli; 19. Arvis Piziks (Lat), MemoryCard-Jack& Jones; 20. Olivier Perraudeau (F), Bonjour, all s.t.

OTHERS: 24. Ullrich; 33. Olano; **38. Armstrong; 39. Hincapie;** 40. Michele Bartoli (I), Mapei-Quick Step; 41. Pantani; 45.

Jeroen Blijlevens (Nl), Polti; **46. Julich;** 56. Zülle; 61. Jalabert; 62. **Hamilton; 68. McRae;** 107. Rodriguez; **117. Livingston; 120. Vaughters; 153. Andreu,** all s.t.

OVERALL: 1. Millar, 210.5km in 5:05:00; **2. Armstrong, at 0:04;** 3. Jalabert, at 0:15; 4. Ullrich, at 0:16; 5. Cañada, at 0:18.

STAGE 3
Loudon–Nantes. July 3.

1. Steels, 161.5km in 3:37:51 (44.480 kph); 2. Wüst; 3. Zabel; 4. Koerts; 5. O'Grady; 6. Nazon; 7. Simon; 8. Kirsipuu ; 9. Vainsteins; 10. Pieri; 11. Stefano Zanini (I), Mapei-Quick Step; 12. Jacky Durand (F), Lotto-Adecco; 13. Klemencic; 14. Emmanuel Magnien (F), La Française des Jeux; 15. Massimo Apollonio (I), Vini Caldirola; 16. McEwen; 17. Frank Hoj (Dk), La Française des Jeux; 18. Ullrich; 19. Mengin; 20. Perraudeau, all s.t.

OTHERS: 25. Jalabert (F), s.t.; **27. Rodriguez, at 0:09;** 28. Olano; 36. Virenque; 45. Zülle; **46. Julich;** 47. Bartoli; **59. McRae; 61. Andreu;** 62. Escartin; **64. Armstrong;** 66. Hincapie; 69. Vasseur; 72. Ekimov; **75. Livingston;** 84. Vandenbroucke; 99. Pantani; 102. **Hamilton; 110. Vaughters,** all s.t.

OVERALL: 1. Millar, 372km in 8:43:09; **2. Armstrong, at 0:04;** 3. Jalabert, at 0:06; 4. Ullrich, at 0:07; 5. Cañada, at 0:18; 6. Zülle, at 0:22; 7. Ekimov, at 0:23; 8. Borgheresi, at 0:29; 9. Voigt, at 0:30; 10. **Hamilton,** at 0:35.

OTHERS: 25. Livingston, at 0:58; 28. Rodriguez, at 1:00; **32. McRae, at 1:05; 33. Vaughters, at 1:06;** 34. Joachim, at 1:07; 38. Vandenbroucke, at 1:09; **46. Hincapie, at 1:13; 55. Julich, at 1:19;** 63. Boogerd, at 1:27; 73. Virenque, at 1:33; 75. Escartin, at 1:34; 139. Pantani, at 2:18; **148. Andreu, at 2:29.**

STAGE 4
Team Time Trial. July 4.

1. ONCE-Deutsche Bank, 70km in 1:25:35 (49.074 kph); 2. U.S. Postal Service, 1:26:21; 3. Telekom, 1:27:01; 4. Crédit Agricole, 1:27:07; 5. Rabobank, 1:27:47; 6. Festina Watches, 1:27:51; 7. Cofidis, 1:28:28; 8. Mapei-Quick Step, 1:28:53; 9. Mercatone Uno-Albacom, 1:29:09; 10. MemoryCard-Jack & Jones, 1:29:14; 11. Ag2R Prevoyance, 1:29:52; 12. Banesto, 1:29:58; 13. Polti, 1:30:14; 14. Kelme-Costa Blanca, 1:30:43; 15. Saeco-Valli & Valli, 1:30:49; 16. Lotto-Adecco, 1:30:55; 17. Farm Frites, 1:31:18; 18. Vini Caldirola-Sidermec, 1:31:30; 19. La Française des Jeux, 1:31:42; 20. Bonjour, 1:32:20.

OVERALL: 1. Jalabert, 10:09:10; 2. Cañada, at 0:12; **3. Armstrong, at 0:24;** 4. Olano, at 0:35; 5. Ekimov, at 0:43; 6.

Nicolas Jalabert (F), ONCE-Deutsche Bank, at 0:49; 7. Gutierrez, s.t.; 8. Marcos Serrano (Sp), ONCE-Deutsche Bank, at 0:52; 9. Miguel Angel Peña (Sp), ONCE-Deutsche Bank, at 0:54; 10. **Hamilton, at 0:55.**

STAGE 5
Vannes–Vitre. July 5.
1. Wüst, 202km in 4:19:05 (46.780 kph); 2. Zabel; 3. Zanini; 4. Steels; 5. Salvatore Commesso (I),Saeco-Valli & Valli; 6. McEwen; 7. Koerts; 8. O'Grady; 9. Vainsteins; 10. Magnien, all s.t.

OTHERS: 22. Vandenbroucke; **25. Armstrong; 26. Hincapie; 28. Julich, all s.t.;** 31. Olano, at 0:08; **33. Rodriguez;** 34. Voight, both s.t.; 39. Virenque, at 0:10; 53. Zülle; **57. Hamilton;** 58. Escartin; 59. Laurent Jalabert; 60. Pantani; **65. McRae;** 75. Livingston; **77. Vaughters;** 98 Dekker; **165. Andreu, all s.t.**

OVERALL: 1. Jalabert, 644km 14:28:25; 2. Cañada, at 0:12; 3. **Armstrong,** at 0:14; 4. Olano, at 0:35; 5. Ekimov, at 0:43; 6. Nicolas Jalabert, at 0:49; 7. Gutierrez, s.t.; 8. Peter Luttenberger (A), ONCE-Deutsche Bank, at 0:51; 9. Serrano, at 0:52; 10. Peña, at 0:54.

STAGE 6
Vitré–Tours. July 6.
1. Leon Van Bon (Nl), Rabobank, 198.5km in 4:28:06 (44.423 kph); 2. Zberg; 3. Magnien; 4. Servais Knaven (Nl), Farm Frites; 5. Piziks; 6. Alberto Elli (I), Telekom; 7. Fabrice Gougot (F), Credit Agricole; 8. Commesso; 9. Durand; 10. Jose Luis Arrieta (Sp), Banesto, all s.t..

OTHERS: 27. Olano, at 7:49; 33. Jalabert; **35. Armstrong;** 39. Pantani; **51. Hamilton;** 52. Virenque; 56. Ullrich; **59. Julich;** 61. Boogerd; 65. Zülle; **66. Vaughters;** 73. Hincapie; 82. McRae; 85. Escartin; 95. Bartoli; 104. Aerts; **105. Livingston; 117. Andreu;** 139. Vandenbroucke; **147. Rodriguez, all s.t.;** 173. Kirsipuu,at 22:26; 176. O'Grady, s.t.

OVERALL: 1. Elli, 842.5km in 18:58:40; 2. Gougot, at 0:12; 3. Wauters, at 1:17; 4. Chanteur, at 2:56; 5. Arrieta, at 3:08; 6. Durand, at 3:27; 7. Commesso, at 3:52; 8. Knaven, at 4:31; 9. Piziks, at 4:38; 10.Jalabert, at 5:40.

STAGE 7
Tours–Limoges. July 7.
1. Christophe Agnolutto (F), Ag2R Prévoyance, 205.5km in 5:11:41 (39.559 kph); 2. Wüst, at 1:11; 3. Zabel; 4. Vainsteins; 5. Klemencic; 6. Paolo Bettini (I), Mapei-Quick Step; 7. Koerts; 8. Zanini; 9. Enrico Cassini (I), Polti; 10. Glenn Magnusson (S), Farm Frites.

OTHERS: 22. Pantani, s.t.; 26. Jalabert; 27. Boogerd; 37. Virenque; 41. Ullrich; 43. Aerts; **46. Hincapie;** 48. Zülle; **52. Julich; 54. Hamilton; 61. Vaughters;** 63. Vandenbroucke; **64. McRae;** 73. Olano; 74. **Livingston;** 86. Bartoli; 88. Ekimov; **90. Rodriguez;** 96. Escartin; 143. Steels, all s.t.; **173. Andreu, at 2:32.**

OVERALL: 1. Elli, 1084km in 24:11:32; 2. Gougot, at 0:12; 3. Wauters, at 1:17; 4. Chanteur, at 2:56; 5. Arrieta, at3:08; 6. Durand, at 3:27; 7. Commesso, at 3:52; 8. Knaven, at 4:31; 9. Piziks, at 4:38; 10. Jalabert, at 5:40.

STAGE 8
Limoge–Villenueve-Sur-Lot. July 8.
1. Dekker, 203.5km in 4:22:14 (46.561 kph); 2. Xavier Jan (F), La Francaise des Jeux, at 0:52; 3. Vicente Garcia-Acosta (Sp), Banesto, at 0:56; **4. Rodriguez, at 0:58;** 5. Pieri; 6. Bart Voskamp (Nl), Polti; 7. Didier Rous (F), Bonjour, all s.t.; 8. Mauro Radaelli (I), Vini Caldirola-Sidermec, at 1:36; 9. Nicolay Bo Larsen (Dk), MemoryCard-Jack & Jones, at 1:36; 10. Michael Sandstod (Dk), MemoryCard-Jack & Jones, at 1:43.

OTHERS: 33. Pantani, at 5:42; 39. Ullrich.; 40. Boogerd; 45. Olano; 46. Jalabert; **57. Julich; 66. Armstrong; 72. Vaughters; 83. Hincapie; 92. Hamilton; 107. Livingston;** 160. Andreu, all s.t.

OVERALL: 1. Elli, 1251.5km in 28:39:28; 2. Gougot, at 0:12; 3. Wauters, at 1:17; 4. Chanteur, at 2:56; 5. Arrieta, at 3:08; 6. Voigt, at 3:17; 7. Durand, at 3:21; 8. Commesso, at 3:52; 9. Knaven, at 4:31; 10. Piziks, at 4:38.

STAGE 9
Agen–Dax. July 9.
1. Bettini, 181km in 4:29:06 (40.356 kph); 2. Geert Verheyen (B), Lotto-Adecco; 3. José Angel Vidal (Sp), Kelme-Costa Blanca; 4. Rous; 5. Zabel; 6. Vainsteins; 7. Cassani; 8. Piziks; 9. Zanini; 10. Klemencic, all s.t.

OTHERS: 38. Rodriguez; 39. Pantani; 44. Olano; 47. **Armstrong;** 48. Ullrich; 49. Jalabert; **52. Hincapie; 61. Julich;** 67. Escartin; **69. Vaughters;** 72. Zülle; 75. Boogerd; 81. Millar; **82. Andreu;** 84. Vandenbroucke ; **85. McRae; 86. Hamilton; 109. Livingston, all s.t.;** 164. Ekimov, at 1:32.

OVERALL: 1. Elli,1432.5km in 28:39:28; 2. Gougot, at 0:12; 3. Wauters, at 1:17; 4. Chanteur, at 2:56; 5. Arrieta, at 3:08; 6. Durand, at 3:17; 7. Voigt, s.t.; 8. Commesso, at 3:52; 9. Knaven, at 4:31; 10. Piziks, at 4:38.

WEEK 2

Back to the Future

Back in 1970, Eddy Merckx was at the height of his fame and dominance. He already was leading the 57th Tour de France by many minutes when stage 14 came along: Gap to the top of Mont Ventoux. The Belgian had vowed that he would make one of his typical solo breaks, to honor his former teammate and friend, Tom Simpson, who died when climbing the Ventoux three years earlier.

Merckx duly made his attack at the foot of the mighty mountain, and was on his own with 8km still to climb. Less than two kilometers from the top, with early-evening sunshine casting long shadows across the Ventoux's stark, white rocky slopes, Merckx reached the granite monument where Simpson fell, making the sign of the cross as he passed by.

On winning the stage, Merckx was mobbed by the media, and, looking pale, he climbed a platform for a TV interview. "It's not possible ... I'm suffocating ..." was all he could say before passing out. Merckx was carried to an ambulance, an oxygen mask placed over his mouth and nose. There, runner-up Martin Van den Bossche also needed oxygen, after making a big effort in the thin air to chase after Merckx, 6263 feet above the hazy plains of Provence.

Their blackouts were eerily similar to Simpson's—the British cyclist who, on a blisteringly hot day, literally rode himself to a standstill, collapsed and died within sight of the summit. Always an aggressive and ambitious rider, Simpson had pushed his body too far—alcohol and amphetamines were blamed after an autopsy. His death was a catalyst for the introduction of drug tests in cycling.

Because of what happened to Merckx, and, of course, Simpson, the Tour organizers were wary to end another road stage atop the giant Ventoux. There were two other stages to its summit. In 1972, Merckx rode more conservatively and didn't counter a late attack by a young Bernard Thévenet, and in 1987, Jean-François Bernard won a Tour time trial up the Ventoux. So this second week of the 2000 Tour would see the famed mountain play host to a road stage for the first time in 28 years.

The inclusion of the legendary peak wasn't the only retro-like feature of the 87th Tour de France that was announced at a press conference in Paris, October 21, 1999. Race organizer Jean-Marie Leblanc also revealed several other kickbacks to the race's great traditions—including that team time trial in the opening week.

Leblanc was pleased that the TTT had brought back into the Tour limelight the leading French rider, Laurent Jalabert.

World No. 1 had been Jalabert's calling card for most of the past five years. So it was a big shock when the UCI World Rankings issued just before the Tour showed that the 31-year-old Frenchman was in 15th place! The reason? Jalabert was keeping a promise to focus on the Tour, and had scaled back his usual schedule of spring races. He didn't even bother to show up for his national championship the Sunday before the Tour.

For such a talented racer, who won the 1995 Vuelta and has finished fourth at both the Giro and Tour, it's remarkable that this was the first time that Jalabert had made the Tour podium a goal. It was quite a change for a man who said he had had it up to here with racing in France when he quit the Tour in 1998, after leading the rider protests against police tactics in that year's anti-drugs purge. We thought we had seen the last of Jalabert as he drove away in his ONCE team car, munching an ice cream.

Well, he came back!

In the opening week of this 87th Tour de France, Jalabert came third in the opening time trial, and then pulled his ONCE-Deutsche Bank squad to a dominating win in the stage 4 team time trial. So Jalabert was back in the Tour lead for the first time in five years.

He remembered the last time. "I don't want to lose the yellow jersey the same way I did in '95," he said on July 4. It will be remembered that Jalabert wore the jersey for two days in 1995 before crashing into the barriers near the end of the fourth stage into Le Havre.

This year, it looked likely that Jalabert would still be wearing the yellow jersey entering the mountains on July 10; but tactical considerations saw him lose it at Tours, and by the time the race reached Dax he was in 14th place, 5:40 behind new leader Alberto Elli. On the list of favorites, however, Jalabert still had a 14-second advantage on Lance

Armstrong, and 57 seconds on Jan Ullrich.

Besides Jalabert, Armstrong and Ullrich, the riders best placed to shoot at the final podium in Paris appeared to be Banesto's Abraham Olano (19 seconds down on Armstrong), Crédit Agricole's Jonathan Vaughters (1:58 behind Armstrong) and Festina's Joseba Beloki (2:18 behind the American). Almost certainly out of the hunt were last year's runners-up: Banesto's Alex Zülle (4:05 behind Armstrong) and Kelme-Costa Blanca's Fernando Escartin (at 6:02).

The dark horse, of course, was Marco Pantani. As in his winning Tour of 1998, *Il Pirata* was riding a canny race, following wheels and limiting his losses after nine stages to 5:12 on Armstrong. He overcame a similar deficit to win the Tour in 1998, and he could do it again.

By now, the Tour was in the deep southwest of France, on the edge of the Pyrénées—and that's where the race was headed for stage 10. The Hautacam mountaintop finish was where Miguel Induráin in 1994 and Bjarne Riis in '96 virtually clinched their overall Tour wins. There wasn't a second stage in the Pyrénées, but after a transitional stage to Revel and a transfer to Avignon, the climbing continued with the much-awaited Mont Ventoux finish. That would be followed by another stage of transition, through the beautiful countryside of Provence to Draguignan—where the Tour would begin a long south-north trek through the French Alps.

The trek would open with a retro stage that included the legendary climbs of the Col d'Allos, Col de Vars and Col d'Izoard; it had been 50 years since these three passes had been included in the same stage. The next alpine stage would be no less daunting: a 168km haul over the Galibier and Madeleine mountains to the 17km, 8-percent uphill finish to Courchevel—where the race would stop for its second rest day.

STAGE 10
Dax–Hautacam (Lourdes) • July 10

Strike Out!

STUNNING! MONUMENTAL! IMPERIAL! PRODIGIOUS! MAJESTIC! INCREDIBLE! CHOOSE WHICHEVER adjective you like, and none of them comes close to describing Lance Armstrong's transcendent ride at Hautacam. Everyone was stunned: veteran race followers, the fans and, most importantly, the other contenders. In a little over half an hour of uphill racing, at the end of a day of rugged climbing and apocalyptic weather, Armstrong pretty much put the 87th Tour de France on ice.

The lean, long American didn't win this stage 10—that honor went to a very brave Basque named Javier Otxoa, after a marathon breakaway—but in Tour history books, Hautacam 2000 will be forever synonymous with Armstrong. He rode with fire in his legs and vengeance in his eyes. It was an emphatic response to those who had questioned his 1999 Tour victory, believing that no one could transform himself from a classics rider into a Tour winner without some unnatural help. His ride also answered those who said that the 1999 Tour wasn't particularly competitive, because past winners Pantani and Ullrich weren't in the field. Well, they were there now, and Armstrong again dominated. Those doubters could no longer question the Texan's efficacy....

When Armstrong awoke that morning in the Hotel Calicea at Dax, rain was pelting down on the small lake outside his window. A gale was blowing, whipping the water into wavelets and bending tree branches as if they were performing a bizarre ballet. The Texan, who races at his best in tough conditions, probably had a smile on his face.

A few rooms away in the same hotel, Ullrich was not so pleased: He likes hot weather, as it was for most of the 1997 Tour he won; and is not fond of rain—he lost the 1998 Tour to Pantani on a day of cold, wet rain in the Alps. Now, in 2000, Ullrich was hoping that the weather for this gigantic stage through the Pyrénées would be better than forecast.

Well, after the early-morning storm, the rain did stop and the sun came out briefly;

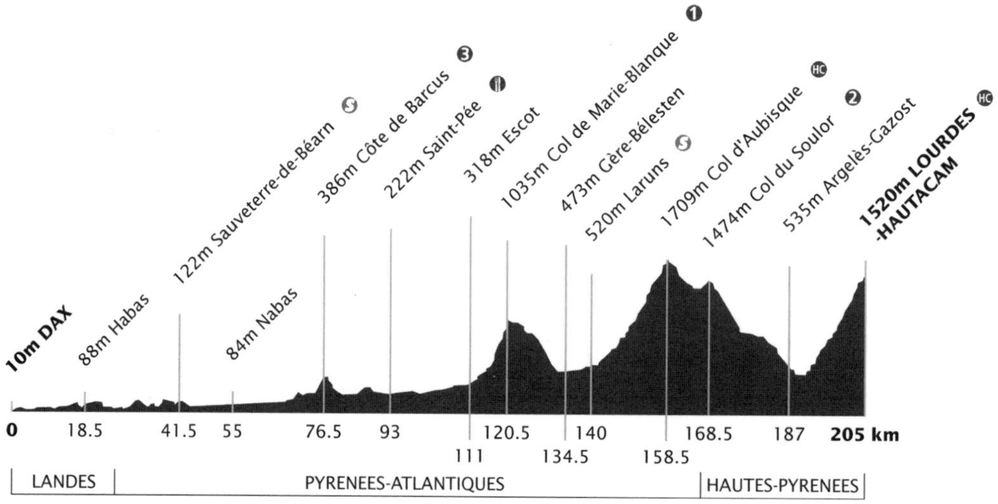

but there weren't many clear spells in the day's mix of heavy showers, strong winds, and mists in the mountains.

Armstrong's confidence and focus were clear, even before the start in Dax. He generally avoids the crush of TV and radio crews that hover around each day's sign-in podium, often by being the last man to ride up to the start, when the media has usually moved on. In Dax, however, he avoided any possible distraction. Still in tights and sneakers, he strolled 100 feet from the back door of his team camper to the metal barriers behind the podium. There, after a gendarme took apart the barriers for him, Armstrong walked up the back steps and was signing in before anyone noticed. He quickly retraced his steps, a broad smile on his face, as he shook hands with a friend.

Others weren't so relaxed. Pantani took a nervous peek at the weather when he briefly opened the door of the Mercatone Uno camper. And Ullrich didn't leave his team bus until the very last minute.

Typifying the riders' mood was the wry look on the face of Colorado's Jonathan Vaughters, who was finally getting a chance to tackle a Tour mountain stage. "I don't particularly like this weather," said the rail-thin climber, whose Crédit Agricole directeur sportif Roger Legeay was expecting him to finish in the top five at this Tour. "I've not ridden up Hautacam … but the hard thing will be getting there. There are some tricky descents before we get there."

The first of those tricky descents flowed beneath Vaughters's wheels two hours into the stage: a sweeping downhill across a green, mist-shrouded hillside to the village of Barcus. The American was safely in the main peloton, still 160-strong, just after they had cruised over the day's first summit, a winding, fairly steep Cat. 3 lined with tall hedgerows and dripping oak trees.

Eleven minutes ahead of them was a three-man attack that had been started by the aggressive Durand, 33km and one hour into the stage. The Frenchman was joined 20km later by Belgian Nico Mattan of Cofidis and Kelme's Otxoa. Riding well together on the narrow, twisting back roads through the verdant foothills of the Pyrénées, they continued to gain time, reaching the feed zone at St. Pee almost 17 minutes ahead of the pack.

Here, the Banesto riders moved to the head of the peloton and increased the tempo. They couldn't let the break continue to steal five-minute chunks, if they wanted their on-form climber José-Maria Jiménez to have a shot at the stage win. Indeed, the Spanish team's acceleration turned the tide, and the gap was down to 16:20 at the foot of the Col de Marie-Blanque—this Tour's first major mountain.

The Marie-Blanque is an "old fashioned" climb. It simply heads up a narrow side valley, following a small creek on a one-lane road that gets progressively steeper, before angling across a bare mountainside with pitches of 14 and 16 percent in the final 4km. Its difficulty was multiplied by the steady rain and a swirling mist hanging over the pine trees at the summit.

In those last 4km, Durand was dropped from the break and lost four minutes, while Mattan managed to keep Otxoa in sight, and rejoined him over the summit. Behind, attacks by Colombian Santiago Botero of Kelme, Frenchman Pascal Hervé of Polti, and the Spaniards Daniel Atienza of Saeco and Francisco Mancebo of Banesto exploded the peloton.

Race leader Elli was among those dropped, but he could feel pleased that his teammate Ullrich was one of the 30 riders in the main pack of leaders. Perhaps the Telekom leader would take over Elli's yellow jersey by the end of the day....

That denouement was still three hours away—which meant a lot of racing (and suffering) lay ahead. A quick analysis showed that Kelme (for team leaders Escartin and Heras), Banesto (for Jiménez and Zülle) and Polti (for Virenque) were throwing down the gauntlet. The riders they had in the chase group were there for two reasons: to allow their respective leaders to follow wheels in the group until they were ready to make a move; and to act as potential bridging targets if and when their leaders attacked.

This strategy would be demonstrated to perfection on the upcoming climb, the mighty Aubisque; but first came the dangerous descent of the Marie-Blanque—in the rain. There are three parts to this descent, the first two in the trees, the last down an open mountainside; and what they have in common are unpredictable turns. These proved the undoing first of Durand and Hervé, who were both chasing hard, riding at the limit, and then Vaughters.

The American, wearing a helmet, skidded on one of the lower turns and slid into a retaining wall, hitting his head. With blood flowing from cuts on his face, Vaughters got back on his bike—before momentarily losing consciousness. The ambulance had to be called up. His race was over. Once again, he had lost his chance to show his climbing form. In 1998, a bad crash before the Tour prevented him from starting; and in '99, he crashed out in the Passage du Gois pileup on stage 2. This time, Vaughters was fortunately not badly injured, but he was bitterly disappointed. He would have to wait another year.

While Vaughters was on his way to the hospital, the leaders were already on the 16km-long Aubisque, where contrasting strategies were being played out. The Postal team's Hamilton and Livingston were setting a hard tempo on the early slopes to prevent attacks, while Banesto, Kelme and Polti were trying to break it apart.

At first, Armstrong's two lieutenants seemed to be winning the battle, but both were suffering. Hamilton later said that the crash he suffered the day before bruised his right leg, "so I was favoring the left one." Livingston explained that "the first week was different this year: Tyler and I both did a lot of chasing, so I'm more tired … and the weather didn't help." Indeed, both Postal's climbers were suffering from the cold wind and heavy rain. "I was physically shivering on the Aubisque," added Hamilton.

When the two Americans dropped back, the expected attacks came from Banesto's Jiménez, Polti's Virenque (linking up with Hervé), Kelme's Escartin and Heras, Festina's Beloki and Mapei's Beltran. These men came together, before Beltran then Virenque jumped away before the top—still 10 minutes behind Otxoa (who had now dropped Mattan for good).

As Armstrong neared the Aubisque's mist-shrouded summit in a group of 20 riders, he was experiencing "a little bit of a crisis."

"I didn't have any teammates left," Armstrong explained. "Ullrich had Guerini. Pantani seemed to be waiting. So my only choice was to wait … (though) I didn't like to give guys like Escartin two minutes."

Still, that's what happened. After the long, three-tier descent via the Col du Soulor—the downhill where Armstrong crashed heavily in training two months' earlier—the Texan's group was 2:05 behind a group that included Escartin, Virenque, Heras, Botero, Jiménez, Mancebo and Beloki, which in turn was 8:25 behind Otxoa.

✸

Up ahead, the mist had cleared to reveal the whole of the 13km Hautacam climb: the first half averaging 7.5 percent on erratic roads that once dead-ended at ancient hillside villages, the second half averaging 8.2 percent on a better graded road leading to the Hautacam ski station. Thick crowds had been waiting here all day in the rain and wind. Now they were about to be rewarded with the defining moments of the 2000 Tour.

As Armstrong had predicted, the spectacular finale was launched by Pantani—a fiercely proud competitor who had come to this Tour to win. And that showed when he made his attack just 1km into the climb. Another man with ambition, Zülle, reacted first, and then had the spunk to counterattack.

Behind these two, Armstrong quickly assessed the opposition, saw that Ullrich wasn't looking great, and smoothly rose out of his saddle to surge onto Pantani's wheel. This was only the beginning of a spectacular pursuit match, with the yellow jersey as the ultimate prize.

Tyler 's diary
July 10
Lourdes

This is going to be short because it's been a long day. The 2000 Tour de France has officially begun for the U.S. Postal Service team. For a while, it seemed like this day would never get here. The first stages can have such a strange effect on you. Being patient—which means waiting for the smartest opportunities that make the most sense strategically—can be as torturous as the physical punishment of this race. Finally, the waiting game ended today … and we are on our way.

When we heard the weather forecast for today's stage, no one was too psyched—except Lance. In fact, when he heard the news he practically started doing a rain dance, hoping it would be torrential. He got his wish. When he woke up this morning and saw water teeming from the sky, he was downright giddy. Lance is the ultimate tough guy. He likes his challenges big.

The ride to the start was pretty quiet. I think we were all preoccupied, knowing what opportunities stood before us—and that we'd all have to ride to our potential under less than ideal circumstances, given the rain.

For the ninth stage out of 10, it rained. We were dumped on intermittently throughout the whole day. Aside from the painted lines on the roads getting slick, there are a number of other things to be aware of when the streets are soaked. I found myself sliding sideways more than once on manhole covers and metal grates. You can't even see them coming when the rain is driving into your eyes.

Like a bad head wind, the rain and cold are tough on smaller guys like me. I was actually shivering during the climb up the Col d'Aubisque. This is one of the downsides of training to climb. Your body gets so lean it barely has anything left to shield you from the elements. And because I was battling the cold, I lacked the extra 5 percent I needed to help respond to the attacks once they started. It would have been better if I could have stayed with Lance until the top of the Aubisque … but on a day like today, your body cannot always do what your brain tells it to.

Kevin, Lance and I rode our new Trek climbing bikes today after taking them for a test run during stage 9. And while this may sound like a shameless plug, I do have to say we all think these bikes are great. Mine even withstood a massive pileup on Sunday. But none of that is as impressive as what Lance proved—that Trek lightweights go uphill fast.

It's great to see Lance back in yellow. Today, he proved to everyone that he is in a league of his own. It's kind of funny to think back to two weeks ago, when some were questioning whether Lance could show any class against the more recent Tour winners—and now people are shaking their heads wondering if he could ever be stopped. It's safe to say he's punched a huge stamp on his credibility. Not that a Tour champion should have to, though….

We're going to do everything we can to keep him there. So, tomorrow, we begin the task of defending the jersey. Wish us luck—because we're just getting going.

The defending champion almost looked as if he were doing one of his famous South of France training rides up the Col de la Madone: maintaining the highest possible cadence on the lowest possible gear. The difference was that whenever he caught a rider, or a group, he would sit in for a few moments, and then launch another out-of-the-saddle sprint.

After disposing of Zülle, then Pantani with 10km to go, Armstrong next came up to the seven men chasing Otxoa. He took a longer rest here before going to the head of the line, and then, looking back at the others, he accelerated again. Virenque tried to go with the American, but soon gave up, and was replaced by Jiménez. The Spanish climber was in a gear several notches higher than Armstrong, and he had to make a huge lunging effort to close a tiny gap. Once there, Jiménez simply followed—no mean task on a road that had pitches of 11 percent.

Now, only the courageous Otxoa was ahead of them: 4:58 with 5km to go ... 3:21 with 3km left ... and, after Armstrong had dropped Jiménez, 2:14 at 2km. It looked possible that Armstrong would even catch Otxoa—but the man who had been leading the race for 150km wasn't about to concede. He was hurting, his style was awry, his breath was short ... and it all meant nothing. For he could now scent his first-ever victory as a pro.

Otxoa started the final climb 10:30 ahead of Armstrong. He kept 41 seconds on the line. But Armstrong was more interested in the time he had gained on his expected rivals for the overall prize: 1:20 on Escartin, 3:05 on Zülle, 3:19 on Ullrich, and 5:10 on Pantani, who had bonked.

Emphatic. No doubt. No doubters....

Magnificent.

Pyrénées Take Their Toll

As in every Tour de France, the brutal change from rolling across the plains on a high 53x11 gear to spinning up mountains on a low 39x23 exercised its considerable damage. Nine riders were forced to quit the race on this one stage, and the battle for the yellow jersey turned into a one-man-show: Lance Armstrong against the climbers.

Among the nine who dropped out was Belgian hope Frank Vandenbroucke, who had been considered an outsider to win the Tour. Vandenbroucke was suffering with tendinitis in his left knee, and when he was dropped on the Marie-Blanque, the day's first major climb—at the same time as sprinters Tom Steels and Jaan Kirsipuu—the young Belgian knew he wouldn't finish the stage.

In the battle for the overall victory, only Ullrich and Zülle managed to stay in the picture, while the other expected threats—Pantani, Olano, Jalabert and Julich—simply crumpled when Armstrong stepped on the gas with 12km of the Hautacam climb to go. Both Zulle and Ullrich lost "only" three minutes to the magnificent Texan, while the others simply weren't ready for this tough, tough day. Olano lost almost seven minutes, Jalabert eight minutes and Julich, suffering from the cold, 12 minutes.

Who then, besides Ullrich (in second at 4:14) and Zulle (13th at 7:22), was left to challenge Armstrong's supremacy? The short answer was: climbers. The men to watch on the Mont Ventoux stage (three days away) and the three hard stages in the Alps looked likely to be Festina's Joseba Beloki (sixth at 5:23), Mapei's Beltran (seventh overall at 6:13), Banesto's Jiménez (ninth at 6:21), Polti's Virenque (11th at 6:59), and Kelme's Heras (15th at 7:33) and Escartin (17th at 7:34). Except for Frenchman Virenque, all of those climbers are Spanish, and this is a reflection of the growing talent pool in Spain over the past two years. And that pool would have been much bigger had the Euskaltel and Vitalicio squads been invited to compete in this Tour.

Interestingly in the race for the white jersey—restricted to riders 25 and under—Spain's Francisco Mancebo of Banesto (who was 11th on the stage) had taken the overall lead, 4:13 ahead of this Tour's first stage winner, David Millar of Cofidis.

STAGE 11
Bagnères-de-Bigorre–Revel • July 11

Dekker II

WITH THE GENERAL CLASSIFICATION HAVING BEEN REWRITTEN BY ONE STAGE IN THE PYRÉNÉES, AND only a handful of riders now in contention for the yellow jersey, everyone was expecting a different type of race on this rolling stage across the Midi. They forgot to tell Dekker.

The tall Dutchman, who had already conducted three long breakaways, taking one of them to a stage victory at Villeneuve-sur-Lot, was ready to go again. Ready and motivated, having lost the polka-dot climbers' jersey to Otxoa the previous day. This stage, with its six minor climbs, offered Dekker a chance to claim back some of his lost ground.

Well, that's what was assumed when he attacked on the first KoM, the Cat. 3 Côte de Mauvezin, just 15km into this 218.5km stage. He went over the summit ahead of

Virenque, Otxoa and Botero, the main contenders in the climbers' competition. And seeing as there was a Cat. 4 climb right after, it was no surprise when Dekker continued his effort on the descent, where he was joined by Kelme's Botero. By the top of the next little hill, they were 14 seconds ahead of the chasing Vicente Garcia-Acosta of Banesto and Javier Pascual-Llorente of Kelme, with the pack at 28 seconds.

Surely, Dekker wasn't intending to "go-all-the-way" once more? If so, wouldn't it make sense to wait for the two chasers and have two more riders willing to share the work? Perhaps. But Dekker was on a mission. Even though heavy rain was falling, he knew that the bad weather would probably discourage any concerted chase from the pack. And, more importantly, he could feel the wind at his back as he and Botero headed along narrow, hilly back roads, parallel to the cloud-covered Pyrénées.

A pursuit was started by the ONCE team, which needed to restore some of its respect after disappointing performances the day before by its leaders Zülle and Jalabert. The Spanish squad quickly caught Garcia-Acosta and Pascual-Llorente, and cut the gap on Dekker and Botero to 22 seconds. This brought Banesto and Armstrong's Postal Service team to the front—and the gap began opening again.

Okay, said the Postals, these two guys aren't dangerous, let them go.

Nobody argued with that assessment, and the gap steadily grew: 2:15 one hour into the stage; 9:30 after two hours; and 13:45 after three hours—at which point the Postal team slightly increased the tempo of the peloton, to stop the gap growing too much. But it was still more than 12 minutes at 35km from the finish, so Dekker had a good chance of winning a second stage….

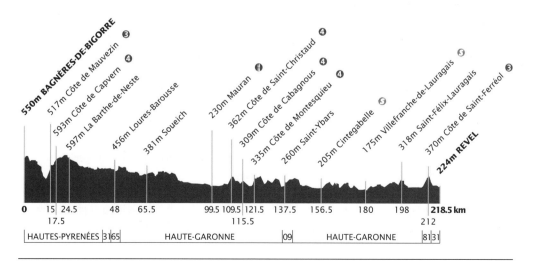

Fred's diary
July 11
Toulouse

You can't believe what a hard time I'm having trying to log on to the Internet. As an American, I'm used to big hotels and having easy access to the Web. Not so easy here in France, where some hotels aren't as good as I would like them to be. This is the third time I've had a problem trying to file my diary piece.

I know you're thinking that the Tour is the biggest bike race in the world and that they treat us like kings. Not! I can tell you it doesn't compare with the accommodations we get on events like the Tour de Langkawi in Malaysia, where we stay at luxury hotels.

Last night, where we stayed in Lourdes, they brought in a 10-inch TV for us, and they had to plug it into an outlet in the bathroom! But the funniest part of the hotel was its maze of hallways. It seems that they had added extensions every few years, and each time added corners. It was hard just to find the way back to your room.

Tonight's hotel in Toulouse is not a whole lot better. Chann and I are again in a room that measures about 10 by 10. There's just enough room for two beds—small beds!—and our suitcases.

I guess I sound a bit bitter. Truth is, I've had two days of wind and rain, and feel in need of a little pampering. That will have to wait, though, until tomorrow, our first rest day.

Plan is, we're leaving at 8:30 in the morning and have a 350km drive to Avignon. We wanted to do the drive after today's stage, and stay at the hotel in Avignon for three days instead of two.

But the Tour people heard about us wanting to change hotels, and our managers were told today that any team that didn't stay in the hotels booked for tonight would be thrown out of the race—it's one of the race rules. So here we are.

We travel by team bus tomorrow, so it'll be possible to get some sleep. On Mapei, we have this really big bus, which is great. The only problem is getting to some of the stages. This morning, we had a little problem coming into the start. We had to drive into this narrow street with cars packed on both sides—and the bus got stuck. Luckily, the cars are small in Europe, so our staff could pick them up and move them one by one! We managed to get through—after moving 200 meters in about 20 minutes.

In today's race, I was tired, not feeling well, and almost got dropped on the last climb. If you weren't in the front, you were fighting in the wind. I said to myself that if I can make it to the top, I'll be okay. When I saw this banner from about 400 meters away, I made myself stay in the group, thinking it was the top. But when we got closer, I saw it was the 1km-to-the-top sign—and I knew I wouldn't make it.

Luckily, the climb leveled off. That gave me the chance to get back among the team cars and sprint onto the peloton, before the descent. There were still about 6km to go, so I was sprinting out of every corner, and I made it back to the front. I wanted to go for the sprint, even though I knew it was only for about 10th place.

At one point, with 2km to go, everyone was in the gutter. I was looking for Zabel's wheel and was going for it, when I saw that the guy on his wheel was Lance—and I knew he wouldn't give it up! So my teammates then took me to the finish, and Bettini led me out. I was in good position for the sprint ... but my legs were done.

The 29-year-old Dekker is in his eighth season with the Dutch team managed by Jan Raas [now Rabobank, previously WordPerfect and Novell], and most of his two dozen victories have come in second-tier stage races like the Tour of Sweden and Tour of Denmark. The lowest point of his career came in October 1999, when he tested over the 50-percent hematocrit limit at the world's in Verona, Italy.

"That was a horrible time," recalled Dekker, who protested his innocence. He was in danger of losing his job, as Rabobank has a firm policy that any of its riders who test positive at the anti-doping control are cut. But a hematocrit test is not definitive, so Rabobank formed a three-man commission—including a respected heart specialist and a hematologist—to investigate Dekker's case and do more tests on his blood sample. After three months, their verdict was: no evidence of Dekker having used prohibited substances. He was back on the team, and began the 2000 season keen to prove himself again on the bike. That chance was taken away when he crashed and broke his collarbone before the spring classics; but he returned to racing in late May, still with something to prove.

Botero also has had problems with medical controls—and came to the Tour with something to prove. He tested positive four times last year for high testosterone counts—a problem that has since been shown to be a characteristic common to his father and grandfather, too. But although he was later issued a certificate from the UCI to validate this, the Colombian was suspended for nine months, and did not return to racing until a month before the Tour.

On a finishing circuit at Revel, Botero tried three times to drop Dekker on the easy Côte de St. Ferréol, but the Dutchman was too strong and then cleverly controlled the final sprint from the front.

It seemed almost rote for Dekker to lead the stage for 203km and win again; but to average almost 43 kph on hilly, rugged back roads was another remarkable athletic feat. For proof, you only needed to look at some of the weary riders who rode into Revel at day's end. More than half the field had been spit out the back when Banesto increased the pack's pace several notches in the final 35km, splitting the peloton into eight separate groups spread over 10 minutes. Everyone was indeed glad to see the finish ... and ready to enjoy the Tour's first rest day.

And Dekker? He was probably already thinking about that well-known saying: never two without three. Hmmm....

Chann's diary
July 11
Avignon

Did you ever want to know what Tour de France competitors do on their rest days in between stages? First of all, I do not know why they have rest days—except to transfer us from one side of the country to the other. These days-off totally throw off everyone's race rhythm, and we just sit around and try not to eat too much all day. Every Euro director will tell that if you stuff yourself on rest day, you will be blocked for the next day's stage.

The other important key factor is your training ride: You have to ride at least two hours with a little effort, and some guys like to do up to four hours with motorpacing. Bartoli asked me if I wanted to join him for an hour behind the car, but I opted out, in favor of more relaxed training.

This Tour is not going that well for me, but I am keeping a positive outlook towards the future, and know that nothing ever comes without a fight. The Giro and the Tour have proven to be very difficult to blend together, and next season I will definitely focus on only one of them. But for now, I have to give my best and look out for all of the guys who are on form on the team. I am sure that we have another win coming, and as always, I want to play a vital role in it.

The Postal boys are riding very strong for Lance, and I believe that their performance has a lot to do with the strong connection that Lance has with his director Johan Bruynel. They prepare for this race more precisely than any other team. Our team will remain focused on winning stages, and try to pull off a mountain-stage win.

Time for a Rest

Some very weary riders rolled into Revel, at the end of what was the longest stage yet of this Tour de France. It was not only the 218.5km from Bagnères-de-Bigorre to Revel that caused the damage, but the constant climbs on a difficult route between the Pyrénées and the edge of the Massif Central, along with a super-fast finale.

With 40km of the stage still to go, the main field was still together, 13 minutes down on the two-man breakaway. Neither eventual stage winner Dekker nor his companion Botero was a danger to Armstrong's yellow jersey; but their big lead was having an effect on one of the other classifications: the team race.

At the start of the day, Dekker's Rabobank team was leading by 6:49 over second-place Banesto, with Botero's Kelme-Costa Blanca squad in sixth place, at 17:51. Banesto wanted to keep its second place, and also prevent Rabobank and Kelme from taking too much time. So when Banesto riders went to the front of the pack—taking over from Armstrong's Postal team—they immediately increased the pace.

Blown by a strong west wind, Banesto increased the speed several notches, cutting the two leaders' advantage to only five minutes on the line—and splitting the pack into eight groups spread over 10 minutes. In the back two groups were sprinters Tom Steels, Marcel Wüst and Robbie McEwen, which allowed Erik Zabel (who took the sprint for 10th place on the stage) to increase his lead in the green jersey classification from 17 to 37 points over Wüst.

Two more riders dropped, leaving 160 riders from the original start list of 180. All of them would enjoy the Tour's first rest day Wednesday, after driving the 350km from their hotels in Toulouse to Avignon. They would then take a leg-loosening training ride of about two hours—preparing themselves for the Tour's next big obstacle: the climb of Mont Ventoux....

REST DAY
Avignon • July 12

Ventoux: The Windy Mountain

ADVERSE WEATHER HAS RARELY AFFECTED THE TOUR DE FRANCE, BUT THERE WAS A CHANCE THAT stage 12, to the 6263-foot summit of Mont Ventoux, would finish lower down the mountain. The reason? The Ventoux was living up to its name—which translated from the French means the windy peak.

July 12 was an official rest day, and the 160 riders remaining in the race traveled from Toulouse in the morning before taking training rides from their hotels around the base of the Ventoux. The infamous Mistral wind was blowing down the Rhône Valley, making riding difficult; but race officials who drove to the top of the mountain reported much tougher conditions: wind gusts of up to 150 kph (almost 100 mph), early-morning temperatures in the 30s Fahrenheit and snow on the ground.

Already, a decision had been made not to install the big tent that was to house the press center near the mountain's summit. Instead, most journalists would remain in the start town of Carpentras, where the press center was set up for Wednesday's rest day.

Stage 12 wouldn't be cancelled, but depending on the wind, the stage finish could be brought down from the summit to the Chalet Reynard turn, 6.5km and 1600 feet lower. Chalet Reynard has previously seen stage finishes of the Paris-Nice race in March—when the road to the peak is usually snowbound

Only four road stages of the Tour had previously ended at the Ventoux summit, all of them won by brilliant climbers. Luxembourger Charly Gaul opened the series in 1958;

Tyler's diary
July 12
St. Paul-Trois Châteaux

Rest days are usually anything but restful. But today, I did find time to take a nap. There always seems to be too much action on these days that are supposedly set-aside for recuperation. For starters, there is usually a transfer of some sort—and today was no exception. We bunked down in Toulouse last night, and drove to the Avignon area this morning.

After the drive, we headed out for a short training ride, to shake the cobwebs from our legs. Like last year, we were greeted in the parking lot by a tour group and scads of journalists. Both entourages traveled with us during the first few kilometers of our ride—until Johan finally declared, "Enough!"

Then there are usually a bunch of interviews scheduled on rest days. Still, today was fairly manageable. The team is doing a great job of giving Lance some space. It's a smart move. As far as I'm concerned, he should be rolled up in some bubble-wrap and tucked away in a safe place where no one can touch him. People tend to forget that guys only get good at this sport if they stay focused. Cramming 100 interviews into an afternoon and shaking hands with every Tom, Dick and Harry doesn't bode well for focus. So Lance is right to be keeping that stuff to a minimum.

We've made our third trip of the season to a small hotel called L'Esplan, which is located about 40km north of Mont Ventoux. We first traveled here during our pre-Tour training camp in May, and returned during the Dauphiné Libéré. And now we're back for the Tour de France. It's odd enough to visit the same town twice in one season, but visiting the same hotel three times is almost unheard of. Crazier still is that we will be here for two nights this time. A rarity during the Tour. It's almost cause to unpack.

A lot of people are saying that the Tour is "over." Anyone declaring this hasn't taken a very detailed inventory of the course profiles facing us during the next 10 stages. We have a lot of work to do before this train pulls into Paris. Not to mention a lot of hills to climb. Wait a minute, did I say hills? I meant to say big f—ing mountains. With so much in front of us, we are all a little hesitant to use the "o" word.

Tomorrow we will climb Mont Ventoux. I'm hoping there's still a little good karma left on the road to the top, as I will be repaying a portion of my debt to Sir Lance. This is a special climb for pro cyclists, and I can't think of a better circumstance to be returning under than defending the yellow jersey. Keep your fingers crossed that we'll be working the same kind of magic that we did in June.

Frenchman Raymond Poulidor won in 1965; Belgian Eddy Merckx in 1970; and Frenchman Bernard Thévenet in 1972. Hot weather was a factor in each of those years, not the wind.

In the 1967 Tour, temperatures were so hot—more than 100 degrees Fahrenheit—they contributed to one of the saddest episodes in Tour history. After being dropped from the front group of leaders, British star Tom Simpson collapsed on his bike 1.5km from the Ventoux summit, and died before reaching the hospital in Avignon. His death was caused by a combination of heat stroke, and traces of alcohol and amphetamines in his blood. A granite monument to Simpson now stands on the rocky slope above the spot where he died.

The 2000 Tour leader Armstrong made reference to Simpson when he assessed the possible impact of the Ventoux stage on this year's race. "It's a very special and mystical climb," he said. "By mystical, I mean it looks more like the moon than it does a mountain. It's only 1900 meters at the top, but it feels (higher). There is no air up there. Maybe because there's no vegetation there ... it's a strange place."

Armstrong, who had reconnoitered all of the race's mountains, said the Ventoux "is the hardest climb of this year's Tour de France," and he wasn't sure what tactics he would adopt during the stage. "I might have to improvise," he stated. His strategy would depend on how his rivals—particularly the Spanish climbers Jiménez of Banesto, Escartin of Kelme and Beloki of Festina—attacked the stage.

A firm ally for Armstrong would be his U.S. Postal teammate Hamilton, who won the Ventoux mountaintop finish in June's Dauphiné Libéré race, and said on this rest day that he was recovering from the injuries he suffered in a crash the previous Sunday: a heavily bruised right leg and chest.

Before the Ventoux (and its hopefully 21km of climbing), the riders would ride 128km on a zig-zag stage 12 route from Carpentras that would take them over the 2057-foot Col de Murs, 2395-foot Côte de Javon, 3267-foot Col de Notre Dame des Abeilles and the 1131-foot Côte de Mormoiron. With the full Ventoux, that made for almost 11,000 feet of climbing in about 91 miles.

It looked like being a very tough day, wind or no wind.

STAGE 12

Carpentras–Mont Ventoux • July 13

A Day on the Mountain

THE RIDERS HAD FELT ITS PRESENCE DURING THEIR TRAINING RIDES ON THE REST DAY: IT FLOATED IN the distance like a white saddleback whale on a sea of green vineyards.

They had heard talk about it on television: the mythical mountain where Tom Simpson died in 1967, and champions Charly Gaul and Eddy Merckx took stage wins on their way to victories in the Tour.

They had seen its details in the race bible: 21km of climbing at 7.6 percent, an elevation gain of 1600 meters (5249 feet), and steepest pitches of 13, 14 and 15 percent.

And now, it had arrived: the race to the top of Mont Ventoux.

Although this relatively short stage of 149km started in Carpentras, only 15km from the mountain's base, it seemed to take forever to reach the Ventoux. That had a lot to do with the complicated course, which first headed away from the famed mountain, before taking a circuitous counterclockwise loop across the windswept plains and along the roller-coaster back roads of Provence.

The first distant view of the giant peak came from a small ridge 20km into the stage—where the field had just come together after an intense bout of racing, pushed by a three-quarter tail wind that had split the pack into three big echelons.

The next clear view of the mountain came from a narrow road climbing away from the pocket-sized vineyards toward a thin forest of cork oak trees at 29km—where the day's first attacks were forming and a dozen riders were chasing back through the team cars after a pileup.

Then, heading toward an exquisitely beautiful valley, the peloton had its first close-up view of the mountain, across fields of aromatic lavender and burnished wheat. This is where a nine-man break that had formed on the fast, sinuous downhill from the Col de Murs was in the process of taking a 4:50 lead over a Postal-led pack.

The break contained some of the favorites' "advance" men: Kelme's Botero for Escartin and Heras; Telekom's Vinokourov for Ullrich; Polti's Hervé for Virenque; and Banesto's Garcia-Acosta and José Luis Arrieta for Jiménez and Zülle. The two Banesto leaders were both motivated for this stage—Jiménez confident after his third-place finish at Hautacam, and Zülle believing he could again take time out of Ullrich and move into the top 10. But if Jiménez were to have a shot at the stage win, they couldn't allow the break's lead to get out of hand. So Banesto directeur sportif Eusebio Unzue now made some firm orders: The team will start chasing … Garcia-Acosta will stop working in the break … and Arrieta will drop back to the peloton to help his teammates close the gap.

The injection of pace from Banesto, helped by the gusting wind, came on the first, wide-open slopes of the day's third Cat. 2 climb, the Col de Notre Dame des Abeilles. In the next 35km—over the plateau-like summit, down the long swooping into-the-wind descent, and along a twisting country road through the Vaucluse vineyards—the gap fell by three minutes. So when the break began climbing the first easy slopes of the Ventoux, it was only 1:35 ahead of the pack, instead of five minutes or more.

Five kilometers into the climb, where the narrow road turns left, away from the lines of grape vines and into a tight, pine-clad limestone hollow, the grade suddenly zooms from 3 percent to 9 percent. Within a kilometer, Botero and Vinokourov rode away from the break, and Postal's Hamilton took over from Banesto at the head of the pack. The American—who won the stage to the Ventoux summit in the Dauphiné Libéré a month earlier—went so fast that only a handful of riders could hold his wheel. Among those dropped, ironically, were Banesto's Jiménez and Zülle, along with Festina's Christophe Moreau, the Frenchman who was lying in third overall.

By the time Hamilton finished his impressive stint, and teammate Livingston took over, Botero and Vinokourov had been caught, while the only men left with Armstrong and Livingston were Ullrich, Heras, Beloki and Pantani. And "Pantani was just coming off the group when I dropped off," Hamilton later said.

Heras then put in a probing attack, which caused Vinokourov and Livingston to be

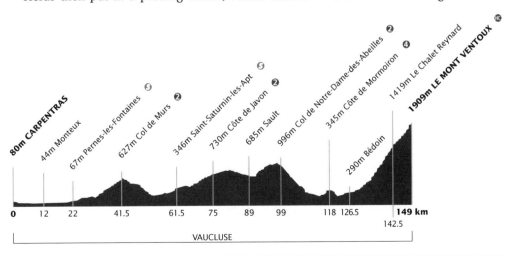

dropped, and saw Pantani lose about 25 meters. Now the only ones with Armstrong were Heras, Ullrich, Virenque, Beloki and Botero.

Pantani was receiving huge support from the fans packed solidly on both sides of the road; but catching back was proving a difficult task. He wasn't losing ground, though. From 100 meters back, he was simply matching the pace set by the "steady Ullrich," who led the break.

The grade, too, becomes more even on the 4km-long stretch before the famous turn at Chalet Reynard, 6.5km from the top. Ah, the turn.... There were perhaps 10,000 of the Ventoux's estimated 300,000 spectators watching from a natural amphitheater above the turn—which took the leaders away from the shelter of the trees and out into the wind howling across the bare, scree-like ridge. It felt more like Everest than the Ventoux, but the sunny skies allowed the stage to continue to the summit.

Almost immediately, the pace slowed, and Pantani came back up to the lead group: the strongest seven men in the race.

Virenque was the next to attack, but he was easily countered. Then, 5.5km from the summit, Pantani put in the first of what would prove to be a whole series of accelerations. The third of these saw Virenque drop back; and the fourth was answered only by Botero. Together, the Italian and Colombian moved 11 seconds ahead.

Pantani surged again, dropping Botero; and at the same time, Armstrong finally made the charge everyone was expecting. The man in the yellow jersey rose out of the saddle, virtually sprinting, and went quickly past Botero before joining Pantani with about 3km still to go.

If things unfolded as they had at Hautacam, Armstrong's next surge would take him solo; but Pantani later said he was now feeling better than he did in the Pyrénées, "although it's not the real Pantani."

Real or not, the shaven-headed one was making a good impersonation of Pantani '98, as he pulled back onto Armstrong's wheel. They then briefly spoke, and settled into sharing a steadier tempo—although the Texan was doing the stronger pulls—until, with 1km to go, they led the chasing Ullrich and Beloki by 30 seconds.

That gap pretty much stayed, as the two leaders and two chasers all struggled against the fierce wind, gusting to 70 kph, on the last 10-percent pitch. The rider in yellow and his rival in pink then made the steep right turn toward the finish line.

Everyone expected a final encounter between the two men who had conquered the mountain. But, anticlimactically, Armstrong didn't contest the sprint, and a gasping Pantani crossed the finish line as a winner for the first time since he left the 1999 Giro d'Italia in disgrace.

Why did Armstrong give up his chance of winning the stage? "I thought it was the right thing to do, the classy thing to do," the Texan later said. "I like Pantani and I respect him. And I know the last 12 months have been tough for him."

And now the Italian was back … even if it weren't the "real" Pantani.

Another Destructive Day

A couple of days before the Ventoux, Armstrong was asked whether he minded not winning the stage at Hautacam. He replied, "I've been second three times so far (in this Tour). The most important thing is to win in Paris. If that means getting five times second, that's okay." Well, after this one, it was already four times second: the stage 1 time trial at Futuroscope; stage 4 team time trial at St. Nazaire; stage 10 mountaintop finish at Hautacam; and, now, stage 12 mountaintop finish on Mont Ventoux.

He may have conceded the stage to a resurgent Marco Pantani, but Armstrong was again the dominant figure of this relatively short stage. In effect, it was a stage played out on the one climb, the 21km-long Ventoux. The four climbs before the Ventoux were relatively easy and ridden at a steady tempo behind the pace-setting of first the U.S. Postal Service and then Banesto.

Banesto was hoping for an eventual stage win by one of its Spanish climbers, José Maria Jiménez or Francisco Mancebo—which didn't happen. In fact, not only did Banesto not take the stage, it also lost any hopes of a place on the Paris podium, when team leader Zülle was dropped with Jiménez as soon the grade steepened on the Ventoux, 15km from the summit. Zülle recovered somewhat to finish in 18th place, alongside the 1999 third-place finisher, Escartin, Dropping another three minutes, though, put Zülle and Escartin respectively into 13th and 14th overall, almost 11 minutes behind Armstrong.

Dropped at the same time as Zülle and Escartin—when Postal's Hamilton and Livingston were forcing the pace—was Moreau. With the help of two Festina teammates, Moreau recovered to place 10th, but he lost third place overall to his Basque teammate Beloki, one of Spain's up-and-coming stars, who finished a remarkable third by outsprinting Ullrich.

On a day that Spain saw poor performances from its expected stars Escartin, Olano, Jiménez and Casero, the younger Spanish climbers all came through strongly. Besides Beloki, Kelme's Heras rode to sixth place (and seventh overall), while the leading under-25 rider, Mancebo, had as an impressive finish as he did at Hautacam, to take eighth—the place he also now held overall.

Tyler's diary
July 13
St. Paul-Trois Châteaux

Today was not the day we were expecting. The weather reports we were hearing were pretty hairy. There were such high winds on the top of Mont Ventoux yesterday, serious consideration had been given to shortening the stage. The press area was moved to the bottom of the mountain and the hospitality venues weren't even set up at the summit. I imagine it was a tough day for the journalists and VIPs…

Hamilton doing his part to protect the yellow jersey.

Luckily, things turned out okay. The sun was shining and it was actually pretty warm at the start in Carpentras compared to the last few days. But the wind was our enemy again, whipping like the famous Mistrals that plague Provence in the wintertime. You could tell that the temperatures were dropping along the race route by what the fans along the sides of the road were wearing. We started out being cheered on by some daring women in bikinis

and wound up being surrounded by people in ski parkas and gloves at the finish.

Our team rode extremely well together today; everyone did their fair share. We half-expected some big challenges, and we got them early on in the stage. A few teams had been remarking to the press that they thought Lance's only weakness was his team. And after Hautacam they might have been justified in questioning us. As a result, we were approached by a lot of reporters this morning who had heard some buzz about Lance "being isolated today"—which basically meant that other teams were talking about putting the hurt on us, so Lance would have to fend for himself at the finish. A few riders did indeed try to make good on this promise; but we controlled things pretty well.

It was a good feeling to return to Ventoux and see the people lining the route. They were going nuts. I don't know if this mountain brings out the best in me or what, but I actually felt pretty good today despite the wind.

After I pulled off from the front, I saw some friends from home along the route: Chris Davenport, once the world champion extreme skier, was on hand today with his wife Jesse. He ran alongside me for a bit and gave me the race update. It's always great to see familiar faces at races—especially at a race like this. Every little thing is a motivator—from the American flags on the side of the road to knowing that an old friend is on hand to cheer for you. It makes an incredible difference.

The strong wind was a big factor on the climb. It was behind the riders on the opening 14km, encouraging the major splits, and was a cross- and head wind after that. And by the top, combined with unseasonable cold temperatures, the fierce northwest wind put the wind chill at around the mid-30s Fahrenheit.

Pantani's time for the 21km Ventoux climb was 58:53 (an average of 21.4 kph), which was 2:02 slower than the climb record set in an individual time trial at the 1999 Dauphiné Libéré by Vaughters. It's unfortunate that Vaughters wasn't here for this historic stage, having crashed out of the Tour in the Pyrénées, as he may well have been up there contending with the Belokis, Herases and Mancebos.

Following Vaughters, Chann McRae became the second American to crash out of the Tour. He had a first fall when he was involved in a pileup just before the little town of St. Didier, 26km into the stage. "My bike was wrecked and I could only get the 52x19," McRae said. "I was chasing back very fast up the first climb, when I tried to race between a team car and a Vini Caldirola rider. My front wheel hit his back wheel, and I went down again. I fell on my right side.

"I had to wait about three minutes for the second team car to come up with my spare bike. I was chasing again, and caught a couple of riders ... one was Kirsipuu. My director Marc Sergeant told me to stay with them. But they both quit, and I was in a lot of pain—my right glute is twice as big as my left, and so I was pedaling with the left leg.

"I didn't have much choice except to abandon. I wanted to get to Paris, even on poor form, but it wasn't possible."

Besides sprinter Jaan Kirsipuu, two other contenders for the green jersey, Steels and Wüst, dropped out, leaving Zabel with a massive 93-point lead in the points competition. Wüst did not start because of a throat infection and fever; Steels finally gave up after several days of fatigue; and Kirsipuu never really recovered from a pre-Tour crash, followed by another at the end of the first week.

The rest day had just been a stay of execution.

Fred's Diary
July 13
Avignon

Hi guys. I'm back again and I think the rest day was just what I needed. Not only that, but we got to stay in one of France's better hotels, which made my R&R a lot nicer.

Today, the stage profile made it look like it would be a pretty hellish day, knowing that we would end up on Mont Ventoux. My job for the stage was to keep Manuel Beltran, our team leader, out of trouble and at the front at all times. So I was on the line right from the start, when the stuff hit the fan in the crosswinds. We got caught in the last of three groups and had to act fast to get back in the action. Luckily, things came together and we quickly moved up to the front.

During this mess, I found out that two of my teammates were in trouble. I guess Tom Steels got caught at the back and wasn't able to close the gap and had to abandon. And for Chann, things weren't any better: He got caught in the first crash of the day and as he was chasing back on, he had another crash that put him out of the race. At first, he gave it a shot and fought to get back on, but soon realized that he was in too much pain and had to call it quits.

After all that carnage, things seemed to cool down, and it looked like the Postal boys were controlling the race. I was happy with this, as it made my job a lot easier. But then, bad luck struck Mapei once again: Bettini and Bartoli were suffering with stomach problems. This was putting more pressure on me, as I had to take up the slack for the others, but I was good for it.

The last half of the race started to pick up as

Banesto took control of the race—for what reason I still can't figure out. At that point, we were coming into the last couple of climbs and I was almost done and could sit up and ride the *gruppetto*—which is made up of the guys who are just interested in making it to the finish before the time cut.

The gruppettos are so funny sometimes. Everyone is at each other the whole time: Someone is pulling too fast; not enough people are helping at the front; everyone is tired and about to bonk and can't even keep a straight line. Luckily, though, the gruppettos have allowed me some recovery time, because that's the only time we have when we've not been racing at max.

Another thing I found out about gruppettos is that instead of waiting for the group to form once everyone dies, you drop off early and ride your own pace, and when you see the group form, you jump across to it. I guess that makes sense, as I was fresher and just riding the gruppetto to conserve for later.

Without wasting myself, I made it to the finish at the top of the Ventoux—and what a finish it was! It looked like you were on the moon. The other great part was how many people were there to watch us come by. They said at least 300,000 just on the Ventoux—amazing support. At one point, there was a giant screen showing the race, with thousands of people at that one spot....

I can feel Paris getting closer and closer, but at the same time I know it wont be a picnic getting there. Wish me good luck in the Alps.

STAGE 13

Avignon–Draguignan • July 14

Back in Time

WHAT WAS THIS ALL ABOUT? SITTING IN THE TOUR DIRECTOR GENERAL'S RED LANCIA WAS FÉLIX Lévitan. Spotted along the day's course through Provence were banners for Zoetemelk and Van Impe. And seen chatting before the start of the stage in Avignon were Sean Kelly, Steve Bauer and Phil Anderson.

It sure seemed like we were back in the 1970s or '80s, a time when Lévitan ruled the Tour with iron control; Joop Zoetemelk and Lucien Van Impe were perpetual podium contenders; and Kelly, Bauer and Anderson all wore the Tour leader's yellow jersey. That all these personalities came together for stage 13 was quite a coincidence. Or was it?

For one thing, it was highly unusual for a modern Tour de France to be finishing in the heart of Provence (this was the first time that Draguignan would host a stage finish). That's because, in the month of July, South of France hotels are fully booked with tourists, and the roads are chock-a-block with holiday traffic, so an event as huge as today's Tour can't be easily accommodated.

In fact, the last time the Tour had a stage finish in the department of Var was back in 1964, when a road stage to Hyères was won by Jan Janssen and a time trial to Toulon went to Jacques Anquetil. The only other time that comes close was a 1973 Tour stage won by Spaniard Vicente Lopez-Carril in Nice—where the Tour started in 1981. Lévitan was the race director in all those years; Van Impe and Zoetemelk were contenders in 1973; and Anderson and Kelly were hot in 1981.

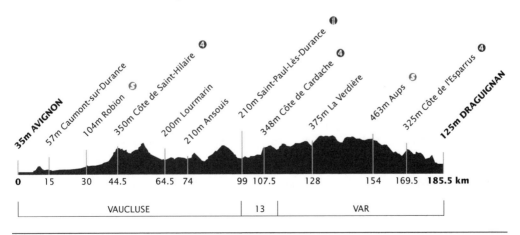

So how did Draguignan manage to host a stage this year? Well, hotels were a problem: The 20 teams were scattered in nine different towns, including the distant Cannes, and a large part of the race entourage stayed in Toulon, 100km away. As for today's traffic in these parts, the majority uses the A4 autoroute, so a stage that used back roads that parallel the highway was practicable. Besides, business traffic on this Friday afternoon was minimal, because it was the 14th of July, Bastille Day.

Being the French national holiday only added to the stage's old-fashioned feel. The huge crowds were in a festive mood, happy to see the race after so many years' absence, and many folks waved banners proclaiming: "Vive le Tour" ("Long live the Tour"). The French fans also would be thrilled if a Frenchman won the stage on *le quatorze juillet*— as was done most recently by Vincent Barteau at Marseille in 1989, and Laurent Brochard at Loudenvielle in 1997....

One team in particular seemed the best equipped to repeat this feat: Bonjour. Made up of all French riders, eight of whom were still in the race, Bonjour so far had had a disappointing Tour. It was time to break out.

An hour and 46km into the stage, it was Bonjour leader Robin who headed the first of the day's breaks to gain more than 15 seconds, before being caught. Then, on a highly technical descent from the Luberon ridge, twisting down a limestone gorge, Robin's teammate Rous joined an attack by Laurent Jalabert's brother, Nicolas. The two Frenchmen gained 40 seconds before Rous dropped Jalabert on one of the incessant hills, and decided to push on alone. There were 114km of the 185.5km stage remaining.

Rous, who was one of the Festina riders thrown out of the 1998 Tour on drugs charges, has made a strong return to racing this year with Bonjour, and is the main reason why his team received a wild-card invitation to the race. In April, Rous won the French classic Paris-Camembert, in a solo break ahead of runner-up Armstrong. In May, he won the Midi Libre stage race. So surely, this strong time trialist—who won the epic Vosges stage of the 1997 Tour in a long solo break—was thinking he could now come through again.

After 28km of this solo attack, Rous crossed the broad Durance River with the wind still at his back, he was a minute ahead of a 12-man chase group, and five minutes ahead of the pack.

With the prospect of another two hours in the saddle, Rous should probably have waited for the chasers; and if he had been racing back in the 1980s, he most likely would have—especially since Bonjour also had a rider in the chase group: 1999 French champion François Simon.

But through the "miracle" of modern radio communications, Bonjour team director Jean-René Bernaudeau was told by Simon that the group of 12 wasn't working well together; and so Bernaudeau encouraged Rous to carry on with his break.

Sure, the big crowds massed along the hilly course in the cool late-afternoon sunshine loved seeing a Frenchman alone in the lead, but even they could sense it was futile: Rous never had more than 1:05 on the chasers, and he was caught after riding solo for 56km.

Then, when an attack was made from the front group by Rous's former Festina colleague Hervé—now with Polti—only two of the leaders went with him: ONCE's Nicolas Jalabert and Banesto's Garcia-Acosta. Rous was dropped, while teammate Simon didn't have the strength to chase.

Bonjour's bid had fizzled with 50km still to go. Now it was up to the younger Jalabert or Hervé to make a bid for the stage win. Jalabert is a useful sprinter ... Hervé is a strong climber ... but it was Garcia-Acosta who had the form. On a short uphill 12km from Draguignan, the tall Spanish rider countered an attack by Hervé, and, doing as his director told him, never looked back.

With permission, Garcia-Acosta did take a peek to see if Hervé and Jalabert were in sight, when he rode beneath the kilometer-to-go archway with 30 seconds in hand. And then he was free to celebrate.

"I knew how the French were motivated for today," Garcia-Acosta said, "so I didn't want to risk being in a sprint." He knows all about losing sprints—as he did when finishing second to Mapei's Nardello in the Carpentras stage of the 1998 Tour.

The 27-year-old from San Sebastian is in his seventh season with Banesto, and can now boast of stage wins at both the Tour and the Vuelta. There should be more to come—just as there were for that other Spaniard, Lopez-Carril, who took the first of his three Tour stage wins in Provence in 1973.

Monsieur Lévitan surely agreed.

The Marathon Stage

The 145 riders left in this Tour de France would likely have their alarms set for 6 a.m. Saturday morning, an untimely reminder that Stage 14 could be an eight-hour ride through the French Alps. And though sunshine was forecast, temperatures were likely to be in only the 50s and 60s Fahrenheit, while northerly winds blowing at up to 70 kph

Tyler's diary
July 14
Draguignan

Today, we covered a whole truckload of potentially dangerous attacks. It wasn't until after we rode 90km that things finally settled down and a group of "non-threatening" guys went up the road. From there, the team rode at the front, setting a tempo that kept the break within a reasonable time gap.

There were a ton of people along the race route. They must have all come down off Mont Ventoux to catch the start. They say the Alps are going to be even crazier. I can't imagine it.

Yesterday worked out pretty well for the team. It was a great feeling to be riding at the front from the base of Ventoux. I had been waiting for a month for the opportunity to bust it for Lance. I feel like I did my job fairly well, since by the time I pulled off there weren't too many guys left. At that point I threw it in my easiest gear and rode as easy as possible, to recover for the long stages ahead.

I don't know if it's a rumor or not, but people are talking about snow in the Alps. The weather has been unseasonably cold here in France, and for the most part, it hasn't really felt like summer.

I hope to God people are kidding about snow—or this is going to be the Tour that was decided by Mother Nature?

It's always nice to see a few familiar faces along the race route. And sometimes, it's just good to know that a friend from home is out on the sidelines somewhere. My first cycling coach is out roaming the roadways of France, but I have yet to spot him. I keep thinking he will appear in his CCB jersey. So if you are reading this, Steve Pucci, put on your pink-and-blue so I can find you.

I was sad to hear that our compatriot Chann McRae left the Tour de France yesterday. He had ridden strongly in the Giro, and I was hoping to see him put in a good effort in France as well. But two crashes in one day can be a little much, at the speed and difficulty that this race moves at. Hopefully, Chann will recover well and return next year to take revenge.

We've got a long day ahead of us tomorrow. Almost 250km of racing over some pretty big bumps. Channel those strength- and survival-vibes our way. We're going to need them.

(44 mph) would make it feel much colder on the highest peaks.

The stage would feature four categorized climbs. The first, the Cat. 2 Côte de Canjuers, began right from the start in Draguignan, and would be a gentle warm-up for the other three: the infamous Cat. 1 Col d'Allos at 127km, Cat. 1 Col de Vars at 177.5km and hors-categorie Col d'Izoard at 228km. From the Izoard's 7742-foot summit, the riders would face a 20km downhill run into Briançon, followed by a steep climb of 1.5km to the finish at 249.5km. The total amount of climbing for the stage: 17,400 feet.

The Allos-Vars-Izoard trilogy hadn't been used at the Tour for more than 50 years. In 1948 and 1949, there was a Cannes to Briançon stage each year, 25km longer than the Draguignan to Briançon course. Both of those stages were won by Italian legend Gino Bartali. He won solo the first time, on his way to winning his second Tour; and he was in a two-man break with teammate Fausto Coppi in 1949, a Tour that Coppi went on to win.

Back then, the three giant climbs were on dirt roads, which added enormously to the challenges. Today's roads are well surfaced, but the ruggedness of the route remains. No one was expecting this Tour's top two, Armstrong and Ullrich, to go on a long breakaway like Bartali and Coppi. Experts were predicting a similar scenario to stage 10 in the Pyrénées, when a long-distance breakaway resulted in a win for Kelme's Otxoa.

The expected unfavorable winds for stage 14 would make it tough for a similar break to succeed. So the most likely scenario was a battle royal on the Izoard, where Armstrong and Ullrich would probably have to reply to the attacks of Ventoux winner Pantani. Now in 13th place overall, Pantani would start the stage 4:34 behind third-placed Joseba Beloki of Festina. It was not an insurmountable handicap for the Italian climber, who appeared to be getting stronger every day.

It would be another difficult day for Armstrong's Postal Service teammates, who again have to control the pace of the peloton for most of the marathon stage. And if any of the four Spanish climbers in the top 10 overall (Beloki, Beltran, Heras or Mancebo) made attacks on the Allos or Vars, it also could be a very dangerous day for Armstrong.

STAGE 14

Draguignan–Briançon • July 15

Stalemate

WHEN YOU'VE ALREADY BEEN IN THE SADDLE FOR SIX HOURS, YOU'RE FEELING THE PAIN OF CLIMBING the day's second major mountain pass, and you're facing another chase to rejoin the pack and then pull it for as long as you can, traditions don't count for much. Sure, this may have been the first time in 50-some years that the Tour de France had included the legendary trilogy of the Col d'Allos, Col de Vars and Col d'Izoard in the same stage, but the only thing that mattered to Postal's Benoît Joachim at this moment was getting to the top of the Col de Vars as fast as he could. The wind was gusting in his face, the grade a steady 8 percent, and he knew there was no glory waiting for him on the other side of the near-7000-foot peak—just more hard work.

Team riders like Joachim, Frankie Andreu, Viatcheslav Ekimov and George Hincapie weren't getting a whole lot of publicity at this Tour. But every day, they were being called upon to control the race for Armstrong in marathon tempo sessions, or defend the yellow jersey in sudden high-speed pursuits. And their teamwork was never more needed than on this gargantuan, eight-hour haul from Provence to the heart of the Alps. From that morning's team meeting in Draguignan, the Postal riders knew what their tasks would be; but cycling strategy is rarely predictable, so they didn't know when and where their day's work would really begin … or end.

Thankfully, from Joachim's point of view, the wind was blowing against the peloton as it headed north into the stark, limestone foothills of Haute Provence. Head winds discourage early breaks, and so the Postal riders didn't have any "control" duties to perform for the first three hours of stage 14.

At a steady average of 27 kph (less than 17 mph), there was plenty of time to chat with colleagues—an easy task for the 24-year-old Joachim, the first Luxembourger to ride the Tour in 16 years, who is fluent in five languages. There was time to study the day's stage profile and see that there were two feed zones today, the first of them coming up at St. André-les-Alpes, after 73km. There was time to admire the towering cliffs of the Verdon Canyon, as the race headed upstream past crowds gathered at riverside campsites. And there was time to think about the hard work that lay ahead.

It came soon enough.

As the Verdon valley widened, along with its road, Joachim and the Postal squad went to the front, increasing the tempo to 32 kph against the wind. Riding as a team at a steady speed at the front discourages breakaways—and it's easier to ride at an even pace like this than have to chase down attacks.

The strategy worked this time, and nobody made a move off the front until they reached the tin-roofed village of Allos, where the course turned right, leaving the valley bottom, to wind its way steeply on a narrow, bumpy road up the bare mountainside. This was the last 6km of the Col d'Allos, and the attack by Pascual-Llorente was just the opening salvo from a Kelme team that was intent on winning another stage.

In fact, it wasn't long before its stage 10 winner Otxoa was dancing away up the climb, followed by teammate Botero, while four Banesto men were also among the 10 riders that eventually took up the chase after Pascual-Llorente.

None of the race favorites made a move, though, until Virenque sprinted out of the Postal-led pack. This provoked a sharp acceleration, causing Pantani to momentarily drop back, later saying he had some breathing problems.

Pantani, like the rest of those dropped, easily rejoined on the steep, technical 18km descent, where the race came back together. And as often happens in stages of this length and difficulty, the key move happened in a valley.

On leaving the crowd-packed streets of Barcelonnette, Banesto's Jon Odriozola accelerated with Rabobank's Maarten Den Bakker, while five others (Kelme's Pascual-Llorente, Banesto's Dariusz Baranowski, Saeco's Paolo Savoldelli, Bonjour's Rous and Telekom's Jens Heppner) joined them on the flat 20km run up the remote, rocky Ubaye

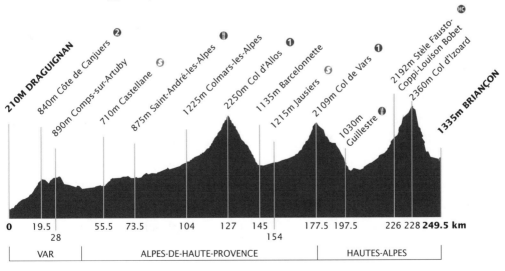

valley. None of the seven was a potential G.C. threat, and they reached the foot of the 10km Col de Vars 3:40 ahead of the pack—still led by the Postal team.

The strength shown by Armstrong's men to control the attacks on the Allos ascent had put a throttle on the race, and it seemed clear that the protagonists were going to wait for the final, most difficult climb—the Izoard—to make their moves.

Back in 1949, when the roads were dirt and long mountain stages like this turned into a war of attrition, the Vars was the climb where Italian greats Gino Bartali and Fausto Coppi began their now-legendary break that saw them reach Briançon five minutes ahead of their nearest challenger. Here, in 2000, the only man to attack was the Tour's lone Colombian, Botero, who had already shown he was suited to long breakaways. This time, he was 80km and two mountain passes from the finish when he rode away from the pack, climbing strongly between high cliffs and then across a grassy hillside toward the bare summit of the Vars.

Botero, 27, is not your prototypical Colombian climber. He's certainly not another Luis Herrera, the petite, dark-skinned Indian from a family of flower growers, who won three Tour mountain stages in the 1980s. Botero, a city boy from Medellin with an economics degree, has fair hair, is 6 feet tall and weighs 152 pounds. He was much bigger than that when he first started cycling.

"I was a track racer," Botero said. "Then I started training with the national road team on 100km rides; they said I was a strong climber and should try road racing." He lost 20 pounds, proved he could time trial as well as climb, and in 1996 turned pro with the Kelme team in Spain.

The Colombian already had shown his versatility in this Tour, in his marathon break with Dekker on the road to Revel and fifth place on Mont Ventoux. Starting this stage, Botero was only 19th on G.C., more than 12 minutes down on Armstrong, so his escape on the Col de Vars was not seen as a big threat. Botero made the most of his freedom, and by the summit, he was only 1:20 behind the leaders, headed by Heppner, and a minute or so ahead of a pack that was showing signs of fatigue from an already long day.

Postal's Hincapie reflected the general state of the peloton: "I'd been riding tempo on the climb, but dropped back. I didn't want to blow," said the American, who went over the top some 40 seconds back of the Armstrong group. "Benoît was behind me."

Now, after the rapid, untechnical descent on smooth roads, the race would climb through the day's second feed zone in the medieval town of Guillestre, then drop into the infamous Queyras gorge—the almost flat 15km approach to the base of the Col d'Izoard.

It was vital that Postal's Joachim and Hincapie be leading here, to protect teammates Hamilton and Livingston from the wind before they led Armstrong up the early parts of the mountain ahead.

They did their duty, with Joachim leading the pack for most of the descent and through the gorge.

Meanwhile, Botero used his time-trial strength and track skills to negotiate the descent faster than anyone else. He joined the break just as the seven leaders grabbed their musette bags at the feed. The gap was now 3:38, and would increase to five minutes before they turned sharp left, into the wind, to start the 14km-long Izoard climb.

The Izoard has three distinct parts: the first third on a straight road that climbs past alpine meadows and through the mountain village of Arvieux; a middle section of switchbacks, climbing at 10 percent through a low forest of piñon pines; and a top section across the rocky moonscape of the so-called Casse Déserte and then up a final zig-zag to the 7742-foot summit.

The wind was blowing wickedly against the race on the first part, and it was here that Botero and Baranowski broke away from the lead group, pursued by Savoldelli; while Vini Caldirola veteran Roberto Conti—the former Pantani lieutenant—made a solo attack from the Armstrong group, which for now was being led by an excellent Ekimov.

Botero went solo on the steep middle section, and reached the top two minutes ahead of Baranowski and Savoldelli. Behind them, another act in the continuing drama of Tour 2000 was about to be played out.

Hamilton was heading the leaders' group at a ferocious pace as the race headed into the trees, when Pantani made a furious acceleration. Riding out of the saddle in the dashing style that endeared him to Tour crowds through the 1990s, Pantani looked determined to repeat the breakthrough performance he had made on this same climb at the Giro d'Italia a few weeks earlier.

Virenque tried to go with the Italian, but got nowhere. Then, the yellow-jerseyed Armstrong blasted out of the group and crossed the 100-meter gap as easily as he had on the Ventoux, two days earlier. There were still 6km to climb, and it seemed that Pantani and Armstrong were about to do an encore of the duet they had played on the Giant of Provence.

Within five minutes, they caught Conti, and Armstrong took advantage of this situation to launch a surprise counterattack. Was the Texan about to repeat the show he put on at Hautacam?

Well, he did catch and pass the riders who had been dropped from the earlier break;

Tyler's diary
July 15
Briançon

The team rode exceptionally well today. At the base of the final decent we still had eight of our nine guys up front. This was really good news for Kevin and I as we headed into the final climb—the Izoard—because it meant we would have reinforcements with us as we got going. It was my job to set a tempo during the early part of the climb just like on the Ventoux. Shortly after I pulled off and Kevin took over, Pantani attacked and Lance went with him. The rest was up to them to duke out. But I think the team did a pretty good job of keeping Lance fresh for as long as possible.

We all made it to Briançon, so now we can check off one of the hardest days of the Tour from our to-do list. It's good to have a long day like today behind us. It's also nice to see that we've made the "big left turn" north. It's a bit of morale booster—although tomorrow won't be a piece of cake by any means. More shark's teeth in the profile.

In case you were wondering what it's like in Briançon, it's worth noting that we are so far in the boondocks that my cell phone can't pick up any reception. On a cell-friendly continent like Europe, that's saying something.

Thanks to everyone who has sent me e-mail and support. I want you to know that your interest in the sport and this race does a lot for our morale. Hopefully you aren't offended that I haven't written back. I'd love to respond to everyone who writes in, but for the moment I can only concentrate on writing these words every day.

# # #

Fred's Diary
July 15
Briançon

There was no need for stage 14 to be so long. From the neutral start to the finish, we were on our bike for almost nine hours—I am not joking. It didn't help that the race went over Cat. 1 or hors-categorie climbs, all with a head wind. For the first time, it looked like the usually too-aggressive riders were showing a little caution. I think it was a smart move by those I sometimes think are a little crazy in the head, even if they are very strong.

We rode at a moderate pace against the wind for about 100km. At one point, I was told, the director of the Tour de France told Team Polti that he would give a prize to the first person to attack. I guess he was getting worried—because the race doesn't get much press when we take it easy—but no one fell for his tricks. I was happy that everyone was feeling their tired legs, too.

Finally, Postal took over before the Col d'Allos and controlled it over the top. I got dropped on the last couple of kilometers of the climb, to end up chasing like a crazy man on the descent. It went downhill forever, and I felt like I was driving a Formula 1 car on a winding road at a very fast speed—except you never knew what to expect if you hadn't pre-ridden the course.

I finally caught back up at the base of Col de Vars, where I went straight for the gruppetto again. I did my little trick of sitting up before the gruppetto and waiting for it to form and then catching back on. It still works, as long as I have some legs left.

From here on, it was all about survival: I knew this would be the longest day on my bike in my life, and I'd also have to ride over the hardest climbs yet. I think the distance was slowly getting to me, as I kept on forgetting to eat. You have to realize that normally you would have three full meals in the time we did this race!

The last climb, Col d'Izoard, was tough, as the approach was windy and it felt like it went on forever. Once we reached the steeper parts, it was actually easier, as the switchbacks gave a bit of recovery. I knew the race was really to the top, as the last 20km were downhill—or so I thought. We did our fast descent into Briançon and then discovered a steep, 1.5km climb leading into the finish that really pissed me off. I was ready to kill whoever designed this course.

As you can see, I'm pretty tired, and I am told that it's going to get even worse. I will make it to Paris, though, despite the efforts of the race organizers ... so look for my next entry, if I can get online.

and he did honor the tradition of the race leader passing alone the famed memorial silhouettes of former Tour winners Coppi and Louison Bobet in the Casse Déserte; but when he reached the kilometer-to-go sign, Armstrong still had Pascual-Llorente stuck to his wheel, and only an 11-second gap on nine chasers (Virenque, Pantani, Beloki, Moreau, Hervé, Ullrich, Guerini, Escartin and Heras).

So it was a stalemate, rather than a checkmate. Nonetheless, Armstrong had achieved his main goal: showing his strength and maintaining his grip on the yellow jersey.

Still to come was a 20km descent and a stiff little climb into Briançon. There, alongside the ancient town's impressive stone ramparts, the long day ended in pale evening sunshine, with Botero deservedly winning the stage by 2:30 over Savoldelli, while Pantani sprinted up the 10-percent hill to take third. And Armstrong's faithful teammates? Hamilton, Livingston, Ekimov and Vasseur all finished with a no-longer-contending Zülle, 14 minutes back. Ten minutes later, Joachim and Hincapie arrived in a group with teammate Steffen Kjaergaard. And Andreu came into Briançon with the 50-strong gruppetto, 36:35 back.

It was a hard day's night, and work was done for another day.

---------------------------- ❀ ----------------------------

In the Heart of the Alps

Even Lance Armstrong is feeling the fatigue of day after day of long stages, tough climbs and harsh winds. In his post-stage press conference, after pulling on a new yellow jersey for the fifth stage in a row, he was asked what he thought of the next day's ride to Courchevel. After asking a journalist the length of the stage, and getting an answer of "240km," he said: "I'm not doing another 250km stage. I'd be happy to have 120km stages the rest of the way to Paris ... well, maybe not."

Stage 15 was actually 173.5km, but Armstrong said it would be tougher than the following, much-longer third alpine stage. And he was right. Stage 15 would open with the long haul to the Col du Galibier—the highest mountain climb of the Tour at 8677 feet; was followed by the terribly difficult 19km-long, 8-percent Col de la Madeleine; and ended with the 22km ascent to Courchevel.

The day wouldn't be made any easier by the weather: clouds increasing through the stage, with a temperature of only 5 degrees Centigrade (41 degrees Fahrenheit) forecast for the finish. If Saturday's marathon eight-hour stage was any indication, then Armstrong could expect more attacks from the Spanish teams Kelme and Banesto, and probably another bid from Pantani.

Armstrong said he told the Italian climber during their joint climb of the Col d'Izoard Saturday: "You are the strongest." Asked if that was a mistake, tactically, and would encourage Pantani for the upcoming stages, the race leader replied, "I feel confident with my condition.... If (my comment) motivates him then it does, but I felt it was deserved."

The last time a Tour stage ended in Courchevel, in 1997, the then race leader Ullrich had to call on the help of teammate Bjarne Riis to answer a strong challenge by Virenque on the Madeleine—before going solo on the descent to catch Virenque. The two finished together at Courchevel, with the Frenchman taking the stage.

Armstrong and his Postal team would have to show similar resolve to defend the yellow jersey for the second day in the Alps. It could be the biggest hurdle Armstrong still had to face ... even if the stage was not 240km.

STAGE 15

Briançon–Courchevel • July 16

Moments of Truth

JAN ULLRICH HAS MIXED MEMORIES OF COURCHEVEL. THE FIRST TIME HE SAW THIS FRENCH SKI RESORT and its patchwork of pitch-roofed chalets, lush pine trees and stuccoed hotels, was in 1997. The young German, then 23, was wearing the Tour yellow jersey, and climbing alongside the Frenchman sporting the best climber's jersey, Richard Virenque. The two had fought an epic daylong battle: Virenque attacked with his Festina team from the stage start, powering up the steep slopes of the Col du Glandon, and leaving Ullrich behind over the summit. Ullrich lost a couple of minutes by the valley, and had to call upon Danish teammate Bjarne Riis on the Col de la Madeleine, to take him within bridging distance of the by then solo Virenque. The German wünderkind was so relieved to have defended his lead that he allowed Virenque to take the stage win at Courchevel, 6561 feet above sea level.

Three years later, the Tour was returning to Courchevel on a similar course, with the mighty Madeleine again preceding the 22km-long haul up to the finish. But circumstances were different. Ullrich was now the challenger, and he set out from Briançon with an overall deficit of 4:55 on Armstrong.

Everyone was saying that the race was as good as over, but Ullrich and his Telekom team were not convinced. They could explain their leader's major time loss at Hautacam by pointing to the cold, wet conditions that Ullrich hates. The German had done better on the sunny (but still cool) slopes of Mont Ventoux, conceding only a half-minute to the American, And at Briançon, he had finished in the same time as Armstrong, at the end of what was considered the most grueling of the three alpine stages.

Now, on a day that started out in sunshine, and would not encounter the forecasted cold, cloudy weather, Ullrich was motivated. He has always climbed the Madeleine well.

In his 1996 debut Tour, the Telekom rider rode at the head of the race for then team leader Riis, and went so hard on the Madeleine that he pre-empted any attacks and put several contenders off the back, on that year's decisive stage to Les Arcs. You've already heard about 1997; and in '98, Ullrich rode everyone off his wheel on the Madeleine—except for race leader Pantani—and won the stage in Albertville.

After missing last year's Tour due to injury, Ullrich was almost back to his best form—

or so it appeared.

By the time this stage 15 arrived at the foot of the Madeleine, with 90km of the day's 173.5km completed, Ullrich was part of a big pack that had regrouped in the Maurienne valley, five minutes behind a break of eight that was started by Commesso on the never-ending descent of the Galibier.

The break soon split up on the first switchback slopes of the Madeleine, with four riders remaining in front until the summit: Banesto's Jiménez, Kelme's Otxoa, Mapei's Nardello and Cofidis's Massimiliano Lelli. Commesso and the other three were all passed by the group of favorites, which grew smaller and smaller the higher they went.

Ullrich's confidence was emphasized by the way he made his teammates Bölts, Vinokourov and Guerini set the tempo. Behind the Telekom locomotive, the first passengers were the three Postal climbers—with Livingston in front of the yellow jersey, Hamilton behind—followed by Ullrich. That was the picture seen by the crowds that got thicker as the 19km climb emerged from a pine forest and headed into its final 8km of bold sweeps across a grassy hillside, where shaggy sheep graze in summer and skiers schuss in winter.

Kelme's Escartin had tried an attack just before this, and it was Ullrich who immediately followed the Spanish climber. But Armstrong's men weren't prepared to let the German go.

Then, with the summit starting to beckon, yesterday's winner Botero—now owner of the best climber's polka-dot jersey—went away unopposed on a solo move that took him within 46 seconds of the four leaders by the top.

Behind, Guerini continued to set the pace for the Ullrich-Armstrong group that was down to just 20 riders.

Those numbers thinned dramatically when, 4km from the summit, Polti's Hervé suddenly accelerated with teammate Virenque on his wheel. Ullrich looked strong as he followed, in sharp contrast to the Postal men: Hamilton and Livingston both dropped off, and Armstrong was near the back of the six-man line that was barely able to follow Hervé.

Was it a crisis? "Absolutely not," the race leader later said. "When Pascal Hervé went, it was out of control.... In fact, Virenque asked him to slow down."

That slow-down allowed Beloki and Moreau (then third and fourth on G.C.) to catch back on, and by the summit this group was 1:20 behind the four leaders (who were joined by Botero on the descent), and 42 seconds ahead of the small group containing

Hamilton, Livingston and Guerini. These three team workers were among a couple of dozen riders who rejoined the Armstrong group on the highly technical 25km descent, with some of them taking off in counterattacks.

On reaching the bottom of the deep, narrow Isère valley, the five-man break was 1:40 ahead of five chasers (Banesto's Garcia-Acosta, ONCE's Luttenberger and Serrano, Lotto's Kurt Van de Wouwer and Rabobank's Michael Boogerd), and 3:37 ahead of the 25-strong group of race leaders. Those gaps widened to 2:15 and 4:10 before starting the 22km climb to Courchevel.

Along the valley road—where three of Pantani's Mercatone Uno team led the chase—Armstrong removed the arm warmers he had worn since the start, ready for a finale that would be played out in bright sunshine, even if it would be only 41 degrees Fahrenheit at the high-altitude finish.

The road up to Courchevel—which is actually a series of four mountain villages at 14km, 10km, 8km and 5km from the summit—is a mix of steep switchbacks and flat, or even downhill sections, in between. It's a mountain that suits Ullrich's steady climbing style, and yet, when Pantani made a sharp attack on a steep turn with about 18k to go, the Telekom leader was dropped.

Surely, Ullrich would fight back, as he had done on the Izoard 24 hours earlier. This time, though, the German seemed to be truly suffering. He looked around to see if anyone was in position to help him close the gap. But the only rider there was Banesto's Mancebo, leader of the young riders' classification, who seemed to be having an even harder time than Ullrich.

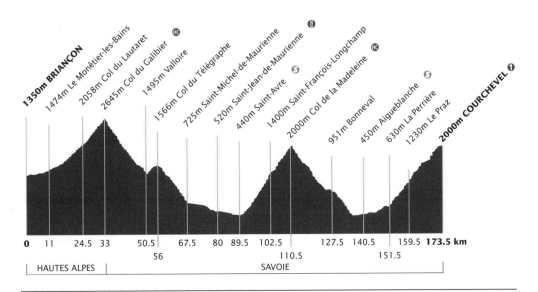

Ahead, the only ones able to go with Pantani were Livingston, Armstrong and Virenque. Pantani, urged on by tens of thousands of Italians who had crossed the nearby border for the weekend, continued his charge. Livingston, his job done, sat up. Then Virenque fell back, once more leaving just Pantani and the race leader together.

The two men looked across at each other, and agreed to work together—Armstrong knowing this would put Ullrich out of range for good, Pantani realizing this would be his best way of catching the leaders, who were still more than two minutes ahead.

In front, Botero, Nardello and Jiménez had dropped the others; and with 10km still to climb, they were 30 seconds ahead of Lelli, and 1:08 ahead of the chasing Pantani and Armstrong, who had been joined by an impressive Heras.

The Pantani-Armstrong-Heras trio continued to close, and were just 35 seconds back when Jiménez attacked from the front three, with 7km left. Riding out of the saddle and pounding a big gear, Jiménez was after the stage win he had failed to get in the Pyrénées. It looked possible when, now solo, the 28-year-old Spaniard still had 35 seconds over the Pantani group with 6km to go.

Then, realizing a stage win was within reach, Pantani made one of his vintage bursts on a sharp right turn heading toward the last of the Courchevel communities. This time, there was no reply from Armstrong—"Pantani was the stronger climber," the American later said.

So Pantani, trying harder than he had in any race for more than a year, set out after Jiménez. He caught him on the steepest pitch of a narrower, bumpier road above the last village, and then, with 2km to go, simply rode away from the Spanish climber toward a spectacular victory.

And Ullrich? Still riding with Mancebo, the former Tour champion was steadily losing ground, having accepted that his yellow-jersey dream was over. Ullrich crossed the finish line on Courchevel's Altiport (a private airfield and heliport) in 15th place, having lost another two-and-a-half minutes to Armstrong.

As for Pantani, he was jubilant. Not only had he achieved a solo win à la Pirata, but he had also overcome his "Armstrong complex." The Italian had said that he wasn't happy that Armstrong had given him the Ventoux stage. And before the stage, Pantani told some reporters, "It hurts me that Armstrong is so strong. I am used to being the patron, especially in the mountains, and so to see someone ride away in front of my own eyes has been hard (for me)...."

Now, in the post-race press conference, he said, "I wanted revenge, and I believe that's what we saw today."

We also saw the enigmatic Italian move up the overall standings into sixth place, only 1:37 behind the man in second place: Ullrich. Did Pantani have something else in mind, besides a stage win, for the last day in the Alps?

Impostors Apprehended

American wrench Greg Miller was riding the Mavic Tour de France neutral support motorcycle behind Marco Pantani when four activists for Basque freedom jumped into the race at the Courchevel mountaintop finish. "Suddenly, there was this guy in a Kelme jersey coming up real fast. I was thinking, 'No way....' We moved over and let him though, and then realized (he was an impostor)," Miller said. "We blocked him against the barriers.

"Then there was a guy with a Banesto jersey. I saw he didn't have a race number on his bike, so I used a wheel to knock him off his bike into the barriers." That protester needed hospital treatment.

A third protester, wearing the polka-dot jersey, was also stopped. But the fourth one, in a yellow jersey, slipped through and sprinted in behind a chase group, raising his arms in "victory." He was seen later being taken away in handcuffs by the police.

The Race for Second

If there were still any doubts, they were erased in the exciting finale of this 15th stage: Barring accidents, Lance Armstrong was going to win a second Tour de France. At the same time, the details on whom would join him on the final podium the following Sunday were thrown into even more confusion.

The logical favorite for second place, Ullrich, was getting weaker rather than stronger as the race wore on. while Pantani was going the other way. It was possible that the two former Tour winners would be the final runners-up to the defending champion in Paris, but they still had to overcome three surprising challengers: Festina pair Christophe Moreau of France and Joseba Beloki of Spain, and Kelme's Roberto Heras, also Spanish.

Only 1:37 separated sixth-placed Pantani from second-placed Ullrich, a margin that the Italian climber could wipe out on Tuesday. After a second rest day on Monday, Pantani had a chance to move into second overall on the Courchevel to Morzine moun-

Tyler's diary
July 16
Courchevel

You see some funny things at bike races. One day it's a group of fans dressed up like cavemen; the next day, it's political messages painted on the roads. But today's antics should make all the highlight reels.

First, there was a guy dressed in a Kelme jersey, who jumped out of the crowds and rode with Pantani. The announcers were fumbling through their notes looking for his number and trying to figure out who he was. When they realized he couldn't hang with Marco they tried to cover up their mistake.

The next race crasher joined the group that was about two minutes down. This guy was really ballsy: He was wearing a yellow jersey. Not only did he join the race, but also he zipped up his shirt and crossed the finish line blowing kisses and raising his arms in victory.

The team had a good day today. Kevin and I were able to hang with Lance a little longer than yesterday. Having the numbers at the end is good on two levels: First, Lance can't be isolated by other teams. Second, if your team has more guys up front for the big stuff, it kills the morale of the other teams.

We're staying at the top of Courchevel tonight, which is kind of cool. We'll be sleeping at 6500 feet. It's a neat area. I like visiting places that remind me of my ski-racing days, and you definitely get that sense up here. Even though it's July, we're surrounded by white caps.

Tomorrow, we rest … and then we get back to the business of climbing.

tain stage, which is similar to the one that took him to a spectacular solo win in 1997.

That year, after almost quitting the race with low morale the day before, he rode away from all the other race leaders on the closing climb, the hors-categorie Col de Joux-Plane, and even increased his winning margin on the rapid descent to the line. The Joux-Plane would be the last of five climbs on Tuesday, and it was one of the steepest of the whole Tour, averaging 8.5 percent for 11.8km. Only 12km of downhill separates the 5577-foot summit from the finish.

After taking 3:21 out of Ullrich on stage 15, a similar margin would take Pantani 1:44 ahead of the German before the one remaining time trial. To keep off Ullrich on his home turf—the time trial route would go within five miles of the German's hometown of Merdingen— would be a difficult task, something that Pantani acknowledged.

Besides Ullrich, both Beloki and Moreau are strong time trialists, so they too were both candidates for the podium. Beloki was currently in third, two seconds behind Ullrich and 1:35 ahead of Pantani, while Moreau was in fourth, 0:54 after the German and 0:41 ahead of the Italian.

Such close margins after a succession of tough mountain stages is rare indeed.

Fred's diary
July 17
Courchevel

This morning I woke up to loud music next door. I was about to go and ask whomever it was to turn it down, when I found out it was already 10 a.m. I was actually happy to see that I was able to sleep in that long. Breakfast was very relaxed, as there was no pressure of being anywhere at any special time.

A nice easy ride on the indoor trainer was done in our room, overlooking a lake. Not a bad spot for an indoor ride; it made it that much sweeter.

I'm glad that the last two weeks have gone by, as they have been some of the hardest I've ever experienced. I have seen many things happen that have changed cycling for me.

Now, it looks to me like everyone is pretty much settled into where they belong, knowing that most likely Lance will be in yellow in Paris. He still won't let himself believe that is true, but I think his competitors believe it. The strangest thing for me is seeing how many superstars have cracked this year.

In the gruppetto of this last stage, we had guys like Zülle, Olano and Jalabert to add to the guys left behind to suffer. It has shown me how cycling is a delicate sport, where being the best doesn't always mean you win.

Yesterday, I witnessed a sight that definitely surprised me. It all started on the climb to the Col du Galibier, where it looked like everyone was content to just make it over the top together. Then Jalabert decided to go on the attack, which was probably an unusual sight, as that sort of move is generally made by the underdogs looking for an opportunity.

Jalabert's effort did not impress anyone in the field, as it was making a hard day even harder. Everyone chased him down, and when he was caught he was called nasty names. Then, when it felt like we were all content, he did it again—and this time Postal took control and brought him back. Lance went up to him and pointed his index finger at his face and just called out, "Jaja!"—as if to say, "This is your first warning; don't do it again."

Jalabert responded with: "This is what cycling is about." It was something I had never seen before: how the powerhouses put each other in their place.

Well, it seems like the heat is on and everyone is looking for their spots in the peloton. As I ride the gruppettos, I see riders just wanting to make it to Paris and wondering what awaits them the next day. For me, it has been an easier job, as I have been comfortable making the gruppettos and looking for my opportunity later in the Tour. That is not to say that I have not been doing my share of suffering. But I think it's about minimizing the suffering, not stopping it, because I don't care where you are in the standings, everyone is suffering just as bad.

Time to go and enjoy the rest of my rest day. See you all later.

Tyler's diary
July 17
Courchevel

I have to say that we kind of lucked out during our second rest day. First, we're staying at a great hotel. It's usually only open four months out of every year, but because the Tour came to town, they opened for two days this summer to accommodate us. It's been the best hotel we've stayed in yet. The other benny of the day was the fact that there was no transfer. We finished the race yesterday and rolled over to our hotels. Piece of cake.

Our training ride this morning became quite a spectacle. We drove the 22 kilometers down to the base of Courchevel to do a nice easy ride on flat roads. But when we pulled over on the side of the road to get out and get on our bikes things turned into a circus. Cars just stopped in the road and people started swarming around the cars. Needless to say, traffic came to a standstill. Nothing like the yellow jersey to cause an impromptu blockade. I've never seen anything like it.

Things were so nuts back at our hotel that a security guard had to be brought in to man the front door. The lobby turned into a free for all. Lots of well wishers were looking for a chance to meet the man in yellow. And it seemed that for every fanatic, there were two journalists. We all tried to pitch in and cover a few interviews for Lance, because there was no way he was going to make the rounds and speak to everyone who wanted a minute of his time today. It would have been impossible.

TOUR DE FRANCE, July 10–16.

STAGE 10
Dax–Lourdes-Hautacam. July 10.
1. Javier Otxoa (Sp), Kelme-Costa Blanca, 205km in 6:09:32 (33.285 kph); **2. Armstrong, at 0:42**; 3. Jiménez, at 1:13; 4. Virenque, at 1:57; 5. Manuel Beltran (Sp), Mapei-Quick Step, s.t.; 6. Escartin, at 2:02; 7. Roberto Heras (Sp), Kelme-Costa Blanca, s.t.; 8. Christophe Moreau (F), Festina, at 3:05; 9. Beloki, at 3:35; 10. Zülle, at 3:47.

OTHERS: 21. Pantani, at 5:52; 23. Olano, at 7:26; 24. Savoldelli; 28. Jalabert, at 8:45; 34. Wauters, at 10:27; 36. Millar, at 10:51; **39. Hamilton, at 12:02; 41. Julich, at 12:40; 71. Livingston, at 25:44; 72. Hincapie, s.t.;** 82. Bettini, at 28:21; 99. Elli, at 31:59; **101. McRae, at 31:59; 140. Rodriguez, at 36:33; 144. Andreu, s.t.**

ABANDONED: **Vaughters,** Vandenbroucke.

OVERALL: 1. Armstrong, 1637.5km in 39:24:30; 2. Ullrich, at 4:14; 3. Moreau, at 5:10; 4. Wauters, at 5:18; 5. Luttenberger, at 5:21; 6. Beloki, at 5:23; 7. Beltran, at 5:44; 8. Otxoa, at 6:13; 9. Jiménez, at 6:21; 10. Angel Casero (Sp), Festina, at 6:55.

STAGE 11
Bagnères-de-Bigorre–Revel. July 11.
1. Dekker, 218.5km in 5:05:47 (42.873 kph); 2. Santiago Botero (Col), Kelme-Costa Blanca, s.t.; 3. Rik Verbrugghe (B), Lotto-Adecco, at 4:51; 4. Millar; 5. Mancebo; 6. Vinokourov; 7. David Etxebarria (Sp), ONCE-Deutsche Bank; 8. Aerts; 9. Bartoli, all s.t.; 10. Zabel, at 5:05.

OTHERS: **15. Rodriguez, at 5:05; 20. Julich; 23. Ullrich; 24. Armstrong;** 26. Jalabert; 28. Boogerd; 30. Zülle; 32. Olano; 43. Pantani; **46. Livingston; 54. Hamilton, all s.t.; 96. Andreu, at 10:16; 97. Hincapie; 100. McRae, all s.t.**

OVERALL: 1. Armstrong, 1856km in 44:35:22; 2. Ullrich, at 4:14; 3. Moreau, at 5:10; 4. Wauters, at 5:18; 5.

Luttenberger, at 5:21; 6. Beloki, at 5:23; 7. Beltran, at 5:44; 8. Otxoa, at 6:13; 9. Jiménez, at 6:21; 10. Casero, at 6:55.

STAGE 12
Carpentras–Le Mont Ventoux. July 13.

1. Pantani, 149km in 4:15:11 (35.033 kph); **2. Armstrong, s.t.;** 3. Beloki, at 0:25; 4. Ullrich,at 0:29; 5. Botero, at 0:48; 6. Heras, s.t. 7. Virenque, at 1:17; 8. Mancebo, at 1:23; 9. Beltran, at 1:29; 10. Moreau, at 1:31.

OTHERS: 29. Julich, at 6:45; 44. Hamilton, at 7:51; 52. Livingston, at 10:07; 76. Zabel, at 17:05; **79. Hincapie, s.t.;** 80. Arrieta, s.t.; 95. Millar, s.t.; **130. Andreu, s.t.; 131. Rodriguez, s.t.**

OVERALL: 1. Armstrong, 2005km in 48:50:21; 2. Ullrich, at 4:55; 3. Beloki, at 5:52, 4. Moreau, at 6:53; 5. Beltran, at 7:25, 6. Virenque, at 8:28; 7. Heras, at 8:33, 8. Mancebo, at 9:42; 9. Otxoa, 9:46; 10. Luttenberger, at 10:01.

STAGE 13
Avignon–Draguignan. July 14.

1. Garcia-Acosta, 185.5 in 4:03:02 (45.796 kph); 2. Nicolas Jalabert, at 0:25; 3. Pascal Hervé (F), Polti, at 0:27; 4. Guido Trentin (I), Vini Caldirola, at 0:57; 5. Stéphane Heulot (F), La Française des Jeux, s.t.; 6. McEwen, at 4:00; 7. Simon; 8. Anthony Morin (F), Crédit Agricole.; 9. Agnolutto; 10. Wauters, all s.t.

OTHERS: 27. Armstrong, at 10:06; 29. Pantani; 33. Jalabert; **52. Julich;** 55. **Livingston;** 59. Escartin; **65. Hamilton;** 69. Savoldelli; 75. **Zülle; 110. Hincapie, all s.t.; 122. Andreu, at 10:44; 135. Rodriguez, at 11:08.**

ABANDONED: Bettini; Casero; Laurent Dufaux (Swi), Saeco-Valli & Valli; Lauri Aus (Est), AG2R Prévoyance; Peña; Bartoli.

OVERALL: 1. Armstrong, 2190.5km in 53:03:29; 2. Ullrich; at 4:55; 3. Beloki; at 5:52; 4. Wauters, at 6:03; 5. Moreau, at 6:53; 6. Beltran, at 7:25; 7. Virenque, at 8:28; 8. Heras, at 8:33; 9. Mancebo, at 9:42; 10. Otxoa, at 9:46.

STAGE 14
Draguignan–Briançon. July 15.

1. Botero, 249.5km in 7:56:13 (31.435 kph); 2. Savoldelli, at 2:30; 3. Pantani, at 2:46, 4. Escartin, at 2:49; 5. Virenque; 6. Moreau, both s.t; **7. Armstrong, at 2:51,** 8. Heras; 9. Ullrich; 10. Beloki, all s.t.

OTHERS: 47. Olano, at 10:20; 52. Zülle, at 14:06; **53. Hamilton, at 14:06;** 55. **Livingston,** at 14:16; 56. Ekimov, at 14:39; 67. **Hincapie, at 23:55; 79. Julich, at 27:56;** 123. Jalabert, at 36:35; **138. Rodriguez, at 36:35; 141. Andreu, at 36:52.**

ABANDONED: Verbrugghe; Steffen Wesemann (G), Telekom; Sandstod; Heulot.

OVERALL: 1. Armstrong, 2440km in 61:02:33; 2. Ullrich, at 4:55; 3. Beloki, at 5:52; 4. Moreau, at 6:51; 5. Virenque, at 8:26; 6. Heras, at 8:33; 7. Beltran, at 9:33; 8. Botero, at 10:00, 9. Pantani, at 10:13, 10. Mancebo at 10:17.

STAGE 15
Briançon–Courchevel. July 16.

1. Pantani, 173.5km in 5:34:46 (31.096 kph); 2. Jimenez, at 0:41; 3. Heras, at 0:50; **4. Armstrong, s.t.;** 5. Nardello, at 1:00; 6. Botero, at 1:09; 7. Massimiliano Lelli (I), Cofidis, at 2:17; 8. Escartin, at 2:21; 9. Moreau, at 2:21; 10. Virenque, at 2:21.

OTHERS: 33. Hamilton, at 11:18; 36. Livingston, at 13:23; 45. Julich, at 22:17; 68. Andreu, at 35:56; 73. Hincapie; 102. Rodriguez, both s.t.

ABANDONED: Van Bon; Arturas Kasputis (Lit), AG2R; Etxebarria.

OVERALL: 1. Armstrong, 2613.5km in 66:38:09; 2. Ullrich at 7:26; 3. Beloki, at 7:28; 4. Moreau, at 8:22; 5. Heras, at 8:25; 6. Pantani, at 9:03; 7. Virenque, at 9:57; 8. Botero, at 10:09; 9. Escartin, at 12:27; 10. Mancebo, at 12:43.

THE
2000
TOUR DE FRANCE
THROUGH THE LENS OF
GRAHAM WATSON

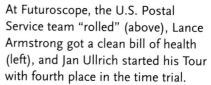

At Futuroscope, the U.S. Postal
Service team "rolled" (above), Lance
Armstrong got a clean bill of health
(left), and Jan Ullrich started his Tour
with fourth place in the time trial.

Time trial winner David Millar (left) got a taste for yellow in the opening stages, and Tom Steels (above) almost lost the win at Loudun to fast-finishing Stuart O'Grady (at far left).

NEXT PAGE: The team time trial-winning ONCE-Deutsche Bank squad was penalized 20 seconds because its team car (in center) got too close to the riders on the St. Nazaire bridge.

Mixed week for sprinters: Marcel Wüst celebrated his first-ever Tour stage win at Vitré (above left), while O'Grady (right) raced 80km with a broken collarbone before being hospitalized at Tours.

(opposite) Michele Bartoli, Alex Zülle, Giuseppe Guerini, Ullrich and Michael Boogerd head the pack on the Aubisque, and Javier Otxoa (below) won stage 10 at Hautacam, Erik Dekker scored the second of three stage wins at Revel (above).

On his way to glory: Armstrong first dropped Marco Pantani (below), then closed the two-minute gap on the Escartin-Virenque group on the climb to Hautacam (main photo).

There's a reason why the Ventoux is also
known as Mont Chauve—the "Bald Mountain."

The "real" Pantani came to life to win at Courchevel (left), while Armstrong raced at 54 kph to take his stage in Mulhouse (right).

At Troyes (opposite), Erik Zabel tangoed his way to victory ahead of Robbie McEwen (right) and Jeroen Blijlevens (left), but the German was fooled in Paris (above) by Mapei, which sprung Stefano Zanini to the win. Later, the Champs-Elysées saw American fans celebrate (lower left), along with podium finishers Ullrich, Armstrong and Joseba Beloki.

Greg LeMond set the trend with first son Geoffrey a decade ago; now its baby Luke David Armstrong getting the royal treatment.

WEEK 3

Heading for Paris

Lance Armstrong in 1999 restored pride to the Tour de France following its drug-related scandals of 1998. He was now just one week away from what should be an even more impressive victory. Armstrong's "miracle" story of winning the '99 Tour only two years after overcoming an advanced case of testicular cancer that had spread to his abdomen, lungs and brain, brought him worldwide fame. In 1999, the 28-year-old American had restored the three-week Tour's athletic legitimacy. But there were still skeptics who believed that no one could win what is arguably the world's toughest sports event without some form of artificial aid.

A couple of days before the Courchevel rest day, the sponsor of cycling's No. 1 team Mapei, Giorgio Squinzi, said in an interview with French sports daily *L'Équipe*: "I'm not suspicious of anyone in particular, but I think that today no one is capable of winning the Tour de France with a natural hematocrit level." He was intimating that to be competitive in the Tour, a cyclist has to use Epogen, the artificial red-blood-cell enhancer—even though riders' urine samples at this Tour were being frozen for testing when an EPO test had been perfected.

Squinzi's comments did not faze Armstrong, who commented. "You have a few people in the sport who don't have a filter in their brain. I (have) to live with that...."

Armstrong was more concerned with the challenges still to come, particular from Jan Ullrich. "He's the biggest talent in cycling," said the Texan. "He can still win the Tour de France ... there's still a week to go."

Going into the last alpine stage, Armstrong enjoyed an overall lead of 7:26 over run-ner-up Ullrich, while Marco Pantani, in sixth. was 1:37 behind Ullrich. The prospect of a battle between the Tour's last three winners was accentuated by the war of words that had been going on between Pantani and Armstrong. Both men said they aimed to win the next day's stage from Courchevel to Morzine, which included the Saisies, Aravis, Colombière and Joux-Plane climbs.

The race would then head into Switzerland, over the Col des Mosses, into Lausanne—to celebrate the centennial of the Union Cycliste Internationale, which is based there. Then came another marathon stage of 246.5km, through Switzerland into Germany, for a finish at Freiburg, close to Ullrich's home in Merdingen. And from here, the only long time trial—58.5km to Mulhouse, back in France—would be the Tour's final showdown.

The last two stages looked likely to see the sprinters back in action, with the Tour's longest stage to Troyes, in the Champagne district, followed by the final day's celebra-tions in Paris. There, the stage would start at the foot of the Eiffel Tower, with the tradi-tional laps around the Champs-Elysées being preceded by three 30km loops on the boule-vards of the French capital.

Asked in Courchevel about his expectations for the final week, Armstrong replied, "The objective is to win, period. Not to win by a specific amount of time—one second is enough."

Indeed, there was still plenty of racing to go....

STAGE 16

Courchevel–Morzine • July 18

Running on Empty

WHAT STARTED OUT AS A FRIENDLY GESTURE BY ARMSTRONG, LED TO AN UNFORTUNATE WAR OF WORDS with Pantani, and ultimately boomeranged on both protagonists on this final alpine stage.

The "feud" began when Armstrong didn't contest the stage 12 finish on Mont Ventoux, and Pantani showed his distaste for the race leader's benevolence by not rais-ing his hands to mark his stage win. Pantani then upset Armstrong with statements in the press that intimated that the American wasn't the strongest on the Ventoux.

In one version, Pantani said, "When he said to me, '*Vitesse, vitesse*,' to get me to accel-erate, he was trying to provoke me. Then he tried to go away alone, but found himself out in the head wind and couldn't do it—that put him in a new dimension in my eyes...."

Having read such quotes, Armstrong said at his press conference on the rest day in Courchevel: "The last few days, his actions and words are a little disappointing.... It's unfortunate that he's showing his true colors." He went on to say: "*Elefantino* has another day (to win a stage), and I would be lying if I didn't say it [winning the stage] was at the back of my mind."

In turn, Pantani—who prefers his Pirata moniker—said, "If (Armstrong) believes that it's all over, he's mistaken. In any case, he isn't finished with me."

It wasn't the first time that Pantani had felt put down in this Tour. He had been angered by a comment made earlier in the race by five-time Tour winner Bernard Hinault, who, when asked what he thought of Pantani's chances in the Tour, replied: "He should focus on stage wins and the polka-dot jersey."

The Italian climber has a different opinion of his potential. He says that winning the 1998 Tour defined him as a person, and that he returned to the sport in May at the Giro for one reason: to prepare for the Tour de France. Now, he was up to sixth place on G.C., and there was one more mountain stage—a stage very similar to the one he took with a solo move in 1997.

With that in mind, and remembering what Pantani said about his epic break on the Galibier to win the '98 Tour ("This was my destiny"), it wasn't a stretch to think that the Italian would try something bold on this 16th stage.

✖

Having had a rest day to recover from his Courchevel win, Il Pirata was full of confidence at the start of the stage, which would open with a 20km downhill to the Isère valley. But his day did not start off well when, just after the descent began, there was a pileup on a bend. Three men went down: Serrano, Botero and Pantani, and when Serrano didn't get up, he was taken to the hospital. Meanwhile, Pantani's whole team waited for him, and brought him back to the peloton after a 6km chase.

There were four major climbs awaiting. If Pantani delayed his expected attack until the last one, the very difficult Col de Joux-Plane, it was argued that he might be able to make up his 1:37 deficit on Ullrich and move into second place overall ... until the stage 19 time trial. If he wanted to achieve something more decisive? Well, no one knew.

And no one expected the Radio Tour announcement at the foot of the very first climb, the Col des Saisies: "An attack by No. 71, Pantani of Mercatone Uno."

"I wanted to explode the Tour without worrying about the consequences," Pantani later said. "I had nothing to lose."

With 130km still to race, it appeared to be a very rash move. But bold moves sometimes produce unexpected results.

Here on the Saisies—a serpentine ascent between alpine meadows overlooked by the snowy splendor of western Europe's highest peak, 15,772-foot Mont Blanc—the Tour did threaten to break apart.

Pantani's sharp acceleration took him clear of the peloton, and across a 1:15 gap to two earlier breakaways: Saeco's Commesso and, as always, Kelme's Pascual-Llorente. Then, with the lead at 27 seconds, six strong climbers raced away from the quickly disintegrating pack: Kelme's Heras and Botero, Polti's Virenque and Hervé, Festina's Beloki, and Banesto's Baranowski.

If these strong climbers could manage to link up with Pantani and Pascual-Llorente, then the Tour really could explode. And for a while, that looked possible: About 6km into the 15km climb, the six chasers were halfway across the half-minute gap to Pantani. But Telekom then put Guerini and Vinokourov to work, prior to team leader Ullrich surging across to the Beloki group. That, in turn, provoked a stepped-up pursuit led by Postal's Hamilton and Livingston … and the chasers regrouped.

Pantani continued his solo attack, and was 35 seconds ahead when first Escartin, and then Hervé jumped away. They caught Pascual-Llorente, and by the Saisies summit were 32 seconds behind Pantani, with the race leader's group—now only 28-strong—at 1:03.

The Postals seemed to have the situation under control, but Armstrong had lost his

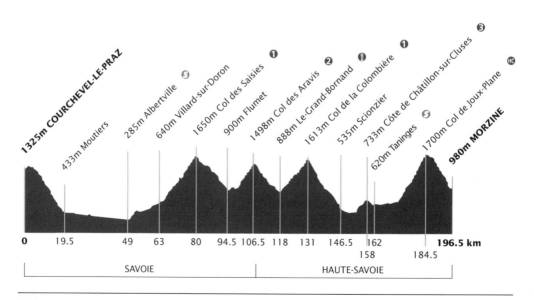

teammates on the climb—except for Hamilton and Livingston, who were happy that one of Armstrong's pals, David Millar of Cofidis, had put in some strong pulls on the top section of the Saisies.

By the start of the second climb, the abrupt Col des Aravis, Escartin and Hervé were with Pantani, and their lead was 1:10. Inspired by the huge crowds thrilled to see him on the rampage, Pantani was not giving in, even though Hervé was just sitting on the back (under orders from Polti leader Virenque) and Escartin was giving only perfunctory pulls.

The time gap remained the same all the way up the 8km Aravis, the match in effect being Pantani at the front against Hamilton behind. On reaching the next valley, however, a right turn brought with it a tail wind, and the tide started to turn.

After the gap dropped to 55 seconds, when Pantani changed bikes in the feed zone, it quickly opened up again. Il Pirata thumped his way up the Col de la Madeleine on the big ring, and halfway up the 12km climb, heading across an open mountainside, his lead was 1:40.

Behind, Hamilton was keeping on the pressure ... and the gap started to drop again. "When it started coming down," said Hamilton, "I had to soft pedal, so we didn't catch them too quickly."

The end came at the foot of the fast and long Colombière descent. Pantani's brash (it could be called foolish) 81km break had lasted for two-and-a-half hours. He had nothing to show for it, except for his bravado and the fact that he had weakened Armstrong's lieutenants in the long chase.

Pantani was cooked though ("I hadn't been able to eat properly ... the stomach pain soon weakened me"), and he was dropped as soon as the group began the Joux-Plane climb, 23km from the stage finish. Accompanied by teammates Marco Velo and Marcello Siboni, he would ride into Morzine more than 13 minutes down. That evening, he was on his way home to Cesenatico.

❁

While Pantani was languishing on the Joux-Plane, Armstrong seemed to be flourishing. After Hamilton and then Livingston had given their best in the first steep kilometer, only eight riders were left with the Texan. That became seven when a gasping Moreau fell off the pace ... and then, at the front of the group, Kelme's Heras made a massive effort that only Armstrong and Virenque could go with.

Ullrich managed to close the gap, then dropped back again, unable to hold the fierce

Tyler's diary
July 18
Morzine

Today was one of those days people are going to be talking about for a while. It was unusual from the get-go—and terribly sad. We stopped after the neutral section at kilometer zero, which is usually the official starting point, to pay tribute to a 12-year-old boy who died after being stricken by a Tour de France publicity car. It was a very sad moment indeed. None of us can imagine what his family must be going through right now. If you get the chance, please keep them in your thoughts.

It didn't take long to get back to business, as tension was already high before today's start. The newspapers were having a field day over comments Lance made yesterday regarding the Mont Ventoux stage and his feelings about Marco Pantani. Evidently, Lance was reacting to a quote Pantani had made about "not being through with making Armstrong suffer." Lance responded by saying that giving the Ventoux stage to Pantani was a mistake and that he regretted the move.

It was no surprise to any of us that today's main objective would be getting Lance across the line first. But Marco had other ideas and attacked on the first climb. He gained a minute on us and stayed out front for the larger part of the stage, which put us on the ropes a bit. Everyone on the team was working up front from the time the attack was launched. Because of this effort, we wound up burning through some of our guys sooner than we would have liked. This left Kevin

and me at the front with Lance. After deciding to save Kevin for the final climb, I began manning the front—and wound up staying there for almost four hours. Talk about a long day.

When we reached the final climb and the serious attacks of the day were firing like loaded guns, Lance realized that he hadn't eaten enough. Unfortunately, Kevin and I were already well spent and nowhere in sight to help him. But I'll give him credit—tons of it. He stayed calm and rode a steady pace to the finish. He said it was the hardest day on the bike of his entire life. But he hung in there and conceded less than a minute-and-a-half to Ullrich. In the scheme of things, this is no huge deal. He still has over five minutes of padding. Considering things could have been much worse, I'd say it went rather well today. I've seen guys lose 10 minutes in a heartbeat after bonking. But Lance stayed the course—a good sign for the future.

Because the team split up after the first climb, we weren't able to regroup until dinner tonight. Then, war stories about today's stage were traded left and right. Perhaps the topper of the day was Frankie's recounting of a deer hitting La Française des Jeux's Frédéric Guesdon. Luckily, he wasn't hurt. The deer, however, is on his way to the morgue. After seeing wild horses on the Aubisque, I thought we had seen everything. But this was surely a once-in-a-lifetime happening—although I'm kind of glad I missed it.

pace. Heras, the 26-year-old Spaniard who placed third in both the Giro and Vuelta in 1999, made another acceleration. This time he went solo, and started eating up his deficit on another young hope, Italian Guido Trentin of Vini Caldirola, who began the climb in a three-man attack that had established a 2:40 lead in the valley.

By the time Heras had caught Trentin, about 6km from the summit, he had a 24-second gap on Virenque and Armstrong—who had been rejoined by Ullrich. The German was looking better now, sitting in the saddle and setting a tempo that had both Virenque and Armstrong standing on the pedals to follow.

Then it happened: The yellow jersey started to drift slowly back from Virenque and Ullrich. The German peeked back, and his eyes grew wider: "I was really surprised to drop Armstrong because he had been so strong since the start (of the climb). Truthfully, at first, I didn't believe it...."

Nor could anyone else. The only time that Armstrong had been remotely in trouble in his 1999 victory had been very close to the finish of the Piau-Engaly stage, when he lost nine seconds to Virenque and Zülle in the last 300 meters—at the end of a six-climb day in which he had tired himself with some long solo efforts.

It was soon apparent that this bad patch was very different. Although Armstrong was bravely holding his style, the legs weren't turning at their previous rate; there was no spark in his eyes; and the riders he had dropped were starting to come back up to him—and go past him. The race leader had bonked.

"There's been a few times in the past when I've said, 'This was my worst day on a bike,' " he said later. "But this was the worst day of my life on a bike ... I was prepared to lose three minutes."

As Armstrong slowly climbed the narrow mountain road, riding between mobs of fans, he was first passed by Escartin, then by Beloki and Hervé. And as he reached the summit, five others caught the race leader: Botero, Trentin, Conti, Moreau and Atienza.

In front, Virenque had ridden away from Ullrich, and then caught Heras. The two climbers crested the Joux-Plane 26 seconds ahead of the solo Ullrich; 1:02 ahead of Beloki, Hervé and Escartin; and 2:08 ahead of the Armstrong group.

Virenque went on to win the stage on his own, after Heras crashed into the barriers when he misjudged a blind left turn at the foot of the descent. And Armstrong? He was simply relieved to drop down to Morzine with his small group and learn that he had conceded only 1:37 to Ullrich. The yellow jersey was safe for another day, and there would no longer be a Pantani to stir things up.

Death of a Child

A minute of silence was given before the Tour's 16th stage, to honor a child who died from the injuries he sustained in a collision with a Tour sponsor's vehicle on stage 13. The 12-year-old boy, Philippe Tardi, was the first Tour spectator to be killed in 12 years.

The boy was reportedly on the dirt shoulder, watching the publicity caravan pass through his village of Ginasservis, about 60km from the end of the Avignon-Draguignan stage. He was hit by a vehicle carrying guests of Tour sponsor Sodhexo that went out of control while slaloming its way between publicity vehicles. The driver has been charged with manslaughter. [A judge later recommended a six-month suspended jail sentence, and a two-year loss of his driver's license.]

After the accident, the French national police and race organizers drastically reduced the number of accredited publicity vehicle that could drive on the official Tour route.

Punched Out

There's an expression in boxing that could appropriately be applied to stage 16 of the Tour de France: punched out. It means that after constantly battering an opponent, a boxer has no strength left to strike another blow. That's what it was like by the finish of this stunning five-climb day that took place on the Tour's first day of warm sunshine—conditions that inspired both stage winner Virenque and 1997 Tour winner Ullrich, who was now Armstrong's one remaining challenger for the yellow jersey.

The day was so punishing—very unlike the final mountain stage in most previous Tours—because an extraordinarily determined Pantani decided that the only way he could climb on the podium in Paris was to make a long-distance attack. Well, no one expected him to make that move 130km from the finish, with all the climbs still to go. And when he went, everyone behind knew that they were in for a long, hard day.

Virtually all the team workers were dropped when the chase began. And it was only the long pulls of Armstrong's two remaining teammates, Hamilton and Livingston (sometimes aided by Ullrich's Guerini, Udo Bolts and Vinokourov) that kept the Pantani break in check. And the speed of the race—more than 35 kph on a stage where a 32 kph average could be expected—meant that no one had it easy.

Armstrong was not alone in having his "most difficult day on the bike"—and limiting his losses on Ullrich to 1:37 should be seen as a major achievement. Heras, who looked as though he had the stage win in his pocket when he attacked on the Joux-Plane, suffered enormously in the end. He was shaking out his right leg on the descent to Morzine, apparently cramping, although he later said he was preparing his muscles for a sprint finish with Virenque; and fatigue certainly contributed to his misjudging a sharp, blind turn at the foot of the downhill.

Both Ullrich and Virenque raced to their limit, and even the last-place finisher, big Magnus Backstedt of Crédit Agricole, had to ride as hard as he did when he won a Tour stage in 1998. This time, he was racing to make the time cut—which he did—although the effort saw him doubled over in pain after he crossed the line 39 minutes behind Virenque.

Backstedt wouldn't be pleased to see the profile for stage 17. Although the French Alps were behind them, the 134 survivors of the day's struggle still had a Cat. 2 pass to climb in the Swiss Alps, with a hard 12km circuit to end the stage in Lausanne. And if Ullrich was feeling as good as he did on the Joux-Plane, maybe he'd try to chip some more seconds away from Armstrong's 5:37 lead before Friday's time trial....

STAGE 17

Evian-les-Bains–Lausanne • July 19

A Circuitous Day

ACROSS THE LAKE, THROUGH THE HILLS AND AROUND THE TOWN: THAT WAS PRETTY MUCH THE STORY of stage 17. From the start outside the belle époque casino in the neatly manicured spa town of Evian-les-Bains, you could look east to the low green mountains of Swiss Romandie, where the stage would head for a loop over the easy climb of the Col des Mosses; and then you could look north across the deep shining waters of Lake Geneva, and see the modern white buildings of Lausanne climbing up a hillside where the race would finish.

After three stages in the Alps, all of them fought to the limit, many racers were relieved that the roads would be flatter, easier today. And yet, when a tail wind sprung up off the lake to blow the 133 survivors toward Switzerland, many of those riders were ready to attack and counterattack as if they had never been in the mountains at all. The aggression resulted in an average of 55 kph for the first half-hour: a leg-breaking pace that would come to haunt some of those attackers later that afternoon.

The loop through the hills saw the formation of the day's only real break, started by Cofidis's Lelli over the Mosses climb, and completed by eight others on the mainly descending roads to the day's feed zone at the cheese town of Gruyère.

Although Telekom had Heppner in the break, he was there as insurance should the break stay away. And with a 1:43 lead 50km out of Lausanne, that was a strong possibility. Still, Zabel knew he had a good chance of winning his first Tour stage in three years, with rivals like Steels, Wüst and O'Grady no longer around.

So his Telekom teammates went to the front of the peloton, and rode as hard as they had in the opening week to chase down the break. It wasn't an easy task in a strong wind; but they cut the gap to 45 seconds by the time they reached Vevey, where the route hit the north shore of Lake Geneva.

It was a spectacular sight seeing the silver lake on the left, the green vineyards on the right, and the Telekom pink-and-white-led peloton charging down the smooth black road in between. By the time they reached Lausanne, and its finishing circuit of 12km, all the leaders had been swept up.

Suddenly, the race changed from a Tour stage to a championship-type event, as the circuit had a sizable hill—averaging almost 5 percent for 2.4km—and a fast, twisting downhill back to the lakeside finish. It was a circuit the Rabobank riders remembered from the Tour of Switzerland, and they waited for an opening.

There was no chance on the long climb, where a break by MemoryCard's Bo Hamburger and Cofidis's David Moncoutié was neutralized by Telekom's Vinokourov, and brought back before the summit, 460 feet above the city—thanks to a powerful effort by Bölts and Ullrich, with Zabel on their wheel.

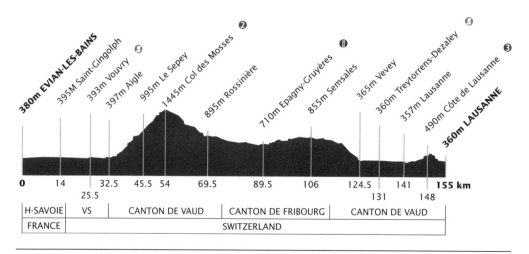

The fast climb split the field, and only 59 riders were now in the front group. When Bölts dropped to the back, Telekom had only Ullrich and Vinokourov to position Zabel for the sprint. The hill had also seen all eight of Armstrong's teammates left behind, so the race leader had no choice but to stick close to the front, in order to avoid being caught in a crash or losing time in a split.

As for Rabobank, it had five men in the lead group, still waiting their chance. With 6km to go, its leader Boogerd shot off the front, hoping to catch out the Telekoms. No luck.

Then Lotto's Mario Aerts bolted clear, inside 4km to go. Next to go was Rabobank's Dekker: Seeing an opening, he took off, surging through one of the many downhill turns. "I sprinted for 200 meters to catch Aerts," Dekker said later. Once there, he immediately started to share pulls with the Belgian.

Their attack was aided by Armstrong and Ullrich being at the front of the line, as neither was taking risks on the turns. And once the chasers reached flatter roads in the last 2km, they momentarily slowed until the group reformed.

Zabel hadn't given up on the win, but with only Ullrich and the over-worked Vinokourov to help him, the two escapees were still 100 meters clear as they reached the final kilometer.

By now the chasers had regrouped, and the gap started to come down. Aerts reacted first to the changing situation and went for a long sprint, hoping to take Dekker by surprise. He didn't fool the Dutchman, but Aerts's burst was just what Dekker needed to launch his own finishing effort, with enough lead to hold off the too-late challenge by Zabel, with Rodriguez taking third.

There was no celebration from Dekker like there had been when he won in Villeneuve-sur-Lot and Revel. This time, there was just a blank look on his face, some tears, and then the only words he could blurt out: "I can't believe it."

Zabel's Troubles

Erik Zabel must be wondering just what he has to do to win another stage of the Tour de France. In Lausanne, for the second time this Tour, he came in second. Zabel took second at Vitré behind fellow German Marcel Wüst in the first week. Zabel also has finished third three times in this Tour. In fact, his last Tour stage win dates back to 1997.

Winning stages came easy at first for the power-packed German sprinter. In his first Tour, in 1995, he soon got the measure of his opponents and at Charleroi on stage 8, he

Fred's diary
Stage 17
Lausanne

My legs were not feeling that great today, but I knew I had to get it together if things ended in a field sprint. For some reason, though, I woke up feeling tired.

Yesterday, I felt that I achieved my goal in the race: getting through the mountain stages with the minimum amount of suffering. as I prepare for the worst. So far, it's worked out. In fact, at times, I felt it was going too easy. A lot of the riders in the gruppetto are living on the edge, and they didn't like it when I tried to push the pace on the climbs. A couple of times, they just let me ride off. But I didn't want to miss the time cut.

Today, it was very fast at the start, and I was trying to cover all the moves. It was crazy. People were attacking when we were going 60 kph. There's no point in riding at 65, 66 kph and gaining 10 meters, so I'd wait until a group had 50 meters, and then jump across. But none of the moves got anywhere.

Then, on the day's main climb, I got dropped, and I was thinking, "Okay, today's going to be another survival day." But I managed to get back on at the KoM. I was hoping that a break would go, so I wouldn't have to do a sprint, I was pleased when Max, my roommate, got across to a break on the descent. He had good legs today.

Telekom had Heppner in the break, and he wasn't working, and then Telekom started chasing. Everyone was fighting for position in the wind. Telekom was going hard, and the rest of us were rotating behind. It was quite a fast pace, just enough to tire the legs.

When the gap started to come down, my teammates were keeping me out of the wind, and I thought, "Oh no, this is great. The only day it's a field sprint, and I don't have the legs. Damnit, I don't know if I can make it."

But for me, the closer I get to the finish, something kicks in and I get fired up. About 10km out, Zanini came up to me and said, "Just follow Zabel." Zanini would usually do the leadout, but he was too tired. Still, all I needed to do was somehow survive the last climb. I saw a sign saying 2km to the top, and I thought I can do that, so I just followed the wheels.

Over the KoM, it was unfortunate that Lance and Ullrich were the ones at the front. When the two guys got away on the descent, Lance and Ullrich were taking it too easy around the turns, because they didn't want to crash. I was right on Zabel's wheel, and saw Lance and Ullrich then give it everything they had.

But they all sat up, and the gap got bigger. Telekom's Vinokourov came up next, and he looked across at me to see if I was going to work—he thought I was still a leadout man. And I said, "I'm not going anywhere."

In the sprint, McEwen came across and I lost Zabel's wheel for a moment, but I got it back in time and took third place. But for me, Zabel went 100 meters too late. And the word is that on tomorrow's stage, Telekom won't ride for him again. So it's likely that a long break will go.

My main goal now is to get the last slot on the Olympic team…. We'll see what I can do.

used his sharp acceleration on a technical uphill finish to take his first stage win. Zabel took a second win at Bordeaux in the final week.

In 1996, the Telekom sprinter showed more confidence. He took stage 3 at Nogent-sur-Oise, again in a tight, technical finish, and a week later earned a much more significant victory at Gap. Zabel was the only sprinter not to get dropped by the lead group on a difficult climb 10km from the finish. That win confirmed Zabel as the best all-around sprinter, and he went on to win the points competition green jersey for the first time.

Perhaps 1997 was Zabel's best Tour. He again took the green jersey, and his friend Jan Ullrich finished with the yellow jersey. Zabel began that Tour by winning stage 3, in a tough uphill finish at Plumelec. Four days later at Bordeaux, Ullrich led out the Telekom sprinter to take his second stage win of the race. Zabel won again the next day at Pau in a spectacularly close finish against all that year's top sprinters.

That win at Pau was more than three years ago, and Zabel hadn't won a Tour stage since, despite continuing to win the green jersey in both 1998 and 1999. And he was on target to win a record fifth green jersey—to beat the four earned by Irishman Sean Kelly.

How come Zabel had not been able to cross the line first at the Tour for so long? One reason was that he has lost some of his pure sprinter qualities, and developed into a much more "complete" athlete—as shown by his three Milan-San Remo victories in the past four years. Then, he suffers from being on a team that had the yellow jersey as its priority. Another reason was exposed at Lausanne.

Zabel was certainly expected to win here, as the local organizers had chosen his image to put on their poster advertising the stage finish ... and it seemed that Telekom was doing everything right. They chased down a nine-man break, by pulling the pack at a 48-kph pace for 55km; but they should have allowed the three survivors from that break to hang out front a little longer.

Instead, the three were caught right on the finish line, with a 12km circuit still to go, and immediately attacks started. Although Telekom put its Vinokourov in a three-man break that formed on the circuit's main climb, all the other Telekom riders were dropped by the summit—except for Zabel and Ullrich, who followed teammate Bölts up the climb. Not even Ullrich could control all the attacks on the tricky descent, and that's where Dekker escaped with Aerts.

Vinokourov (not a lead-out specialist) did all he could to catch the two escapees, but there was still a 20-meter gap to close in the final 100 meters. Zabel probably sprinted faster than he has done since that last stage win in 1997, but he was still two meters

Tyler's diary
July 19
Lausanne

We are spending the night in Switzerland. This is a drag for me, because it means my cell phone doesn't work. I've been putting off signing up for annual service in Nice for as long as possible, and tonight is one of those nights when my procrastinating has caught up with me. But one night out of touch with the rest of the world won't kill me.

The big news of the day obviously was that of Marco Pantani packing his bags and returning home to Italy. Looking back on yesterday's stage to Morzine, it's pretty unbelievable that he thought he could stay away all day. The stage was hard enough without making a suicidal move like going for a break with Escartin and Hervé on the first climb. But he did accomplish one goal yesterday—which was giving us a run for our money. He did a nice job of putting our team to work. Keeping him within a minute's range wasn't so easy over all those climbs.

It was a pretty tough stage today, tougher than I thought it was going to be. First, the UCI vampires paid a visit to Lance, Kevin, Frankie and me this morning. (So much for random testing within the team...) Then attacks were firing from kilometer zero. How many times have we seen that in this race? It's crazy. The pace was so

incredible I couldn't find one single moment for a "nature break." For anyone who knows me and my pea-sized bladder, this is saying something. Needless to say, today was more painful than it looked on paper.

With the critical climbing days behind us, the press is no longer holding back and giving us space to prepare for each day. The start was an absolute madhouse. I did four interviews this morning before lift off. This may not sound like a lot, but if you multiply that number by nine riders and 30 staff you have a lot of yacking going on. I often wonder if everyone gets sick of hearing the same story over and over.

Speaking of press, a German cycling magazine made some rounds on Monday during our rest day in search of the lightest bike in the race. Turns out my new Trek climbing bike was the least heavy they could find at 7.3 kilograms (16 pounds). Spare me the short guy jokes, please. Although I have to say that knowing I was on the lightest machine during the stage to Morzine was a bit of morale-booster for me. In fact, I'd have to say yesterday was my best day at the Tour this year. You can't stay out front for hours if you're not having a good day.

behind Dekker at the line.

Maybe Telekom would do its best to put Zabel in better position on the 246.5km stage 18, which would finish in his home country. There were sure to be hundreds of thousands of German fans on the route leading to Freiburg-im-Breisgau, where there would be no hilly finishing circuit to contend with. Zabel's only remaining opponents were Mapei's Rodriguez, Farm Frites' McEwen and Polti's Jeroen Blijlevens, now that sprinters Wüst, Steels, O'Grady and Kirsipuu were no longer in the race.

STAGE 18

Lausanne–Freiburg-im-Breisgau

Bragging Rights

WHEN YOU'VE BEEN IN A SMALL BREAKAWAY GROUP FOR THE BEST PART OF SIX HOURS AND YOU'RE coming into the finish against a hometown favorite, it helps to have Guido Bontempi on your side. Bontempi is the directeur sportif of the Italian team, Saeco-Valli & Valli, whose rider in the stage 18 break was Salvatore Commesso.

Commesso is one of those riders in the peloton whom you either love or hate. He's 25 and in only his third pro season, but last year rose to instant fame by taking the Italian national road championship, followed by a stage at the Tour de France (winning solo at Albi after attacking a small breakaway group). Commesso doesn't look like a top rider. He weighs a hefty 143 pounds for his five-foot-five height, and has the swagger of a pop star rather than an athlete, an image that's emphasized by his blond-streaked hair and his penchant for heavy jewelry.

Commesso comes from the "poor" South of Italy, from the street-smart city of Naples, yet lives in the "rich" North, outside of cosmopolitan Como. He came into cycling as a track rider, as did many Italian cyclists before him—like Giuseppe Saronni (world champion and Giro winner of the 1980s) … and Bontempi.

Bontempi remains one of the smartest race tacticians around. In a 15-year career as a pro cyclist, he won five stages of the Tour de France and 16 at the Giro, thanks to both a powerful finish and an uncanny sense of positioning. Commesso, too, has a good turn of speed, and a seemingly in-bred aggression.

There's a story going around that on his second visit to the East Coast's First Union race week this June, Commesso pushed an American sprinter off the road when he was upset by his squirrelly riding. Call him cocky, call him whatever you like, but you can't ignore him.

At the Tour, the rotund young Italian had been in more attacks than pretty much anyone else—other than the four other guys he found himself out front with, after only 4km of this marathon 246.5km stage: France's Durand and Robin, Germany's Voigt and Kazakhstan's Vinokourov.

These five "head-bangers" managed to build up a maximum lead of 27:40 by half-distance, and averaged more than 40 kph, into a head wind, on a course that headed through the foothills of Switzerland's Jura and Germany's Black Forest.

This was a big day for the Germans, and it appeared that everyone had taken the afternoon off work to greet the Tour: Massive, partying crowds, fronted by a big oom-pah band, were waiting at the frontier town of Rheinfelden; and the numbers of fans massed on every small hill and in every small village were as big as those seen earlier at the Tour on major mountain climbs and in big cities.

It was on one of those crowd-solid hills with 40km to go, and just after Durand had made his bid for victory, that Commesso charged away with Vinokourov on his wheel. For about 20 minutes, the two held a tenuous lead (between 16 and eight seconds) over the other three—with Bontempi urging Commesso to keep going hard. The advice worked: With 25km left, the gap started to grow, and was more than two minutes when Vino' and Commesso headed into the wide streets of Freiburg.

Vinokourov is a Telekom rider, and virtually every fan here was sporting a Telekom hat or T-shirt or flag or banner: It didn't matter that the man in the front wasn't German.

Having won his share of stages—in events like the Midi Libre and Tour de l'Oise—Vinokourov knew what he was doing when he made an attack about 2km out.

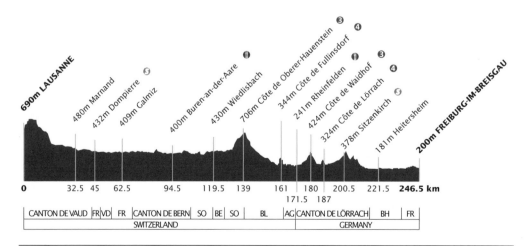

Commesso was quick to chase.

The Telekom man also knew what he was doing when he refused to come by the Italian as the two began finessing for the sprint, 1400 meters from the line. Commesso wanted Vinokourov in front of him, but when he stood still on his pedals at the last turn, 400 meters from home, hoping to get the Telekom man to roll past, Vino' refused to take the bait.

And so, with Bontempi's encouragement, Commesso slowly wound up the pace, started the sprint from the front (now with a tail wind) and kept his opponent out to the right when he accelerated with 100 meters left. But the colorful Italian never let Vinokourov get level with him: He had won another stage of the Tour.

Something else to brag about in the nightclubs, when he was back home in Pusiano.

Time Trial on their Minds

None of the top-10 contenders at this Tour de France did more work than they had to on the long, long stage 18 through Switzerland into Germany. Race leader Lance Armstrong did show his yellow jersey very briefly at the front just 2km into the stage, when he chased up to Spaniards Pascual-Llorente of Kelme and Garcia-Acosta of Banesto, when they went on the attack. Armstrong clearly didn't want the dangerous Spanish teams to again make the day a hard one for his over-worked U.S. Postal squad. He didn't have a problem though with the five men who escaped right after that—the best-placed of the breakaways, Vinokourov, started the day 40 minutes behind Armstrong on G.C.

So why did no one really want to work too much? They wanted to keep their remaining strength intact for the next day's individual time trial from Freiburg across the border into the French city of Mulhouse. It was a stage that Armstrong would dearly love to win, though he would have to be at his best to overcome Ullrich, who not only would have the inspiration of racing in front of his hometown fans—the German lives in the village of Merdingen, 10km west of Freiburg—but also needed a stage win to restore his prestige.

On overall time, Armstrong preceded runner-up Ullrich by 5:37. When Armstrong was asked by an Italian journalist that evening whether that margin would be enough for him to keep the yellow jersey, the Texan look dumfounded. "Are you serious?" he exclaimed. "I thought I won all three time trials last year…. But I am planning to win tomorrow…. Next question."

Besides wanting to win for the prestige, Armstrong would like to prove that his bad

Tyler's diary
July 20
Freiburg

Today was the second longest stage of the Tour. Thankfully, the route was a bit more forgiving—with a little less climbing—than the longest to date, which was to Briançon. However, there was a 7km neutral section that went straight uphill and was kind of outrageous. For sure, it would have been a category climb if it were during the race. I've never seen guys hurting before kilometer zero before. But then, this is the Tour de France....

Even though we pedaled for almost 250km, things went easy for the team. A break of non-threatening riders went away early, which was just fine by us. All the other teams were looking at us, wondering why we weren't starting a chase. But we didn't budge. Finally, the teams with riders in the top 10 had to get organized, when the break was up by 27 minutes. That was just perfect. We held our position at about mid-peloton. It felt like a day off compared to the last few stages.

I've never seen crowds like there were today. The last 35km were jam-packed with spectators. Even the smallest inclines were lined with the kind of crowds you usually see on the classic climbs like Alpe d'Huez. It was practically single-file in some places. Johan warned us to look out for Lance. He told us to "swarm him." Good

thing we did, because at one point, a huge guy was running beside him, spilling his beer and screaming, totally out of control. He almost ran into Frankie. It's great to see enthusiasm for the sport, but today was extreme.

There's a wrap-up TV show called "Velo Club" on France 3 every night. They invite different teams and individual riders to come on the show after each stage. Usually, you'll see the stage winners, the overall leader and select VIPs who are visiting the race. Because we are in Germany tonight, they interviewed the Telekom guys. I've heard that I may make an appearance tomorrow night, to talk about my climbing bike. I guess having the lightest bike at the race is as big a deal to others as it is to me. Cool.

The toughest part of this race is seeing some of your comrades pack it in and head home. It's been a rough ride for some. As it stands right now, the U.S. Postal squad is the only full fleet left. The poor ONCE guys are down to four riders. This is kind of funny, considering that they have three full-size team buses at the Tour—practically private accommodations.

Tomorrow is the time trial. We'll see if I have any juice left to make a good showing. Wish me luck.

patch on the Col de Joux-Plane—when he conceded 1:37 to Ullrich—was no more than that: a brief setback. He also would like to stamp his authority on the Tour just like he did in 1999, when he won the final time trial at Futuroscope.

The next day's 58.5km time trial was completely flat, on long straight roads that should suit Ullrich more than Armstrong, especially as those roads would be lined with perhaps half-a-million of Ullrich's German fans. The wind should not be a factor, as it was forecast to blow from the northwest, mainly favorable on the north-to-south course. But a time trial at the end of a grueling three weeks is as much a test of stamina and character as of intrinsic speed. Armstrong also had the advantage of starting last of the 129 riders, three minutes after Ullrich. If need be, Armstrong would be able to base his schedule on what Ullrich was doing in front of him.

While the Armstrong-Ullrich match was the big attraction of the stage, there was also a tight battle in prospect for the third place on the Paris podium. At the moment, Basque rider Beloki held that spot, just five seconds ahead of fellow Spaniard Heras, 58 seconds ahead of Virenque, and 1:44 ahead of Moreau.

Back on stage 1, a 16.5km time trial, the best of these four was Beloki in 12th place. He was 23 seconds faster than 30th-placed Moreau, and 51 seconds faster than the other two, who finished 71st (Heras) and 72nd (Virenque). However, Moreau had a back problem that day, and a better reference for his time-trial strength was his performance in the 1999 Tour's Metz time-trial stage, when he finished in third place behind Armstrong and Zülle. And over a distance as long as 58.5km, Moreau was certainly capable of making up a 1:44 deficit on a young rider like Beloki. And Virenque, who had gotten stronger as the Tour progressed, couldn't be ruled out.

It looked like being a great stage!

STAGE 19

Freiburg-im-Breisgau–Mulhouse TT • July 21

Battle of the Heavyweights

IF THERE WERE ANY DOUBTS THAT ARMSTRONG AND ULLRICH WERE THE STRONGEST MEN IN THIS TOUR, they were eliminated in just over an hour of furious pedaling along the flat roads of the middle Rhine valley, on this warm, mainly sunny Friday afternoon. This was a prize fight, a battle of the heavyweights of world cycling: Lance "Big Tex" Armstrong vs. Jan "Tourminator"

Ullrich. Not 12 rounds at three minutes a round, but 58.5 kilometers at about 100 revs per minute. The champ vs. the ex-champ. The American star vs. the hometown boy. Ullrich was going for the knockout. Armstrong had a more conservative approach....

Ullrich lives in Merdingen, a village just outside Freiburg that the time trial course would nearly pass through in the opening 10km. Imagine if the Tour had come to Austin, and the course was lined with tens of thousands of Texans all screaming for one man. That's how it was in Freiburg, where the festive crowds were even bigger than on the previous day. And that's how it was all along the 38km section in Germany, on fast, flat roads passing fields of head-high corn, and racing though picturesque villages of half-timbered houses decked with German and Telekom-team flags.

Ullrich, starting three minutes ahead of Armstrong, raced through a tunnel of cheering fans. He wore his world championship rainbow jersey—and a helmet, which showed his seriousness: Ullrich had worn just a turned-back cycling cap to win his world time-trial title the previous October in Italy.

Here, at the Tour, the German started much faster than any rider before him did, and his speed energized his fans. As for Armstrong, dressed in a yellow skinsuit and helmet, he said that he was concerned that the crowds would be out of control: "It only takes one guy to do something devastating...."

But he later reported that the crowds inspired him, too, with their loud applause and shouts of support. "It felt it was also my home, the amount of cheering," the Texan said. "I've never seen so many people for a time trial."

With an overall lead of more than five minutes, Armstrong had no reason to go to the limit, and he agreed with directeur sportif Bruyneel to see how things were going at the first time split, before making a decision on whether to go for the stage win. So, instead of starting in his typical all-out manner, Armstrong reported that he kept looking at his heart-rate monitor, to make sure he was riding under his limit.

The first unofficial check came after 11km. "When I heard I was in the same time as Ullrich, I knew I would have a good ride," said Armstrong. Just how good, we were about to find out.

Once he had been give the green light, the race leader started to pull ahead of Ullrich: two seconds after 15km, five seconds after 20km, 15 seconds after 33km, and 25 seconds after 44km. The first official time split, at 20.5km, showed that his speed to that point was 55.322 kph—considerably faster than the all-time Tour time trial record of 54.545 kph set by Greg LeMond in his famous Versailles-Paris win in 1989, over a distance of 24.5km.

Armstrong is not a pure stylist like Ullrich; the Texan, like LeMond, time trials on his power and energy, and usually does better on courses with lots of turns, ups and downs. He said that he would never attempt the world hour record, because he couldn't imagine "sitting down for an hour." Armstrong was glad there were overpasses on the Freiburg-Mulhouse course, so he was able to stand on the pedals a few times.

Once in the final 15km, Ullrich, on learning that he was losing ground, started to fight back. After being 25 seconds down at 44km, the gap only slightly increased to 27 seconds at 48km and 29 seconds at 52km—and at the end of the long finish straight in Mulhouse, Armstrong hit the line with a winning margin back to 25 seconds.

His final time of 1:05:01 was one second outside a 54 kph average, and 40 seconds off the speed that would have equaled LeMond's record average (over a much shorter distance). Still, it was the fastest road time trial longer than 50km in cycling history.

Ullrich was gracious in defeat, his performance proving that he was indeed close to his best, but not at the level to win the Tour....

Beyond the battle of the two super-champions, there were some other great contests—especially the one for the third spot on the Paris podium.

While climbers Heras and Virenque soon ruled themselves out for that goal with much slower times, the Festina teammates Moreau and Beloki fought to the very last kilometer. Moreau needed to claim back 1:44 on Beloki, if he were to overtake him on G.C. After 20.5km, he had recouped 29 seconds of his deficit. By 44km, the gap was 1:14, and it looked as though the tall French rider was going to do it.

But Beloki was fighting all the way. In the next 8.5km, he cut the gap to 1:11—and after sprinting out of the saddle to the line, the young Spaniard held the final margin to 1:14. He had saved third place by 30 seconds.

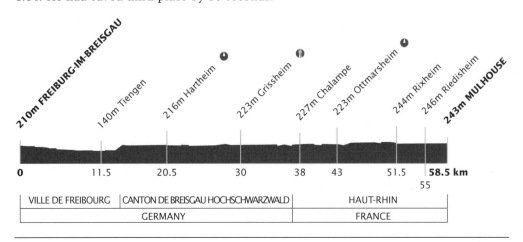

Tyler's diary
July 21
Mulhouse

Lance ended the day saying that something would have been missing if he hadn't won a stage in this year's Tour de France. And while that may not have been the sentiment of his many supporters, it was nice to see the guy hammer one home today. It was his seventh career stage win today. Not bad.

Everyone thinks that the individual time trial, by virtue of its name, is a day off for the domestiques. Not so. I was very much "on the job" today, and had a full list of marching orders this afternoon. For starters, Johan told me to race the first 3km as if they were the last three. After that, I was asked to race the time trial as if it were a 30-40km race, not a 60km race.

The hope was that my early split times, taken every three kilometers, would be a good gauge for Lance. After going full-tilt during the first half of the race, I was expected to fade on my way home. Luckily, I was able to hold on and keep up a decent pace. Hopefully, Lance found the opening splits of use as well.

All in all, it was a much better day than I expected. You never know where your form is going to be after so many long days defending the yellow jersey. But an odd phenomenon occurs for a lot of us during the Tour: We actually ride into better form than we had at the start. Perhaps that was my situation today—or maybe it was just the adrenaline flowing. We'll never know, as this thing called bike racing is far from being an exact science.

Incidentally, Lance raced the second fastest time trial in Tour de France history today. Not too shabby. And I recorded the sixth fastest time ever, so that gives you an idea of how fast the pace was. The top two guys were in a league of their own, for sure. Impressive. Although it's kind of nice to see that Greg LeMond still holds on to the top spot: His epic '89 time trial remains the fastest ever.

Lance is not the only rider at this year's Tour who's living out a dream come true. I was able to catch up with Eric Dekker yesterday and he told me that this is his seventh Tour—and that his three stage wins this year are his first ever. I guess that means there's hope for all of us, if we have the guts to stick it out. Eric is a really nice guy, and he seems to be completely overwhelmed by his success this year. Good for him. It's his kind of story that keeps us all going.

Moreau's fine performance gave him third place on the stage, 2:12 slower than Armstrong; while the race leader's rabbit, Hamilton, took fourth, another 49 seconds back. It was a remarkable performance by the New Englander when his epic defensive rides in the Alps are taken into account, as well as the circumstances of his time trial.

"I like to start slowly," Hamilton said, "but I was riding to establish splits for Lance. I sprinted the first two, three kilometers...." He was given 40km as his flat-out limit, yet he still matched Moreau's speed over the final 15km, and was only 39 seconds slower than his team leader on this final stretch.

Maybe Hamilton is the "heavyweight" of tomorrow. But today, "Big Tex" was king.

Armstrong's Speed

Little things play a big part in the life of Lance Armstrong. On Thursday, he was astonished that an Italian journalist had asked whether the 5:37 margin he held over second-placed Jan Ullrich would be enough for the American to retain the yellow jersey in Friday's time trial. Armstrong's reaction was: "Are you serious?"

Well, when Armstrong walked in the press conference after winning the stage 19 time trial, the first words from his lips were: "Where's the guy who was sitting there yesterday?" He pointed at the empty seat in the front row, and said, "I thought about him a lot today." Whether that made the Tour leader ride faster, he didn't say, but Armstrong did race faster than anyone before over a distance longer than 50km, and defeated Ullrich by 25 seconds.

Over the flat 58.5km course, Armstrong averaged almost exactly 54 kph (actually 53.986 kph), which is 1.637 kph faster than the fastest ever achieved by Miguel Induráin, who completed the 64km Tours-Blois stage of the 1992 Tour de France at 52.349 kph.

The fastest regular time trial in Tour history remains the 54.545 kph average achieved in 1989 by Greg LeMond over a much shorter 24.5km, between Versailles and Paris. That course was downhill for the first half, included a couple of short downs and ups on underpass ramps alongside the Seine River, and then made the 1km climb and downhill on the smooth cobblestones of the Champs-Elysées. The wind was favorable, except for the uphill part of the Champs-Elysées. LeMond used aero' bars for that time trial—which was the first year they had appeared at the Tour.

To compare that 1989 course with stage 19's between Freiburg and Mulhouse is difficult. This course had only a few slight ups and downs, one of which was an overpass. The wind was generally favorable, and the temperature was as warm as that in 1989 in Paris. Perhaps an indication of how fast Armstrong went, you need only look at his time to the 20.5km time split: The Texan did that opening stretch in 22:14, at an average of 55.322 kph (34.375 mph). And that section included a fair number of turns leaving the city of Freiburg and one of the course's longer uphills. At times, Armstrong was turning the pedals at 120 rpm, although his average cadence was between 104 and 105 rpm.

Armstrong now had only two stages to get through before winning his second consecutive Tour. The 254.5km stage 20 from Belfort to Troyes would include three Cat. 4 climbs in the middle part of the route, along with dozens of uncategorized hills. The weather for this longest stage was forecast to be sunny and warm, up to 80 degrees Fahrenheit at the finish, with a favorable breeze. Ideal conditions for another long breakaway.

STAGE 20
Belfort–Troyes • July 22

Nearly ... Not Quite ... Victory!

ASK ANY RIDER WHAT WAS THE HIGHLIGHT OF THIS, THE LONGEST STAGE OF THE 2000 TOUR DE FRANCE, and you would get very different answers.

If you asked a college graduate such as Tyler Hamilton, he might say it was the all-white round-towered church designed by Le Corbusier that he saw sitting high on a hillside at Ronchamp, soon after leaving the Belfort start.

A country boy like Frenchman Jacky Durand might point out the sweeping fields of wheat being harvested on the wide-open plains of the Haute-Marne region.

A political buff such as the erudite Colombian Santiago Botero, who has a namesake sculptor living in Paris, would probably mention the enormous Cross of Lorraine memorial to General De Gaulle, peeking over a stand of trees at Colombey-les-Deux-Eglises, home of the late French president.

And a wine connoisseur like Italian Massimiliano Mori would draw your attention to the terraced vineyards near the finish in Troyes that produce a pleasantly dry champagne.

But you would have heard no mention of the stage's sights from the mouths of Michael Boogerd, François Simon, Jeroen Blijlevens or Erik Zabel. Those four men only had eyes for the race—for very different reasons.

Boogerd had started this Tour as one of the outsiders, hoping to at least repeat his fifth-place finish of 1998, when he proudly wore the Dutch national champion's jersey. Instead, he had struggled in the second tier for the entire three weeks, and now was lying in an anonymous 19th place, 42 minutes behind Armstrong.

At least he felt he was going to finish the Tour, with the prospect of good form for August's World Cup races, and the later world's. He had been strong enough to attack in the Lausanne finale, but after the marathon stage to Freiburg, he got sick and had a poor time trial, vomiting during his ride. But at least he was going to finish the Tour....

Then, 63km into the 254.5km stage 20, a VIP car trying to drive past the peloton caused a crash. Boogerd came down and remained lying in the road, his bike shattered, his neck lacerated. He was taken to the hospital for stitches. He wasn't going to make it into Paris.

While Boogerd was crashing, the 1999 French champion Simon was preparing to attack. This was going to be his big day: the stage ending in his hometown.

Simon is the last of four brothers from Troyes who have all been pro cyclists. The best known was Pascal Simon, who was wearing the yellow jersey in the 1983 Tour when a fall caused a hairline shoulder fracture: He continued racing in the yellow jersey until the pain became too much.

Younger brother François doesn't have quite the same qualities, but he's known as a feisty racer with a good turn of finishing speed. And on this day, he felt inspired. Maybe he could get a stage win for his upstart Bonjour team.

Well, Simon did get into the day's big break, along with fellow French worker Sebastien Hinault of Crédit Agricole and the Pole Grzegorz Gwiazdowski of La Française des Jeux. But the Postal team's tempo kept the trio to a maximum lead of 3:43, and as they reached the outskirts of Troyes, where Simon started seeing road signs pointing to

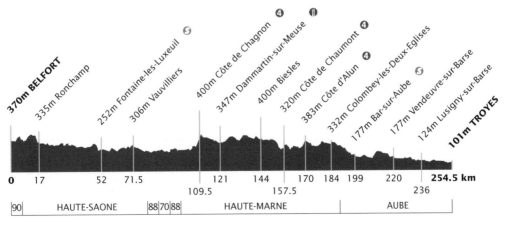

Fred's diary
July 22
Troyes

Paris is almost here. At the start, when I thought about Paris, it felt so far away … and now it's here. It has been a hard Tour de France, but at the same time, I have enjoyed every day. I think I have had my lows and highs, like everyone has, but I will remember them both as something positive.

I guess I missed my last entry, which may make you wonder what is going on with me. Let me tell you, it is crazy during the Tour. I sometimes wonder how we actually have time to race. I have been busy keeping my sponsors and fans happy, and I have been amazed by how many fans I have picked up here. When I climb up these crazy hors-cat climbs, I hear my name time after time, especially when I'm riding next to riders like Zülle or Jalabert.

Yesterday's time trial, for me, was just a tempo ride that turned into a good ride, with 23rd place for the day—and that really surprised me. It never crossed my mind that I would even try in the time trial, but as I kept riding and seeing all the fans, it just motivated me to go on.

In today's stage into Troyes, everyone expected a break to go early on, but at the same time, no one seemed willing to start the action. We rode easy for a good while, until finally a break went up the road. But this one seemed to be a bit too big and missing some key teams to let it stick. It was chased down quickly, and we then settled in for another slow ride that ended when Simon from Bonjour attacked around 140km. That started the fire that didn't stop till the finish.

It came down to the sprint finish that all of us sprinters have been waiting for. This time, both Max and I had good legs, so we decided that he would get a leadout from Zanini, and leave me free to float. But things didn't turn out too well at the finish, as we didn't get in a good formation for the final corner.

After trying to come around Max and Zanini, I found myself just barely squeezing in between them, and that caused us to put Max in a bad spot—and myself at the same time. Zanini was on the right against the barriers, and I had nowhere to go. All I could do was coast across the finish line, while Max was forced to go out on the left into the wind, wasting a valuable sprint to move forward. Not a good day for the Mapei boys, so let's see if we can make up for it tomorrow.

Tomorrow, we start at the Eiffel Tower. The last time I was there was as a tourist with my girlfriend, Annie. I think it will have a different meaning to me after tomorrow, though.

# # #

Tyler's diary
July 22
Troyes

Nothing like having the longest stage of the Tour the day before the finish. Who thinks of this stuff? But we managed to plod our way through it. In fact, it really wasn't that bad. Per usual, there was an early break—and we did our part to set tempo and keep their lead to a minimum. When the gap reached four minutes, the sprinters' teams took over the helm, and we were able to drop into the slipstream. We took advantage of the free ride for the last 50km of the day.

There was one disappointment today: Michael Boogerd crashed out of the race. A Tour de France VIP car–which plays host to sponsors and important guests–tried to make its way through the peloton. The maneuver caused some guys to hit the brakes, and the classic lock-up domino effect ensued. Michael was a casualty at the back. He must have touched wheels with someone in front of him. It's sad to see a guy get robbed of his opportunity to make it to Paris at this stage of the game. But luckily his injuries are fairly minor.

After the finish, I finally made my appearance on France 3's "Velo Club." I was supposed to be on three days ago, but logistical confusion had kept me away from everyone's favorite French wrap-up show. They originally wanted to interview me about my new climbing bike. On the day they requested my participation, I showed up for the interview–but my bike did not. Yesterday, my bike was on hand for the show, but I wasn't. Today, we finally appeared in tandem. But after all that arranging, they didn't even ask me one question about the bike. Pretty funny.

With the end in sight, dinner was a little more relaxed tonight. Make that ridiculously more relaxed. Eating is such a big deal at this race– what you eat, how much you eat, when you eat–it's nuts. But tonight, no one cared. I drank four beers with my dinner and had ice cream for dessert. Totally unheard of behavior at *le Tour*. In fact, the ice cream was such a hit, the kitchen sent out the barrels from the freezer. It was practically a free-for-all.

Tomorrow morning, we travel to Paris aboard the Orient Express. Last year we cruised in on the TGV and they let us take turns driving the train. I'm wondering if they'll be as generous tomorrow.

his village, the gap was down to 15 seconds. Five kilometers still remained, but Simon knew that he had to attack if, in his ninth pro season, he was finally going to win a stage of the Tour.

Racing as hard as he could on roads that he rides most every day in the off-season, Simon did battle. He was still ahead with 4km to go; still clear with 3km remaining; still leading at the 2km marker…. Was it possible that the Telekom, Farm Frites and Polti teams (for sprinters Zabel, McEwen and Blijlevens) were going to screw up?

Simon would have made a great stage winner. But miracles don't happen. He was swept up by the speeding peloton 1800 meters from his goal.

Now it was the sprinters' turn. The first real chance they had had to contest a mass finish since Wüst won at Vitré more than two weeks earlier. In the interim, Blijlevens—a non-factor in the opening stages—had ridden himself into form, and was looking for his first Tour stage win since he triumphed at Cholet in 1998.

Blijlevens's Polti team had worked hard to bring back the break, and now they were trying to get him into a good position in the final straightaway that was a little too narrow, and a little too twisty to favor a fair, straightforward sprint. Blijlevens likes it this way, and has often come through in tight situations to win at the Tour.

This time he had to work a little too much for himself in the lead-up, and he was boxed in with 100 meters left. But somehow he extricated himself, and saw an opening along the right-side barriers with 50 meters to go. He came hurtling though, passing three or four others, and threw his bike at the line … only to look left and see that he was beaten by two who got there first. He thumped his handlebars in frustration. So close, yet so far. Now he'd have to wait for tomorrow's finale in Paris.

While Blijlevens was venting, the man who had won was roaring with joy. It was the rider in the green jersey, the Tour's top sprinter for four consecutive years, who hadn't won a stage for three years. Zabel did it this time—by a wheel over second-place McEwen—thanks to his Telekom teammates leading him out in perfect fashion. He almost blew it, though, by throwing up his hands in celebration, just as Blijlevens was throwing his bike at the line.

It was a great ending to another marathon stage, which had been easier than expected for some, and tough for others. The 128 riders would retain many different memories for many different reasons on their final night's sleep before Paris. The Eiffel Tower was just over the horizon….

Party Time

A more relaxed, but more physically tired Lance Armstrong was about to ride onto the Champs-Elysées wearing the Tour de France yellow jersey. But he wasn't quite ready to claim victory. "I have to stay out of trouble, and I won't be convinced (I've won) until I cross the line," he said.

But once across the line in Paris, Armstrong would be ready to celebrate. And he wouldn't need to buy any champagne for his many guests…. That's because in Troyes Sunday morning, before he and the rest of the 128 riders still in the Tour board the Orient Express train, bound for Paris, Armstrong was due to be presented by the mayor of Troyes with his weight in champagne. That would about 100 bottles of bubbly if the Texan tipped the scales at 72 kilograms (154 pounds).

Besides his immediate family, including his wife Kristin, baby son Luke and mother Linda, Armstrong intimated that a big show business star would join them to celebrate on Sunday. "I don't want to say who it is, as I want to respect their privacy," he said.

Armstrong added that he was "more looking forward" to the end-of-the-Tour festivities than last year. The U.S. Postal Service leader said that in 1999 he was emotionally drained after winning the Tour. "I needed the entire off-season to recover mentally," he said. "This year, I need a break physically, but I'm motivated for the Olympics. That's a big goal."

As for the Champs-Elysées, following the traditional presentations and lap of honor, Armstrong and his team would celebrate at a party similar to the one they had last year at the Orsay museum on the Left Bank of the Seine River.

Asked whether he would now be shooting for a record five Tours de France, Armstrong wouldn't be drawn, but he did say: "I'll be here next year, I can promise you that."

STAGE 21
Paris–Paris (Champs-Elysées) • July 23

Finales

In the shadow of Victorian France's most magnificent structure, the iron-latticed edifice called the Eiffel Tower, two Californians had two good stories to tell. They were chatting before the start of this final stage, which for the first time in Tour history was both starting and finishing in the City of Light. In fact, the finish line on the Champs-Elysées was only a short stroll away, just the other side of the Seine River.

Jeff Pierce has happy memories of that finish line. Now a marketing man for GT, Pierce was a journeyman rider for 7-Eleven back in 1987, the pioneering American team's second year at the Tour. He had no real appreciation of the final stage's tradition as a battleground for the sprinters, and felt like he was just in a regular bike race when he made it into a breakaway in the final kilometers.

"I was just racing," Pierce recalled. "I wasn't thinking about it being on the Champs-Elysées. I was in a small group off the front. We were about to be caught. and everyone started spreading across the road. I was at the back and just put my head down and attacked as hard as I could. When I looked back I had maybe six seconds, and I just kept going."

He kept going—and won the stage!

Pierce remains the only American to win on the Champs-Elysées, other than LeMond in that unforgettable Versailles-Paris time trial of 1989.

Now, there was another Californian who looked capable of winning on the Champs. A sprinter: "Fast Freddy" Rodriguez.

Fred's diary
July 23
Paris

Well, this morning there was an early wake-up call, as we were to catch the Oriental Express train from Troyes to Paris. Let me tell you, it was a long, but very enjoyable ride. We were wined and dined all the way to Paris. The atmosphere was like being in a Western movie, expecting some cowboys to ride by trying to highjack the train.

Once we made it to Paris, I was greeted by all the fans and press awaiting my reactions to making it through my first Tour. I told them it wasn't over, as today was one of the more important days for the team. This was the queen of the sprint stages, so it was very important for us.

I finally was able to meet my girlfriend, Annie, who flew out from California just to see me ride through Paris. It was a sweet feeling to have her with me as I entered the final stage.

Back to the race…. Well, not much happened in the first 60km. It seemed that everyone was very happy just to be there. The rumor was that this was one of the hardest Tours in a while. Great timing that I picked it as my first Tour, right?

Well, eventually, Postal decided to take control around the halfway point, knowing that it was going to get crazy. That gave everyone the green light on the attack-fest. Knowing that we didn't have the numbers, we were willing to gamble on a sprint finish, as the other teams—like Telekom, Farm-Frites and Polti—controlled the race.

The problem with a stage like today is that it's short, fast, the last one, and everyone thinks they can win. It makes it that much harder to stay up front and be comfortable.

Today, we decided to race for Zanini, as he has sacrificed himself so many times for the team. This was the perfect place to thank him for all his work.

Well, it was a crazy finale and the plan was to keep him protected, with Max and myself leading him out for the finish. It worked out perfectly: Max took control around 400 meters from the line, while I followed with Zanini on my wheel.

Max went so fast around the last right corner that I could not hold his wheel. I had to chase hard to make it back on. But I guess everyone behind was feeling the same way, as Zanini was fighting to stay on my wheel.

In last 200 meters, I jumped to the right of Max as Zabel followed, while allowing Zanini to surprise him from the left. I guess you could say he fell for the bait.

I am so happy for Zanini right now: He deserved that win and he proved it, as he came flying by us.

Guys, thanks for following me through my first Tour. I enjoyed recounting it to you, as it allowed me to reflect on and relive each day. Alas, the time has come for me to say good-bye and venture into the Parisian nightlife. Unfortunately, what happens tonight can never be written about.

The U.S. champion, distinctive in his stars-and-stripes jersey, had enjoyed an excellent debut Tour. He'd been a huge factor in getting Mapei teammate Steels his two stage wins at Loudun and Nantes. He had ridden strongly to get in the big break on the stage to Villeneuve-sur-Lot. He had come close with third place at Lausanne. And just the previous day, in Troyes, he finished 15th—despite having been trapped on the barriers after he and his Mapei teammates Max Van Heeswijk and Stefano Zanini messed up their finish. "I didn't even sprint," he said.

Now, under the Eiffel Tower, he was talking about the Champs-Elysées. "We're working for Zanini today," Rodriguez confided. "After all the work he has done for us, he deserves it. So Max and I are going to lead him out. That's our plan."

It wasn't such a crazy plan as it sounded, for two sprinters to lead out a lead-out man. After all, in the final stage of the 1998 Tour, Zanini led out Steels for the win ... and Zanini still came in second.

Three-and-a-half hours after Rodriguez revealed the Mapei plan, it was put to the test. As on the day before, Telekom, Farm Frites and Polti closed down the breaks and were leading the pack as they rounded the turn into the Rue de Rivoli for the last time, 1500 meters from the finish. Mapei had only five men left in the race, and climbers Beltran and Nardello were no use as workers for their three teammates when the field was moving at 65 to 70 kph in a long snaking line. So the three Mapei musketeers had to work for themselves, and key off the efforts of the more-complete sprinters' teams.

Somehow, they managed to get to the front just as they reached the last turn, 400 meters from the line: Van Heeswijk led the line into the Champs, followed by Rodriguez and Zanini, who were followed by a Zabel on fire after his stage 20 breakthrough.

Clearly, Zabel thought Zanini was riding shotgun for Rodriguez, and believed that the

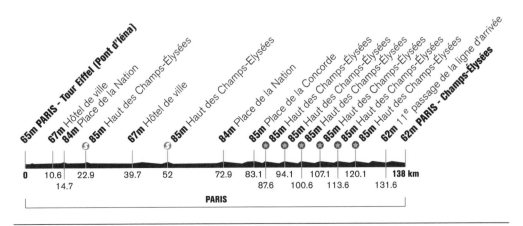

American was about to launch his sprint. So when Zanini peeled off to the left, Zabel quickly latched on to the American's wheel, ready to challenge him in the last 100 meters. You could almost feel the German's horror when Rodriguez eased up, and the solid Zanini sprinted away to the win. Another second place for the green jersey.

Zanini waited until he had crossed the line before believing he had done it. Then his long-jawed face erupted in ecstasy, and his arms shot up in shocking belief, engendering the same reaction in his two teammates. First, fourth and fifth was quite an ending for the three Mapeis.

They weren't the only ones raising their arms, of course. Seventy-six places back, that famous guy from Texas was also celebrating.

Bits and Pieces

Jeroen Blijlevens of Polti, who thumped his bars in anger after finding an opening too late, and just failing to catch stage winner Zabel at Troyes was even angrier in Paris. In the lead-up to the sprint, he got tangled with American Bobby Julich. After they crossed the line in 47th and 53rd places respectively, Blijlevens and Julich got into a fistfight, with the Dutchman drawing blood from the unfortunate American. The result? Blijlevens was thrown out of the race, and did not appear on the official finish list.

That cut the final number to 127 finishers, 14 fewer than last year. Also less than last year was the average speed, although the 39.569 kph average was still the third fastest in Tour history.

Among the less-publicized competitions, Kelme-Costa Blanca won the team race; Francisco Mancebo of Banesto won the best young rider award (25 and under); and Erik Dekker of Rabobank won the super-combativity award (by a single point over best climber winner Santiago Botero of Kelme). In the final prize countdown, as last year, the U.S. Postal Service came out tops, with 2.54 million francs (about $370,000).

Tyler's diary
July 24
Nice

Wow, what a race! I can't believe it's finally over. I'm relieved, to say the least. Finishing a grand tour is a funny thing: It's almost like you never fully realize the magnitude of what you are doing until it's done—which is probably a good thing. As for the pressure of riding for the yellow jersey, it's hard to find the words that best describe the honor, the expectations, the difficulties, the challenges, the excitement…. I could go on forever, yet never capture the experience fully.

As we did last year, we celebrated on Sunday night with a party at the Musée d'Orsay in Paris. There were roughly 250 people in attendance, including riders, family, sponsors and special guests. The surprise of the evening came in the form of actors Robin Williams and Michael J. Fox. Evidently, both gentlemen are fans of cycling and attended the finale on the Champs-Elysées.

Lance put Robin Williams on the spot by making him give an impromptu speech. He seemed unfazed, though, and managed to generate the biggest laughs of the night. But the most poignant moment of the evening came when he stated that seeing the final stage on this year's Tour de France had touched his soul and kicked him in the heart. A very generous statement from an incredible man. We were all floored.

Not to get all name-droppy, but I want to mention that the thrill of my night was when I lucked into meeting Michael J. Fox. He is as funny and humble and genuine as you might imagine. Meeting him and his wife was a huge and unex-pected thrill for me. It was a special evening for all of us.

This morning started early, as my wife and her parents and I were taking a 10 a.m. plane to Nice. You'd think someone who just finished the Tour de France would get more than three hours of sleep, but with the adrenaline flowing and the excitement surrounding the team, it was hard to call it a night. Upon arriving in Nice, we had the brilliant idea of hitting the beach. It took the four of us about three seconds to pass out and fall asleep.

Since the big show has come to a close, I thought it would be fun to recap my highs and lows.

Tour highs:

⁜ Crossing the finish line in Paris right next to Lance—who, by the way, sported a "Texas-sized" grin.

⁜ The Hautacaum mountain stage. Although it was not my best day personally, seeing Lance dominate the way he did was a huge motivator.

⁜ Returning to Mont Ventoux—because it's an epic climb and will always hold a special place in my heart.

⁜ The Courchevel-Morzine stage. While it may sound odd—considering how tough the day
(to page 208)

wound up being for Lance—it was my strongest day of the race. I was able to ride for Lance longer and harder than either one of us thought I could.

✣ The German fans. It almost goes without saying: They've set a new standard in the world of cycling.

✣ The final time trial, because riding the splits for Lance was a huge deal, and feeling good while doing it was an unexpected bonus.

✣ Being the only team to finish with all nine riders—doubters be damned!

Tour lows:

✣ The bridge in the team time trial: four kilometers of pure hell. I'd be happy to never ride that stretch of road again.

✣ Crashing in Dax was a total bummer, considering it was the day before the first critical stage (Hautacaum).

Since I can't think of any other low points, it must have been a good month. It's an honor to ride for a guy like Lance, who seems to be making sports history with every move. We've all been lucky to be a part of it. Thanks for joining in.

And, thanks again for reading. This was fun.

TOUR DE FRANCE, July 18-23.

STAGE 16
Courchevel–Morzine. July 18.
1. Virenque, 196.6km in 5:32:20 (35.476 kph); 2. Ullrich, at 0:24; 3. Heras, at 0:27; 4. Escartin, at 1:09; 5. Beloki, at 1:11; 6. Hervé, at 1:11; 7. Trentin, at 2:01; **8. Armstrong, at 2:01**; 9. Moreau, at 2:01; 10. Botero, at 2:01.

OTHERS: 30. Hamilton, at 12:25; 36. Livingston, at 12:58; 38. Pantani, at 13:44; 43. Olano, at 17:18; **46. Hincapie, at 23:50; 71. Rodriguez, at 30:55; 75. Julich, at 30:55;** 117. Zülle, at 30:55.
DNF: Plaza; Nicolas Jalabert.

OVERALL: 1. Armstrong,2810km in 72:12:30; 2. Ullrich, at 5:37; 3. Beloki, at 6:38; 4. Heras, at 6:43; 5. Virenque, at 7:36; 6. Moreau, at 08:22; 7. Botero, at 10:19; 8. Escartin, at 11:35; 9. Mancebo, at 13:07; 10. Beltran, at 13:08.

STAGE 17
Évian-les-Bains–Lausanne. July 19.
1. Dekker, 155km in 3:24:53; 2. Zabel; **3. Rodriguez**; 4. Simon; 5. McEwen; 6. Aerts; 7. Mori; 8. Vainsteins; 9. Nico Mattan (B) Cofidis.; 10. Moreau, all s.t.

OTHERS: 29. Ullrich; 35. Armstrong; 64. Hamilton; 66. Julich, all s.t.

OVERALL: 1. Armstrong, 2965km in 75:37:23; 2. Ullrich, at 5:37; 3. Beloki, at 6:38; 4. Heras, at 6:43; 5. Virenque, at 7:36; 6. Moreau, at 8:22; 7. Botero, at 10:19; 8. Escartin, at 11:35; 9. Mancebo, at 13:07; 10. Beltran, at 13:08.

STAGE 18
Lausanne–Freibourg-in-Berisgau. July 20.
1. Commesso, 246.5km in 6:08:15 (40.162 kph); 2. Vinokourov, s.t.; 3. Durand, at 1:05; 4. Voigt, at 1:16; 5. Jean-Cyril Robin (F), Bonjour, s.t.; 6. Larsen, at 15:35; 7. Knaven; 8. Thierry Marichal (B), Lotto; 9. Perraudeau, all s.t.; 10. Hamburger, at 15:37.

OTHERS:19. Rodriguez; 34. Armstrong; 42. Ullrich; 51. Hamilton; 59. Hincapie; 68. Olano; 71. Escartin; 86. Livingston; 92. Julich; 98. Jalabert, all s.t.

OVERALL: 1. Armstrong,in 3211.5km in 82:01:48; 2. Ullrich, at 5:37; 3. Beloki, at 6:38; 4. Heras, at 6:43; 5. Virenque, at 7:36; 6. Moreau, at 8:22; 7. Botero, at 10:19; 8. Escartin, at 11:35; 9. Mancebo, at 13:07; 10. Beltran, at 13:08.

STAGE 19
Freiburg-im-Breisgau–Mulhouse Time Trial. July 21.
1. Armstrong, 58.5km in 1:05:01 (53.986 kph); 2. Ullrich, 1:05.26; 3. Moreau, 1:07:13; **4. Hamilton, 1:08:02;** 5. Beloki,

1:08:27:26; 6. Jalabert, 1:08:48; 7. Millar, 1:08:57; 8. Nardello, 1:08:58; 9. Botero, 1:09:00; 10. Trentin, 1:09:17.

OTHERS: 23. Rodriguez, 1:10:43; 32. Julich, 1:11:36; 61. Livingston, 1:13:22; 81. Hincapie, 1:14:06; 104. Andreu, 1:15:11; 125. Boogerd, 1:16:52; 126. Commesso, 1:16:54.

OVERALL: 1. Armstrong, 3270km in 83:06:19; 2. Ullrich, at 6:02; 3. Beloki, at 10:04; 4. Moreau, at 10:34; 5. Heras, at 11:50; 6. Virenque, at 13:26; 7. Botero, at 14:18; 8. Escartin, at 17:21; 9. Mancebo, at 18:09; 10. Nardello, at 18:25.

STAGE 20
Belfort–Troyes. July 22.
1. Zabel, 254.5km in 6:14:13 (40.805 kph); 2. McEwen; 3. Blijlevens; 4. Vainsteins; 5. Van Heeswijk; 6. Mori; 7. Piziks; 8. Magnien; **9. Hincapie**; 10. Mengin, all s.t.

OTHERS: 27. Armstrong; 31. Livingston; 33. Ekimov; 42. Vasseur; **75. Julich; 89. Hamilton, all s.t.; 111. Andreu, at** 2:43; 119. Joachim, at 3:35; 120. Kjaergaard, at 3:35; 121. Commesso, at 4:46.

ABANDONED: Boogerd.

OVERALL: 1. Armstrong, 3524.5 km in 89:20:32; 2. Ullrich, at 6:02; 3. Beloki, at 10:04; 4. Moreau, at 10:34; 5. Heras, at 11:50; 6. Virenque, at 13:26; 7. Botero, at 14:18; 8. Escartin, at 17:21; 9. Mancebo, at 18:09; 10. Nardello, at 18:25.

STAGE 21
Paris Circuit. July 23.
1. Zanini, 138km in 3:12:36 (42.990kph); 2. Zabel; 3. Vainsteins; **4. Rodriguez;** 5. Van Heeswijk; 6. Magnien; 7. Simon; 8. McEwen; 9. Commesso; 10. Piziks, all s.t.

OTHERS: 26. Hincapie; 44. Andreu; 53. Julich; 76. Armstrong; 77. Hamilton; 89. Livingston, all s.t.

87th TOUR DE FRANCE, July 1-23.
Final Overall
1. Lance Armstrong (USA), U.S. Postal Service, 3662.5km in 92:33:08 (39.569 kph); 2. Jan Ullrich (G), Deutsche Telekom, at 06:02; 3. Joseba Beloki (Sp), Festina, at 10:04; 4. Christophe Moreau (F), Festina, at 10:34; 5. Roberto Heras (Sp), Kelme, at 11:50; 6. Richard Virenque (F), Polti, at 13:26; 7. Santiago Botero (Col), Kelme, at 14:18; 8. Fernando Escartin (Sp), Kelme, at 17:21; 9. Francisco Mancebo (Sp), Banesto, at 18:09; 10. Daniele Nardello (I), Mapei-Quick Step, at 18:25; 11. Manuel Beltran (Sp), Mapei-Quick Step, at 21:11; 12. Pascal Herve (F), Polti, at 23:13; 13. Javier Otxoa (Sp), Kelme, at 25:00; 14. Felix Garcia Casas (Sp), Festina, at 32:04; 15. Alex Vinokourov (Kaz), Deutsche Telekom, at 32:26; 16. Roberto Conti (I), Vini Caldirola, at 34:18; 17. Kurt Van de Wouwer (B), Lotto, at 34:29; 18. Guido Trentin (I),

Vini Caldirola, at 35:57; 19. Jean-Cyril Robin (F), Bonjour, at 43:12; 20. Geert Verheyen (B), Lotto, at 46:24; 21. Peter Luttenberger (A), ONCE-Deutsche Bank, at 48:27; 22. Nico Mattan (B), Cofidis, at 50:09; 23. José Maria Jimenez (Sp), Banesto, at 51:45; 24. Grischa Niermann (G), Rabobank, at 52:06; **25. Tyler Hamilton (USA), U.S. Postal Service, at 56:30;** 26. Giuseppe Guerini (I), Deutsche Telekom, at 59:33; 27. Massimiliano Lelli (I), Cofidis, at 1:06:05; 28. Mario Aerts (B), Lotto, at 1:06:44; 29. Daniel Atienza (Sp), Saeco-Valli & Valli, at 1:09:19; 30. Dariusz Baranowski (Pl), Banesto, at 1:09:27; 31. Javier Pascual Llorente (Sp), Kelme, at 1:16:33; 32. Andrei Kivilev (Kaz), AG2R, at 1:17:28; 33. David Cañada (Sp), ONCE-Deutsche Bank at 1:17:44; 34. Abraham Olano (Sp), ONCE-Deutsche Bank, at 1:19:44; 35. Laurent Madouas (F), Festina, at 1:20:40; 36. Bo Hamburger (Dk), Memory Card-Jack & Jones, at 1:21:33; **37. Kevin Livingston (USA), U.S. Postal Service, at 1:23:13;** 38. Enrico Zaina (I), Mercatone Uno, at 1:23:33; 39. Marco Velo (I), Mercatone Uno, at 1:24:21; 40. Jens Heppner (G), Deutsche Telekom, at 1:29:51; 41. Paolo Savoldelli (I), Saeco-Valli & Valli, at 1:32:00; 42. Udo Bölts (G), Deutsche Telekom, at 1:32:33; 43. Marc Wauters (B), Rabobank, at 1:33:34; 44. Roland Meier (Swi), Cofidis, at 1:35:57; 45. Didier Rous (F), Bonjour, at 1:39:55; 46. Marcello Siboni (I), Mercatone Uno, at 1:42:00; 47. Jon Odriozola (Sp), Banesto, at 1:43:22; **48. Bobby Julich (USA), Crédit Agricole, at 1:44:15;** 49. Maarten Den Bakker (Nl), Rabobank, at 1:46:17; 50. José Angel Vidal (Sp), Kelme, at 1:50:59; 51. Erik Dekker (Nl), Rabobank, at 1:51:27; 52. Cedric Vasseur (F), U.S. Postal Service, at 1:55:25; 53. Vicente Garcia-Acosta (Sp), Banesto, at 1:56:31; 54. Laurent Jalabert, at 1:58:47; 55. Viatcheslav Ekimov (Rus), U.S. Postal Service, at 1:59:57; 56. Marc Lotz (Nl), Rabobank, at 2:02:04; 57. Jose Luis Arrieta (Sp), Banesto, at 2:04:21; 58. François Simon (F), Bonjour, at 2:10:08; 59. Ermanno Brignoli (I), Mercatone Uno, at 2:10:28; 60. Jens Voigt (G), Crédit Agricole, at 2:10:37; 61. Erik Zabel (G), Deutsche Telekom, at 2:11:07; 62. David Millar (GB), Cofidis, at 2:13:03; 63. Antonio Tauler (Sp), Kelme, at 2:16:05; 64. Fabio Sacchi (I), Polti, at 2:17:40; **65. George Hincapie (USA), U.S. Postal Service, at 2:20:31;** 66. Christophe Agnolutto (F), AG2R, at 2:23:07; 67. Massimiliano Mori (I), Saeco-Valli & Valli, at 2:24:05; 68. Markus Zberg (Swi), Rabobank, at 2:26:40; 69. Pascal Chanteur (F), AG2R, at 2:27:19; 70. Riccardo Forconi (I), Mercatone Uno, at 2:28:14; 71. Walter Beneteau (F), Bonjour, at 2:28:17; 72. Salvatore Commesso (I), Saeco-Valli & Valli, at 2:28:48; 73. Massimo Podenzana (I), Mercatone Uno, at 2:29:17; 74. Jacky Durand (F), Lotto, at 2:31:48; 75. David Moncoutié (F), Cofidis, at 2:32:26; 76. Xavier Jan (F), La Française des Jeux, at 2:33:55; 77. Koos Moerenhout (Nl), Farm Frites, at 2:34:31; 78. Michel Lafis (S), Farm Frites, at 2:35:52; 79. Paul Van Hyfte (B), Lotto, at 2:36:03; 80. Stefano Zanini (I), Mapei-Quick Step, at 2:36:07; 81. Gilles Maignan (F), AG2R, at 2:36:12; 82. Romans Vainsteins (Lat), Vini Caldirola, at 2:38:10; 83. David Delrieu (F), AG2R, at 2:38:10; 84. Alberto Elli (I), Deutsche Telekom, at 2:40:12; 85. Pavel Padrnos (Cz), Saeco-Valli & Valli, at 2:40:19; **86. Fred Rodriguez (USA), Mapei-Quick Step, at 2:40:19;** 87. Orlando Rodrigues (P), Banesto, at 2:40:31; 88. Sebastien Demarbaix (B), Lotto, at 2:41:19; 89. Steffen Kjaergaard (N), U.S. Postal Service, at 2:44:01; 90. Anthony Morin (F), Credit Agricole, at 2:44:02; 91. Glenn Magnusson (S), Farm Frites, at 2:45:46; 92. Benoit Joachim (Lux), U.S. Postal Service, at 2:45:56; 93. Arvis Piziks (Lat), Memory Card-Jack & Jones, at 2:46:06; 94. Mirco Crepaldi (I), Polti, at 2:48:30; 95. Christophe Mengin (F), La Française des Jeux, at 2:50:21; 96. Mauro Radaelli (I), Vini Caldirola, at 2:51:01; 97. Jaime Hernandez (Sp), Festina, at 2:51:14; 98. Emmanuel Magnien (F), La Française des Jeux, at 2:51:21; 99. Nicolay Bo Larsen (Dk), Memory Card-Jack & Jones, at 2:52:14; 100. Frank Hoj (Dk), La Française des Jeux, at 2:52:46; 101. Thierry Marichal (B), Lotto, at 2:52:52;

102. Massimo Apollonio (I), Vini Caldirola, at 2:54:00; 103. Max Van Heeswijk (Nl), Mapei-Quick Step, at 2:54:50; 104. Gian Matteo Fagnini (I), Deutsche Telekom, at 2:55:45; 105. Andreas Klier (G), Farm Frites, at 2:58:04; 106. Gregory Gwiazdowski (Pl), La Française des Jeux, at 2:58:05; 107. Benoit Salmon (F), AG2R, at 2:59:59; 108. Martin Rittsel (S), Memory Card-Jack & Jones, at 3:00:47; 109. Servais Knaven (Nl), Farm Frites, at 3:02:09; **110. Frankie Andreu (USA), U.S. Postal Service, at 3:02:15;** 111. Pascal Deramé (F), Bonjour, at 3:03:30; 112. Pascal Lino (F), Festina, at 3:03:38; 113. Robbie McEwen (Aus), Farm Frites, at 3:04:28; 114. Simone Borgheresi (I), Mercatone Uno, at 3:04:28; 115. Bart Voskamp (Nl), Polti, at 3:05:17; 116. Frédéric Guesdon (F), La Française des Jeux, at 3:07:16; 117. Tristan Hoffman (Nl), MemoryCard-Jack & Jones, at 3:07:17; 118. Geert Van Bondt (B), Farm Frites, at 3:07:39; 119. Allan Johansen (Dk), MemoryCard-Jack & Jones, at 3:08:22; 120. Anthony Langella (F), Crédit Agricole, at 3:13:40; 121. Serge Baguet (B), Lotto, at 3:17:15; 122. Franck Bouyer (F), Bonjour, at 3:18:37; 123. Magnus Bäckstedt (S), Crédit Agricole, at 3:20:27; 124. Francisco Leon (Sp), Kelme, at 3:22:52; 125. Sebastien Hinault (F), Crédit Agricole, at 3:41:02; 126. Damien Nazon (F), Bonjour, at 3:43:13; 127. Olivier Perraudeau (F), Bonjour, at 3:46:37.

Ejected: Jeroen Blijlevens (Nl), Polti, at 3:20:45.

Points: Zabel

King of the Mountains: Botero

Best young rider : Mancebo

Team: Kelme-Costa Blanca

Combativity: Dekker

PART THREE

REFLECTIONS

Center of Attention

There was a moment on the final day of the 87th Tour de France when Lance Armstrong was very much alone. It wasn't when he stood high on the winner's podium overlooking the Champs-Elysées, clutching a yellow baseball cap to his heart as the chords of the Star Spangled Banner resonated along the most regal avenue in the world. There, looking down, he could see his radiant wife Kristin and jolly nine-month-old son Luke David waiting to join him.

No. Armstrong's separate moment came some four hours earlier on July 23. He was straddling his bicycle, standing in the middle of the cobbled street on the Pont d'Iéna, the fast-flowing Seine River below, the magnificence of the Eiffel Tower rising at his back, and early-afternoon sunshine giving an extra glow to the golden *maillot jaune* he was wearing for the 11th consecutive stage.

Armstrong was alone right then. As a soft breeze caressed his lean, weather-reddened face, he could hear the buzz of excitement in the festive crowds lining the metal barriers; the busy, amped-up techno-music thumping from start-line loudspeakers; and the fusillade of clicking shutters emanating from a double tier of photographers stacked up in front of him.

The focus was all on this man, a 28-year-old Texan whose story is an inspiration for cancer patients all over the world. A father who is bestowing on his son the joy of life that he never received from a father he never knew. A cyclist who was about to be anointed as winner of the Tour de France for the second time in two years.

A Tour de France is won in many different places, at many different times. And, at that moment on a river bridge in Paris, alone with his thoughts, Armstrong could reflect on what had brought him to this triumph. The training. The technical preparations. The team. The family. The coaching. The cancer patients. The climbing tests. The doctors. The diet. The desire. The mental toughness. The tolerance for pain. The tactics. The motivation.

"Mentally, I think you have to love what you do ... what you desire to be," Armstrong said one day, discussing what makes a champion. "There are those who don't have that desire to be a champion.

"I think I was raised with this mentality, not born with it. You're not born with aggression or a killer instinct.... Something shapes you at a young age. Not that I can point to anything that says I would be aggressive....

"My mother taught me to be a fighter, to never quit."

Those qualities came in handy during the 21-stage, 3662.5km odyssey that was about to come to a close. Armstrong had tougher opposition than he did in 1999. The 1997 Tour winner, Jan Ullrich, took second place for a third time, his presence always menacing, if never threatening, once the American had built an impregnable lead. The 1998 winner, Marco Pantani, stretched Armstrong in the mountains with his exuberant, sometimes reckless aggression that finally ended his challenge. And a new generation of Hispanic riders—Joseba Beloki (third overall), Roberto Heras (fifth), Santiago Botero (seventh) and Francisco Mancebo (ninth)—attacked and attacked, forcing Armstrong's U.S. Postal Service team to go on the defensive much more often than they had in 1999.

Despite the seeming ease with which Armstrong built up his 6:02 margin of victory over Ullrich (compared with the 7:37 over Alex Zülle in 1999), there were critical moments when the race hung in the balance.

On the long, windswept crossing of the hump-backed St. Nazaire bridge in the stage 4 team time trial, the Postal squad almost fell apart. The rules require that five riders are needed to qualify for a finishing time, so when the nine-strong team became six as soon as the bridge climb began, the pressure was on. And when first Frankie Andreu and then Tyler Hamilton had trouble staying in contact because of the speed and the wind, Armstrong was in danger of losing serious time. But both of his American teammates came through, and the team finished in a strong second place, producing a 40-second gain for Armstrong over Telekom's Ulllrich.

Another dangerous moment came six days later, when Armstrong had no teammates left with him halfway up the cold, rainswept climb of the Col d'Aubisque, and he had to sit and watch as potential dangermen like Kelme-Costa Blanca's Fernando Escartin, Polti's Richard Virenque and Mapei-Quick Step's Manuel Beltran (along with young bloods Beloki, Botero, Heras and Mancebo) disappeared into the thick mist that swirled around the Pyrenean peak. Armstrong, of course, turned around that "little crisis" on the very next climb, the Montée de Hautacam, where he caught and passed all of those rivals, and added a hefty 3:21 to his lead over Ullrich.

Only once did the German star even remotely challenge the Texan. That was on the last six kilometers of stage 16's Col de Joux-Plane, where Armstrong bonked and lost 1:37 to Ullrich. The American later said, "Joux Plane was the hardest day of my life on a bike. Physically I was empty. I had no energy and no fuel. Mentally, I thought I was at risk of losing the Tour de France."

But that was the last climb of the final mountain stage of the 2000 Tour. By then, it was much too late for Ullrich to change the race's momentum. And as if to prove that the Joux-Plane setback was just a temporary one, three days later between Freiburg and Mulhouse Armstrong pounded his time-trial bike for 58.5km to his only stage win, at a speed that shattered Miguel Induráin's record for a time trial longer than 50km.

That stage win was the seventh of Armstrong's career, and one of the most spectacular. When asked if it were also the most memorable of the seven, the Texan was emphatic that it was not. "Limoges is my most memorable stage win, " he said, "and the most important victory of my career—nothing will ever compare with that."

His Tour stage win at Limoges in 1995 was the one when he honored the memory of his Motorola teammate Fabio Casartelli, who had died in a terrible crash three days earlier. Armstrong confirmed that he rode with the strength of two men that day—his and Casartelli's.

Casartelli's death (consecrated by the stage victory) was an epiphany for Armstrong, after which he better understood the frailty of life and the finality of death. It perhaps helped him to appreciate his own mortality when he was diagnosed with life-threatening testicular cancer just over a year after his stage win at Limoges.

Armstrong's battle with cancer has been dramatically chronicled in his autobiographical book, "It's Not About the Bike," which hit No. 1 in the New York Times non-fiction best-seller list a week after his repeat win at the Tour. His comeback from cancer remains one of the most heroic stories in sports. And that's what allowed him to achieve main-stream fame in 1999.

"Last year, (my comeback) was a big story because I survived the illness and won the Tour de France," Armstrong said in a press conference the day before the 2000 Tour finished, "but every year that I come back and try to do this another year is another year that I've survived the illness. I wish it [cancer] were more of a story or more of an item (this year), but I knew that, I predicted it would be sort of second or third tier."

For the Texan, though, it's a continuing fight. "I don't consider this year a comeback, like last year. I think this year is a confirmation, but I think that's important, in the fight against cancer, because it's a continuation and a confirmation of what I did last year as a cancer survivor making a comeback—especially the fact that everybody was here, everybody was on the start line.

"Physically, it was a harder Tour for me (than last year), and I sit here today as a more tired athlete.... I think everybody in the race is relieved that the race is almost over. Three weeks is a long time for any sporting event, and to finish, whether you finish in first place or 101st place, it's a special feeling to finish a three-week tour. It's a good feeling. I remember when I finished my first Tour de France, there was a real sense of accomplishment there. And I think it changes a rider for the rest of their career."

With two Tour wins behind him, and with the intention of continuing to focus his season on the race for as long as he has "the passion and love for the sport," Armstrong could be headed for the Tour's ultimate record: the five consecutive victories taken by Induráin. When asked if five Tour wins was a possibility, the Texan replied, "Probably not.... I don't think I have the desire to do that."

A few times during the 87th Tour de France, Armstrong was asked a similar question: How would you compare yourself with the race's legendary winners? He was embarrassed by the subject. At one point he even said, "No, I don't think there's any comparison. Take my career, it's been long, I've won many events ... but I don't think I can compare with riders like Eddy Merckx. It would be silly of us to compare. I don't care to compare myself with the greats—I have too much respect for them."

Another time, referring to the Tour's four five-time winners, the Texan said, "I think Merckx, Hinault, Induráin and Anquetil are a lot more talented than I am."

And yet Armstrong's results show that he is well on the way to joining the sport's legends— at least on paper. Only 11 men before him had won back-to-back Tours (see "Back-to-back Tour winners"), and only four of them also won the world road race championship: Greg LeMond, Bernard Hinault, Merckx and Louison Bobet. Admittedly, LeMond and Bobet both won three Tours, the others five, but Armstrong's achievements are not that different—even though there are cultural differences between Armstrong and the great riders of the past.

Bobet was a similar rider to Armstrong in that the Frenchman was first regarded as a stage winner and single-day racer. He made his Tour debut in 1947 at age 22; first won a stage of the Tour in 1948; became the French national champion in 1950; and won his first one-day classic (Milan–San Remo) in 1951. He wasn't regarded as a potential Tour winner until he changed his training methods and began focusing much more on developing his climbing and time-trial skills. In fact, Bobet didn't win the Tour until he was 28, in 1953—the seventh time he had started the race. He won his world title in 1954

In comparison (that word again!), Armstrong debuted in the Tour at age 21, taking his first stage win that same year, along with the U.S. national title and his world championship. So, he began faster than Bobet. The American took his first classic (the Clásica San Sebastian) two years later, and his second (the Flèche Wallonne) in 1996. Armstrong, of course, was diagnosed with cancer that same year, and after overcoming the illness he adopted a very different type of training. He became a better climber and an even stronger time trialist, and won his first Tour at age 27 on his fifth appearance. Now he has won two, and 2001 could see him join Bobet as a three-time Tour winner.

What about the other three greats, you may ask? Well, no one can compare with

BACK–TO–BACK TOUR WINNERS

Lance Armstrong (USA) 1999–2000

Miguel Indurain (Sp) 1991–95

Greg LeMond (USA) 1989–90

Laurent Fignon (F) 1983–84

Bernard Hinault (F) 1981–82, 1978–79

Eddy Merckx (B) 1969–72

Jacques Anquetil (F) 1961–64

Louison Bobet (F) 1953–55

Nicolas Frantz (Lux) 1927–28

Ottavio Bottecchia (I) 1924–25

Philippe Thys (B) 1913–14

Lucien Petit–Breton (F) 1907–08

Merckx: The Belgian super-champion literally won every important race (except Paris–Tours), most of them multiple times. You're right, Lance, it would be silly to even think of a comparison with Merckx.

Next up as a back-to-back Tour winner and world champion was Hinault. Again, like Bobet (and both Frenchman came from the Brittany region), Hinault's first breakthrough was in single-day racing: At age 22, he won two classics back-to-back: Ghent–Wevelgem and Liège–Bastogne–Liège. But Hinault was a smaller, lighter rider than either Bobet or Armstrong, which meant he was a natural climber, and he won the Tour on his debut in 1978 at age 23. His world title came two years later, while he would add the Giro d'Italia, the Vuelta a España, Paris–Roubaix and the Tour of Lombardy to his palmarès before he retired at age 32.

As for LeMond, he was a very different type of cyclist than Armstrong. The Californian came into the sport earlier in his life, immediately mapped out his career—penciling in the ages at which he aimed to win the junior world's, the Olympics, the pro world's and the Tour. His first world pro title came in his third pro season, his first Tour six years into his career. LeMond of course, like Armstrong, had his life interrupted by a near-fatal experience—one from shotgun wounds, the other from cancer. So LeMond didn't earn his back-to-back Tour win until his 10th year of pro racing. And LeMond never won a classic.

Certainly, the ways of cycling have changed, and Armstrong may be right that the sport will never again see all-dominating riders like Merckx and Hinault. Interestingly, one of the first questions posed to Armstrong at the 2000 Tour was: "After your Tour win last year, do you regard yourself as the patron, like an Hinault?" The Texan was a bit taken aback and answered, "I think that the days of a patron in the peloton is something from the past—that's finished. There is no Bernard Hinault in the peloton ... no longer a boss."

Armstrong did say, though, "I'll be back here next year, I can promise you that." And if he were to continue displaying the same absolute confidence, the same dominant attitude, then he would be regarded as the boss—not only by his team, but by his opponents, too.

It was 5:15 p.m. on July 23, 2000 when Armstrong crossed the finish line of the final stage of the Tour de France, to win the world's oldest grand tour by a wide margin. About three hours later, a few hundred miles away in St. Andrews, Scotland, Tiger Woods parred the final hole of the final round of the British Open, to win the world's oldest golf major by a record nine shots.

Two young American winners in two traditional European sports. Both are high achievers, with impeccable reputations. Both are high-profile athletes with major endorsement contracts and the worldwide publicity that comes with them. Both are compassionate people who head up charity foundations. Both are stubborn individuals who know what they want from their respective entourages. And both jealously guard their private lives: the 28-year-old Armstrong married with a wife and young son, the 24-year-old Woods now dating a Californian college graduate.

There are differences, of course. Though Armstrong will likely become the most rewarded cyclist in history in terms of career earnings, Woods competes in a much richer sport and is on his way to becoming the first billionaire athlete. Period.

Comparing their athletic careers, Armstrong was a prodigious young athlete and won the world professional championship when he was only 21; but he didn't achieve true fame in the U.S. until he won the Tour after his comeback from cancer. Woods's fame came rapidly, as soon as he won his first major, the Masters, at age 21, and he has been a center of attention ever since.

While Woods was on his way to completing golf's Grand Slam in Britain that July weekend, Armstrong was talking in France about his fellow Nike-sponsored athlete. "Of all the sports superstars I've met," said Armstrong, with wonder, "Tiger Woods was the most excited to meet Lance Armstrong."

Asked about their relative fame, the Tour winner said, "He's much more visible than a cyclist can possibly be. [Cyclists] wear helmets and sunglasses, so we're a bit hidden. Our faces are not known like a golfer's. When I walk around Nice, or walk around Austin, nobody says anything. That's fine with me. It's better for my family, better for my safety."

Armstrong also said he wasn't comfortable being compared with an athlete who clearly dominates his sport. "He's the best golfer in the world," said the Texan. "I don't know that winning the Tour de France makes me the best cyclist in the world."

Modesty is commendable, but it has become very clear that a second victory at the Tour, closely following the release of his best-selling autobiography, and preceding a second round of TV talk shows, had made Lance Armstrong almost as big a personality as Tiger Woods. And the fact that the Tour winner was on the cover of *Sports Illustrated* the week before Tiger Woods only added to that confirmation.

"It's an honor for a cyclist to be on the cover of *SI*," Armstrong conceded. "It's a big deal. How many times was Greg [LeMond] on the cover? Twice? This is big for cycling in America."

Sure is. Just as the Tiger phenomenon that has swept golf has brought thousands of young people into that sport, the Lance "miracle" story could well bring thousands of new riders into bike racing.

Tiger and Lance. Two good stories. Two great athletes. May they continue for as long as they desire. The center of attention.

Made in the USA

Four American manufacturers supplied bikes at the 2000 Tour, including Trek, which built the bikes that Lance Armstrong rode to victory.

By the time Lance Armstrong finished the prologue time trial at the 1999 Tour de France, word was out that the lively—and winning—time-trial bike he had just ridden was not, as its label suggested, a Trek. Armstrong had grown comfortable with his precisely fit and measured custom titanium Litespeed, manufactured in Tennessee by a small, but growing, framebuilder in the small town of Ooltewah. Trek company officials later conceded that the bike wasn't theirs and then happily pointed to the fact that the vast majority of Armstrong's Tour was spent on their ride—a typical off-the-shelf OCLV carbon-fiber road bike. Still, the Wisconsin bike builder wasn't about to let another opportunity slip by. And well before the 2000 Tour began in Futuroscope, Trek was ready not just with a new time-trial bike, but a new even lighter road bike that—despite its almost drab color—really shined as the Tour hit the mountains.

Armstrong and teammate Tyler Hamilton showed up at the starting line on July 1 with an impressive pair of Trek OCLV TT frames. Both were custom designs, but represented a model the company would release to the public in 2001—albeit in relatively limited numbers.

Trek engineer Doug Cusak said the OCLV design crew redesigned Armstrong's 1999 bike from the ground up. "We started with the geometry that he used during the Tour last year," Cusak explained. "The new bike uses a slacker seat-tube angle, 74 versus 75 degrees. This allowed better aerodynamics in the area directly behind the seat. The head-tube angle is at 73.7 degrees, and was set using the fork rake to give handling on the stable side."

Cusak also made a few small adjustments to the position of the bottom bracket to compensate for the shorter axle-to-race distance resulting from the integrated headset on the bike.

"And finally the chainstays were lengthened to allow for better flow of air around the seat tube and wheel behind the rider," Cusak remarked.

One thing the design initially planned to include was a water reservoir built into the TT bike's down tube. U.S. Postal team mechanic Geoff Brown said that both Armstrong and Hamilton opted not to include the reservoir on their bikes. "It's a nice idea," Brown said on the eve of the Tour opener, "they just weren't sure about it, so we decided not to go with it."

The result was an impressive looking aero' steed that pushed right at the limits of the UCI's new design rules, especially those regulating tubing profile.

Beyond the new frame, Armstrong's bike was pretty much equipped as it had been a year earlier, including the same VisionTech handlebars that he used in 1999. The big difference on that front, of course, is that the pricey hi-tech handlebars didn't sport the stickers of another manufacturer. The small American handlebar manufacturer had signed on as U.S. Postal team sponsor.

Any doubts that the bike would perform were quickly put to rest in Futuroscope when Armstrong rode to a strong second-place behind a surprising performance by Tour rookie David Millar of Cofidis. But it was during the final time trial—a 58.5km grind from Freiburg-im-Breisgau to Mulhouse—that Armstrong and his new ride really proved their mettle. Covering the course in 1:05:01, Armstrong set a blistering pace of 53.986 kph, the second fastest time trial in Tour history and the fastest time ever turned in for a time trial longer than 30km. Not a bad debut for a new bike.

Time trials, of course, are critical to success, but the wide consensus is that the Tour de France is almost always won—or lost—in the mountains. It is a truism that has dictated training schedules and equipment choices for decades. And the mountains also provide the perfect stage for bike builders to showcase their best efforts at crafting lightweight equipment.

Armstrong moved into the yellow jersey on the day the Tour moved into the mountains, stage 10 from Dax to Lourdes-Hautacam. While admittedly "it's not about the bike," even the man who long ago proved that point was himself quite the stickler when it came to selecting the right equipment for the task at hand.

In January 2000, Armstrong approached his bike sponsor with a request to produce a lighter version of his regular-issue Trek 5500. The frame design had remained relatively constant since its inception in 1992. Indeed, it stayed almost unchanged until 1999, when Armstrong's teammate Kevin Livingston became the first member of the squad to try a prototype of the 2000 model, which featured a new 1-1/8-inch steerer and lighter weight carbon in its construction.

With the exception of Livingston, the entire 1999 Postal squad rode the original Trek 5500 OCLV, constructed from 150 GSM Pre-preg carbon—meaning 150 grams of carbon fiber per square meter of material that is pre-impregnated with resin. For 2000, the entire team's standard-issue road bikes were made from 120 GSM Pre-preg carbon and also sported integrated headsets and the aforementioned 1-1/8-inch steerer. The result was a bike that weighed about 150 grams less than 1999's.

But Armstrong wanted something even lighter for the mountain stages. The job fell to Trek engineers Brian Schumann and Jim Colegrove, who said they could whip up something using lighter—albeit far more expensive—materials. The result was that grayish OCLV you undoubtedly saw Armstrong riding when the Tour hit the road to Hautacam.

"It's something we've been thinking about doing for years, but cost was always a factor," Colegrove noted. "The 5900 is based on the exact same design as the 5500—the same geometry, the same spec. The difference is that we used a lighter, higher strength material."

That material—110 GSM Pre-preg carbon—has been available for years, but, as Colegrove pointed out, it was significantly more expensive. The result was an unpainted frame—to save still more weight—that hits the scales at just over a kilo, or 2.2 pounds, which represents another 150-gram cut compared to the intermediate 5500/120.

The biggest savings, however, come from the fork, also made from 110 carbon. The new 345-gram fork weighs 195 grams less than the fork Armstrong used the previous year. And it still has an aluminum steerer.

At the Tour, Armstrong and his two climbing companions, Tyler Hamilton and Kevin Livingston, were riding the new Trek 5900 Super Light. In Armstrong's size, the bike weighs about 7 kilos (15.4 pounds), caressing but not violating the UCI weight limit.

In building the bike, Postal mechanic Dave Lettieri added a carbon seatpost and titanium bottle cages to such "standard" team goodies as French-made TA aluminum cogs and chainrings. However, there were a few things that Armstrong seemed unwilling to tweak. He continued to use the same saddle—a Selle San Marco Concor—and 10-year-old Look-compatible Shimano pedals. Those are areas where Armstrong could probably have saved even more weight, but why tinker with those key points of contact?

Despite the added cost of the new material, Trek was willing to commit the time and resources to producing the frame for the public, especially since the bike made a successful debut at the Tour. At $4500 a pop, it needed to shine on the slopes of Hautacam.

Though Trek didn't change its basic OCLV design until recently, Cannondale was out there changing things faster than anyone could keep up with. In 1998—right around Tour time—the Saeco team phased out the Cannondale CAAD3 technology and began a switch to the CAAD4. At the 2000 Giro d'Italia, Cannondale rolled out its new CAAD5 and then in Futuroscope, it was already time to show off the CAAD6. So what did all this CAAD-ing about mean?

The improvements were noteworthy. All told, the changes made the latest incarnation nearly a full kilo lighter than the CAAD4 used at the 1999 Tour. Much of the weight loss—260 grams—came from the conversion to an all-carbon fork, but there were other changes that collectively added up to greater savings.

To start, the CAAD5 adopted the increasingly popular approach of integrating the headset and its races right into the frame, for a 21-gram savings on the CAAD5. (Most of the bike industry's biggest companies adopted the same set-up in 2000).

The CAAD6 went one step further and did something no one else had yet addressed: integrating the bottom bracket. To begin with, the frame abandons the use of the traditional 1.37 x 24 threads-per-inch interface in favor of an oversized bottom bracket shell. Spinning inside is a 30mm bottom-bracket spindle—about 5mm fatter than the hollow bottom-bracket spindle from Shimano. Remember, you can get away with a lighter material and smaller wall thicknesses when you increase the diameter of the tube.

CAAD6 project engineer Chris Dodman said that the new bottom-bracket spindle weighs about 60 grams; that's 30 grams less than its Dura-Ace counterpart. On top of that, the elimination of standard bottom-bracket cups means additional weight savings. The system uses sealed cartridge bearings that press directly into the frame.

The CAAD6 also incorporates a Dodman-designed crankset that uses hollow crankarms that weigh about 162 grams on the left and 165 grams on the right. Currently, the 7000 series aluminum crankarms are being made in 170mm and 175mm lengths, but not the 180mm lengths popular among taller riders, which is why several Saeco riders did not ride their own versions of the new CAAD6 at the Tour.

"By changing the interface, we've saved about 115 grams just in the bottom bracket over the Dura-Ace set up, and it's at least four-percent stiffer," said Dodman, who stood like a proud father at Futuroscope when Saeco's Paolo Savoldelli and Laurent Dufaux headed down the road to Loudun. He had been working on the design changes for some time, and the two riders—and later the entire team, including stage 18 winner Salvatore Commesso—took on the new bike almost sight unseen.

While Trek and Cannondale are Tour veterans—having been a part of the European peloton since 1997—other American companies were making their own forays into the world's biggest bike race. GT, for example, continued its bike sponsorship of the Belgian Lotto-Adecco squad, which began just prior to the 1999 Tour. The Lottos even added another American sponsor, equipping the team with carbon-rimmed wheels manufactured by Zipp, a composites firm based in Indiana.

But it was Specialized—a company once rooted in road cycling but having a bigger reputation on the mountain-bike side—that made a big splash at the 2000 Tour. Indeed, throughout the very brief history of American bikes at the Tour, the third- and fourth-place finishes of Festina's Joseba Beloki and Christophe Moreau meant that this was the most successful debut of an American brand-named bike in the history of the Tour.

The deal had been in the works since the late summer of 1999. Actually, Specialized president Mike Sinyard—a guy who had started the company by selling Italian bicycle components from the back of his van in the 1970s—and the company's international product manager Lance Bohlen had been considering a sponsorship for much longer, though the hurdles to overcome proved to be formidable. But finally, after shopping around for a team, Specialized landed a contract with Festina, a team emerging from its scandal-plagued appearance at the 1998 Tour and—coincidentally—just about ready to end its contract with its then bike supplier, Peugeot.

With a new custom frame facility, new personnel and even a nice bit of road history in place, Specialized was ready to pick a team. That proved to be something of a challenge. In recent years, several manufacturers have locked in long-term contracts with top teams for increasingly princely sums. Italian biggies like Colnago and Pinarello had signed several teams—in particular, Colnago with Mapei and Pinarello with Telekom. And on the U.S. side, Cannondale had ridden its Saeco deal to unprecedented heights; Trek was enjoying the fruits of its U.S. Postal Service team sponsorship; and GT snagged its last-minute deal with Lotto in 1999. There weren't many slots left.

Specialized talked to the available contenders and, said Bohlen, "We were even close to signing with Kelme and Mobilvetta." Eventually, however, "it became clear that Festina made the most sense."

The two-year Festina deal was likely to go longer than that, said Bohlen. After the drug scandal of 1998, the team was completely reorganized with a slate of new riders, giving it one of the youngest average ages in the peloton. The team had potential both short- and long-term. Sinyard said the team's history didn't dissuade him from considering the deal.

"The team is totally changed. The old staff and most of the old riders are gone," Sinyard pointed out. "Festina's sponsorship depends on the team staying clean. Of all teams out there, this has to be one of the cleanest. They can't afford not to be. They've been caught and they can't afford to let it happen again."

Once a contract was signed with the Festina team, for bicycles and accessories, the company—like any first-time sponsor—was eager to see how its bikes would be received. Well, the feedback may have come a bit sooner than expected.

During the Mediterranean Tour, in the early morning hours of February 9, thieves scaled the fence of a "secure" compound in Marseille, France. They broke into the Festina team van and stole 11 of the team's new Specialized M4s. They'd have taken all 18 if a team mechanic hadn't come downstairs to investigate a noise.

The theft turned an already frenzied effort into a mad rush for the folks at company headquarters in Morgan Hill, California. Even for those companies with big race programs already in place, re-making custom bikes at a moment's notice can be a hassle. For Specialized, the theft came at a time when its new custom program was just coming on line.

"We're right at about 10 frames a week," said Gary Yokota, Specialized's prototype shop director and master framebuilder. The company was already building those 10 custom frames a week and was already scrambling to meet a total team requirement of 75. And then came Marseille.

Well, at least the measurements were on file. Yokota and senior design engineer David Earle had already spent the previous few months working out specs on each Festina rider. Earle traveled to the French squad's training camp in Calpe, Spain, to finalize details with individual riders.

"We had custom bikes for everyone at the camp, and most everyone was satisfied," Earle recalled. "I think there were four or five riders who needed changes. Of all of them, I think Marcel Wüst was the most vocal. He is very concerned about what he rides. We sat down and designed a bike for him at the camp. He seems happy with the result."

But in February, said Bohlen, the focus was back to producing bikes as quickly as possible. "It's a matter of getting everything to everyone and on time."

Ever since he arrived at Specialized in 1993, Bohlen had been pushing for the company to take on a pro road team's bike sponsorship. "It's been an educational—and somewhat humbling—experience," he noted. "We've been wanting—I've been really wanting—to do this for years, but it made sense to wait until we had the new facility, the distribution in place, and the people necessary to do it right. If we'd have done this a year ago, we'd have been in a world of hurt."

The "facility" was part of a building-wide remake of Specialized's corporate headquarters in Morgan Hill, where the company owns two buildings. In 1999, Specialized moved a huge part of its operation—assembly and warehousing—to a new location in Salt Lake City, Utah. Even after leasing out the smaller of the two California buildings, the changes freed up a ton of space for new offices, a design center and Yokota's stomping grounds: the new prototype shop.

By the summer of 1999, Specialized had brought in what it considers the core of the new race program: Yokota, Earle and frame painter extraordinaire Keith Anderson—the man charged with making the bikes stand out in a crowd. Heading the group was a new vice president for engineering, Mike McAndrews. He came to Specialized from RockShox, but considered his years with the Kawasaki and Fox racing programs as the main experience he brought to his new responsibilities at Specialized.

"A race sponsorship doesn't do anyone any good if that's all there is to it," McAndrews suggested. "The racing has to serve a purpose that translates into something tangible as far as product. For S-Works, that should speed up the process as far as development is concerned. I mean, the way we used to have to do it was to design it here, send the drawings to Taiwan, have them prototype it, send it back, work out the bugs, redesign it, send more drawings...."

The entire Specialized sponsorship program was soon to be run through the prototype shop. Even while scrambling to supply the squad with custom M4 road bikes, Earle and Yokota were already working on the Festina team's newest bike, the SL. The lightweight S-Works road frame did not use the M4 manipulated tubing employed in the original team bikes. Instead, it was built around a new 6000-series aluminum tube-set developed in conjunction with Columbus. The "E5" tubing is similar to Columbus's new Starship tube-set, though Bohlen quickly added that the E5 is different because of "proprietary characteristics that I can't go into." *Vive la difference!*

Mystery tubing or not, Yokota had already built a few of the frames in February, and the feed back from the riders who had used them was positive. Weighing in at 1.9 pounds, a 55cm SL could "if properly equipped" make a bike that pushes the limit on the UCI's 14.9-pound minimum weight requirement. "But as far as components, riders tend to favor reliability over weight," Bohlen noted.

By Tour time, the Festina squad was fully equipped. Each rider had a selection of bikes including the M4, custom time-trial bikes and, of course, the new SL.

Wüst was the first of the Festinas to make his mark on the Tour and he did it with his new climbing bike. The personable German sprinter saw an interesting aberration on the course profile of the opening—day time trial in Futuroscope: a small climb with a Cat. 4 rating. No time trialist, Wüst opted for his custom-built SL climbing bike for this other-wise flat TT. Knowing that the climber's jersey would be awarded to the rider who scaled the short climb the fastest, Wüst concentrated all of his efforts on sprinting up the small rise. It worked. Wüst, usually known as a sprinter, had locked up the famed polka-dot jersey for the opening three days of the Tour—because there were no rated climbs for the next three days. Indeed, he kept it longer than expected, even losing it in style, when he won stage 5, the same day he conceded the climber's jersey to Mapei's Paolo Bettini.

The interesting fallout from Wüst's decision was that he and several other Festina rid-ers continued to use the SL throughout the Tour, not only in the mountains. Beloki, on the other hand, used his slightly heavier M4 for the duration of the Tour.

"The deal worked out better for us than we could have imagined," Bohlen said. "A podium spot in our first Tour?"

While bikes were obviously the focus, Specialized used its bike sponsorship as the vehicle for its accessories as well. The team was equipped with Specialized bottles, cages, helmets, gloves and, yup, even those saddles that were designed to mitigate problems of … uhhh … erectile dysfunction brought on by endless hours on the bike.

"We brought Dr. [Roger] Minkow to the camp in Spain," Bohlen said, referring to the designer of Specialized's Body Geometry line of gloves and saddles. "He did his presentation on the impotence risk a rider faces. He used graphics and a computer model of the pelvis. You could have heard a pin drop in the room. I guess it's an important subject for a bunch of guys in their 20s."

Bohlen conceded that the Festina riders were "contractually obligated" to at least try the saddle. "Some might switch, but the reaction has been pretty good," he said.

By Tour time, it became clear that the mass-marketed saddle was too soft and a touch too heavy for most of the team. While a few riders continued to use the original model, Specialized responded to rider concerns and issued a new lighter "Team Issue" version. Of the nine riders on Festina, only three used the more traditional old-style saddle. Apparently, some of the riders had concerns outside of cycling to consider.

Trading Places:
Julich and Beloki

It was the year, it seemed, when almost all of the big names were at the start of the Tour: Armstrong, Ullrich, Pantani, Zülle, Escartin, Vandenbroucke, Jalabert, Olano, Virenque, Julich.... But aside from Armstrong and Ullrich, it turned into a Tour in which many of those same names fizzled out, some struggling badly in the mountains and some dropping out altogether. At the same time, "new" stars emerged. There was no more fitting contrast than between the third-place finisher of 1998, and his successor in 2000....

For Bobby Julich, there was no way to describe the 2000 Tour except as a disappointment. The American entered the race with high hopes, but saw them washed away on the wet, frigid first day in the mountains. After a freezing-cold descent from the Col d'Aubisque on stage 10, Julich suffered terribly on the finishing climb to Hautacam, losing 12 minutes by the end of the stage. He knew his Tour hopes for 2000 were over, and as he continued to struggle, the Crédit Agricole rider began to rethink his Tour objectives.

"When I bonked or froze or whatever happened to me on that descent ... up the Hautacam it was, you know, really facing that G.C. was over, and it was tough to deal with. Mentally and physically, I just wasn't the same since then," Julich said the morning of stage 16, from Courchevel to Morzine. "It's tough.... When I got to the base of the climb and I couldn't even pedal, seeing stars, and it was just starting the climb, I knew that it wasn't gonna work out the way I wanted it to."

And from that point, Julich had to ride through the toughest of his four Tours, losing time every day in the mountains.

"I've never seen the Tour through these eyes before, or through these legs before. It's easy to attack, and easy to wake up in the morning when you're feeling great and really motivated. It's really difficult just to find the morale and push through it when you're not feeling like you should," he said.

"It's disappointing. Sometimes you just want to crawl in a hole and not have anyone recognize you, when you're going up a climb 20 minutes down, when you're used to being in the front attacking," he admitted, staring off into the distance.

"I just didn't see any sort of compensation for the sacrifices that I made. That's the toughest thing, because you hope to see some compensation in terms of results, or just good sensations," Julich continued. "It's not like I'm crazy and I have to expect to win a race just because I trained hard in the winter—but the sensations, I expected to be a little bit better."

Julich's problems actually began before the Tour, when allergies took their toll, and reached their worst right at the end of the Route du Sud in June. But he wasn't making excuses, and accepted that he might have to re-set his Tour ambitions for the future.

"For me, maybe I need to work a little bit more on the mental part. It was difficult to look at the Tour as anything of a success if I wasn't on the podium," Julich said, "and maybe I should cut myself a little bit more of a break, and realize that I can't really compare everything to '98 and my third place."

Julich remained optimistic, though. "This could turn out to be a good thing, because the last three seasons, I've been absolutely unmotivated to race after the Tour. So maybe this will … give me motivation for the end of the season that I haven't had in the last couple of years, to make myself more of a complete cyclist. One thing's for sure, I need to re-evaluate my objectives, and obviously no longer think only of the Tour."

With the stars like Julich falling by the wayside, an improbable Spanish pro emerged, and ended up on the podium in Paris with Armstrong and Ullrich. And, of course, there were many people asking, "Who's Joseba Beloki?"

Sometimes, the phrase "revelation of the Tour" is overused, but considering that this dark-haired, bushy-browed rider had never before completed a three-week Tour, his performance did represent a big breakthrough.

Back in the spring, Beloki's Festina team director Juan Fernandez had called the 26-year-old "the next Spanish hope," and his results gave a hint of that promise: fourth in the Dauphiné Libéré in 1999, winner of Spain's Tour of Asturias in April 2000, and winner of the time trial stage at Switzerland's Tour de Romandie in May.

But Beloki's only grand tour experience before 2000 was a short stint at the 1999 Vuelta, ending with his withdrawal after five days, due to tendinitis. At the time, he was riding for the small Euskaltel–Euskadi operation. The team had given Beloki his first pro contract in 1997—after he had already decided to quit the sport.

That original contract came about largely by chance: Beloki was signed primarily because the Basque team needed a representative from his home region of Alava. But despite his unlikely beginnings as a pro, Beloki showed promise with Euskaltel in 1998 and '99. So much so that when Fernandez became Festina's team director for 2000, he didn't hesitate in signing Beloki.

Come July, Beloki showed why his boss had such confidence in him. Despite being a bundle of nervous energy in his first Tour, the Spaniard was solid, if not spectacular. Almost always with the front group in the mountains, his highlight was a third-place finish atop Mont Ventoux, behind Pantani and Armstrong.

Beloki's climbing prowess had him in third place heading into the final time trial; and on that 58.5km ride from Freiburg-im-Breisgau to Mulhouse, he showed how well he had survived the three-week Tour. He placed an impressive fifth on the day, and held off Festina teammate Christophe Moreau's challenge for the final podium spot in Paris.

"(Beloki) showed his class in the mountains and also in the time trial," said race winner Armstrong. "And he showed that he can ride in the front for a three-week Tour de France."

So there he was, next to Armstrong and Ullrich on the victory stand: a new face. And now nobody will have to ask, "Who's that rider?"

"He will no longer be a surprise," Armstrong confirmed. "This is his arrival. He will be a favorite in the future."

Behind Lance, How the Other Americans Rated

The world knows that Lance Armstrong defended his Tour de France title in commanding fashion, but the rest of the American contingent received even less publicity than they did in 1999. Of the other eight U.S. riders who started the Tour, four were racing for Armstrong on the U.S. Postal Service team, two raced for Crédit Agricole of France and two for Mapei-Quick Step of Italy. Here's how they fared:

Frankie Andreu

Not too many people have started and finished nine Tours. But that's the milestone Frankie Andreu reached in 2000; and for the second time, he rode onto the Champs-Elysèes alongside the race winner. The Postal team's road captain is now the U.S. rider with the most participations at the Tour (ahead of Andy Hampsten), but still two short of the 11 Tours ridden by Canadian Steve Bauer. At 33, Andreu may still have a Tour or two left in his legs; but he will have a stiff task to oust Bauer as the top-scoring North American Tour rider.

Andreu is the prototypical domestique who is always ready to ride hard for his team, whether its pacing Tyler Hamilton back to the peloton after a crash (as he did on stage 2), getting into a long-distance break to give his teammates some respite from chasing (as he did on stage 8), riding tempo to defend the jersey on yet another marathon stage, or being the voice of experience that helped Postal take second place in the team time trial.

Incidentally, that was the fourth time that Andreu has finished second in a Tour stage—twice in TTTs. At this late point in his career, the Michigan veteran is destined probably never to win one … but that's all right.

Overall finish: 110th at 3:02:15. **Overall rating:** 8

Tyler Hamilton

Once again, Tyler Hamilton did exactly what the Postal team asked of him—and more! The only time that the New Englander could be faulted in his lieutenant role for Armstrong was on stage 10, on the cold, wet climb of the mighty Col d'Aubisque. His leader would have liked to have had Hamilton pacing him for a lot longer than a couple of kilometers on the near-one-hour climb, but Armstrong was so strong that day, he wasn't in need of much more assistance. However, if Hamilton hadn't been suffering from the cold weather and the after-effects of a heavy fall the previous afternoon, he might well have helped Armstrong narrow the gap on solo breakaway Javier Otxoa, and enabled the Texan to crown his Hautacam demonstration with the stage win as well as the yellow jersey.

Hamilton more than made up for that minor low point of his Tour. There was his amazing performance on the mountain that Armstrong called "the toughest climb of the Tour"—Mont Ventoux. Hamilton's acceleration on the steepest part of the 20km ascent destroyed many opponents' hopes and set up his leader's later counterattack. But the real high point came a few stages later, on the day that Armstrong had his toughest moments of the Tour—on stage 16.

That day, Hamilton heroically pulled the small group of leaders for three or more hours after Marco Pantani's attack on the first of the stage's five climbs had seen Armstrong lose all of his Postal teammates except for Hamilton and Kevin Livingston.

Another of Hamilton's greatest qualities is his calmness—a quality that proved vital on that alpine stage to Morzine. Without Hamilton's steadying influence, Armstrong certainly would have had to work harder in chasing Pantani. And had that been the case, the effects of the Texan's bonking on the stage's final climb, the Joux–Plane, may well have cost him the yellow jersey. Remember, when Pantani bonked on the Hautacam, he lost more than five minutes to Armstrong in less than 10km.

Despite all of his unselfish work, Hamilton still came through strongly in the final time trial. His fourth-place ride in the Freiburg–Mulhouse stage, at 51.592 kph, was one of the fastest time trials in history. As a comparison, his ride slots between the best two Tour TT performances of Miguel Induráin, both over 64km: 50.539 kph from Périgueux to Bergerac in 1994, and 52.349 kph from Tours to Blois in 1992.

Now 27, and with four Tours behind him, Hamilton looks set to continue his impressive progress.

Overall finish: 25th at 56:30. **Overall rating:** 9

George Hincapie

If he were a member of any other team, George Hincapie would have won a Tour stage in either 1999 or 2000. The native New Yorker is fast approaching his peak in single-day racing, and it is perhaps a little galling for him to be playing the domestique role at the Tour (a role he plays extraordinarily well!) while watching others grab the glory—especially riders like Christophe Agnolutto, Salvatore Commesso or Erik Dekker, who Hincapie regularly sees off in the spring classics.

Hincapie is an emotional rider, but for the past two Tours he has harnessed his ambitions to become a model teammate for Armstrong. Hincapie's speed, strength, endurance and six-foot-three build make him the perfect "motor" for his team leader on the flats; and Hincapie has also progressed in the mountains. He is not a natural climber, but the strong pulls he made on mountain passes like stage 14's Col de Vars are a big part of the Postal team's success formula.

This was Hincapie's sixth Tour, and he has finished all of them except the first, when a crash forced him to pull out. His consistency and reliability make him one of Postal's most important building blocks.

Overall finish: 65th at 2:20:31. **Overall rating:** 9

Bobby Julich

This was Julich's fourth Tour, and he was hoping it would be one in which he would regain the momentum of his third-place finish of 1998. The native Coloradan had high hopes after the stage 4 team time trial, when he led his Crédit Agricole team to an excellent fourth place, only six seconds behind Ullrich's favored Telekom squad. Julich then awaited the first mountain stage, the one to Hautacam.

This proved to be the most decisive stage of the Tour, because of its three major climbs and the cold, wet weather. Despite losing his climbing lieutenant, Jonathan Vaughters, to a crash, Julich appeared to be on his way to a strong finish at Hautacam. On the rugged Col d'Aubisque, he was climbing strongly and easily stayed with the major 21-strong group, along with Armstrong, Ullrich and Pantani. It was at the summit, where clouds were swirling around the riders and the temperature was in the low 40s, that things started to unravel. Julich got an inadequate rain jacket for the long, cold descent, and when the group reached the valley for the immediate ascent toward Hautacam, he was literally frozen. Julich lost 10 minutes in 13km, and his morale disappeared.

His detractors may now have written Julich off as a future Tour contender, but at only 28 his natural ability combined with his Zen-like approach to race preparation mark him as a rider whose best years could still be ahead of him.

Overall finish: 48th at 1:44:15. **Overall rating:** 5

Kevin Livingston

When Livingston crashed on a rainy day in early April at the Tour of the Basque Country, and broke his collarbone in two places, the Missouri native's Tour preparations were shot. To a professional, even a day off the bike can be a handicap; but missing a week or so of riding, and returning to racing only a month before the Tour made it impossible for Livingston to return to the level of climbing excellence he showed in 1999.

So there was no repeat of the heroics he displayed then in pacing Armstrong up the giant Galibier and Tourmalet climbs. Instead, Livingston had to be content with nursing his form, which improved as the race went on. His strongest performance came on the difficult uphill finish to Courchevel, where he was the glue keeping Armstrong stuck to an attacking Pantani—while Ullrich fell off the pace. That was a vital element in Armstrong's overall victory, as that setback for Ullrich allowed the Texan to take a more-than-seven-minute cushion into the next stage, the one that saw Armstrong himself almost come unstuck on the Joux–Plane.

Only 27, Livingston will be returning to the Tour for many years and with greater ambition on a different team: the British-based Linda McCartney squad.

Overall finish: 37th at 1:23:13. **Overall rating:** 8

Chann McRae

Chann McRae's normally serious face had more of a forlorn look on it for much of his first Tour de France—which ended prematurely after he crashed twice within five kilometers, early in stage 12. It was perhaps a timely ending, as the slightly built Texan knew he wasn't performing anywhere near his best.

There was a reason....

In 1999, McRae earned the respect of the mighty Mapei team with his excellent support rides for its leader Pavel Tonkov at the Giro d'Italia and Vuelta a España. As a result, he was slated to ride the Tour in 2000, which meant he would bypass the Giro. Well, he was supposed to, but was called upon at the last minute to ride again for Tonkov in Italy. He did so with distinction.

McRae went home to Texas for a week's break before returning to his Italian base to build up his form for the Tour. Then, a week before the start in Futuroscope, he got a call: He wouldn't be going to France. McRae was heartbroken. He stopped training ... and then, a few days later, he was told he would be going after all.

And so he was thrown like driftwood into the maelstrom that is the Tour. Instead of the careful build-up toward a long-term goal, he was making his Tour debut not knowing if he were truly wanted, and not knowing what was expected of him. The result was one disillusioned athlete who knew that he wasn't ready to tackle two grand tours in quick succession.

Proving that he has a real role to play at the Tour would have to wait, and his move to the U.S.-based Mercury team should help in his evolution.

Overall finish: Abandoned stage 12 **Overall rating:** 4

Fred Rodriguez

If anyone ever embraced the rush of excitement, sense of awe and glare of publicity represented by the Tour de France, then it was Fred Rodriguez. Thrilled to be called up for his first Tour, knowing what was expected of him, and enjoying every day to the full, the darkly handsome Californian made his mark. The fans loved his dashing style, his easily recognizable stars-and-stripes jersey and matching bandanna, and the effervescence with which he raced.

"I want to be in the middle of the whole thing," he said on the first day of the Tour. And he was.

Rodriguez could not have had a more perfect beginning than playing an important role in the Mapei team leadout that helped Tom Steels win the first two road stages. He showed immense talent in getting across to the big break on the stage through the Dordogne—and with greater experience of the Tour's tactical nuances, he might well have won on that windy day to Villeneuve-sur-Lot. Later, he displayed intelligence and patience in getting through the long mountain stages unscathed, pacing himself like a veteran instead of like a young man riding his first grand tour.

It was fitting that Rodriguez ended the Tour with a flourish: third, behind Dekker and Erik Zabel, at Lausanne; a remarkable 23rd place in the stage 19 time trial; and the key man in the Mapei ruse that sprung his teammate Stefano Zanini to victory on the Champs-Elysées. Rodriguez would be back.

Overall finish: 86th at 2:40:19. **Overall rating:** 7

Jonathan Vaughters

He has the aptitude. He has the drive. But so far, Jonathan Vaughters has had neither the luck nor the time to become a true Tour de France rider. Stopped by a crash before he even got to the race in 1998, he has now started two Tours—but each one has ended with him riding away in an ambulance after scary falls. At least this time he managed to complete nine whole stages, as against just two in 1999. At this rate, Vaughters will get to finish a complete Tour by 2002....

The Coloradan went into the 2000 Tour to race for Crédit Agricole teammate Julich, and maybe shoot for a stage win on Mont Ventoux. Things started well enough for Vaughters with a 23rd place in the opening time trial, and an impressive performance in helping his squad take fourth in the team time trial. A week into the race, his directeur sportif Roger Legeay was saying that Vaughters was capable of making the top five in Paris.

That possibility ended abruptly when he skidded off a slick mountain road into a retaining wall while descending the Marie–Blanque pass in the Pyrénées—on the first stage that could have showcased his climbing talents. Yes, Vaughters needs to ride with less hesitancy in wet weather, but at least he proved that he could negotiate the Tour's always-difficult opening week.

He may be progressing in short bursts but, eventually, Vaughters will surely harness all of his potential to become the great Tour rider he was meant to be.

Overall finish: abandoned on stage 10. **Overall rating:** 6

Drugs and the Tour

Ever since the drugs scandal at the 1998 Tour de France, cyclists have been the subject of intense focus by the world's media. Doubts still exist on the level of doping that exists in the sport. New tests are helping to clarify the situation, but they are also creating new controversies.

In its most basic form, cycling is simply and joyfully one of the world's most vigorous and rejuvenating pastimes. A 10- or 20-mile jaunt through the countryside can improve both your body's circulation and your general outlook on life. A ride in the hills, a bit of friendly competition among friends or perhaps a sprint to the edge of town might be tiring, but just adds to the pleasure of it.

Now take that 20-, 30-, or even 50-mile ride and turn it into 120 or 150 miles. Then change that casual "battle" between friends into an epic struggle between the world's best at daily average speeds of up to 50 kph, add rough roads over steep, seemingly unending mountain climbs and then multiply by 21 days, and you have the Tour de France.

The simple fact that human beings, no matter how fit, are being asked to race at an elite athletic level for three weeks can explain why one rider, as he walked up a particularly grueling climb in the 1909 Tour de France—the first one to include the high mountain passes of the Pyrénées—screamed out "Assassins!" at a race official. With that in mind, it shouldn't be all that surprising that cycling at its highest levels has long been linked to the use of drugs—performance-enhancing or otherwise.

In the early days of the sport, riders consumed alcohol, caffeine, strychnine and an array of other drugs that now we know did little to help and much to harm their performance. By the 1940s and '50s, the level of pharmacological awareness among riders had increased, and amphetamines—widely used by soldiers in World War II—became the drug of choice. Drug use was pervasive and looked likely to continue if one took the depressingly cynical comment of five-time Tour winner Jacques Anquetil to heart. The Tour de France, he said, is not won "on mineral water alone."

Doping was a problem largely ignored—and therefore effectively legal—until the mid-1960s. The rules began to change in late 1966; not soon enough, however, to prevent the death of British cyclist Tom Simpson on a brutally hot day on the slopes of Mount Ventoux in the 1967 Tour. He was later found to have a combination of alcohol and amphetamines in his system. Through that tragedy, cycling became the first sport to subject riders to random drug testing during competition. The Olympic movement followed suit and established its first serious drug-control effort at the 1968 Summer Games in Mexico City. Ever since, it has been an ongoing battle between those who test and those who hope to evade detection.

By the mid-1990s, it was clear that the drugs of choice among cyclists willing to cheat had reached incredible levels of sophistication. Riders were no longer "benefiting" from alcohol, amphetamines or the early generations of anabolic steroids. Not only are those substances detectable, their positive effect is both marginal and short-term.

The new pharmacopeia included drugs designed to subtly manipulate the most basic functions of the human body. First and foremost is Erythropoietin—produced in the 1980s by the American pharmaceutical giant Amgen to combat chronic anemia—which boosts red-blood-cell production. Riders believe with some justification that the performance benefit of EPO is huge—as much as 10 to 15 percent. One rider described the difference between a rider on EPO and another of equal talent but not using the drug as tantamount to "the difference between a man and a woman. It's huge."

EPO alone can affect the outcome of a race, but there were other drugs being used, too. Human growth hormone—first developed as a treatment for children suffering from dwarfism—can, in carefully controlled doses, aid in recovery, boost muscle production and "burn" fat. Corticosteroids—a family of drugs with a number of legitimate uses—can reduce inflammation, reduce fatigue and give an exhausted rider a feeling of well-being.

Beyond measurements of their suspicious effects, these drugs have essentially been undetectable. In the absence of proof, many said, it was irresponsible to assert that their use was widespread. But if there had been doubts that the drugs were used, and used in an organized fashion, those doubts were put to rest just before the start of the 1998 Tour de France. That was when a team car belonging to the world's then–No. 1 team, Festina, was stopped by the French police and found to be carrying more than 400 vials of drugs, including EPO, growth hormone, corticosteroids and even amphetamines.

The ensuing scandal has swirled around cycling in general and the Tour in particular, ever since. In early 1999, the International Olympic Committee held a three-day conference on doping in sport, after which it issued a weak mission statement, but interestingly also committed some $25 million to "the battle against doping in sport."

The infusion of cash added a sense of urgency to efforts already underway to develop a means of detecting the undetectable. On the eve of the '99 Tour, the UCI rolled out two new experimental tests: one for the presence of corticosteroids and another for the presence of oxygenated perfluorodecalin (PFC), a super oxygenating chemical designed for trauma patients in emergency rooms with no immediate access to a blood transfusion. Lifesaving if used as it should be, it was life-threatening to a healthy adult trying to use it for a competitive advantage. Once thought to be the subject of experimentation among some riders, its dangers and, perhaps more significantly, lack of real benefit, the drug disappeared from the peloton by the time a test appeared. Not surprisingly, no riders were listed as "positive" for PFCs.

So, too, was the case for the new test for corticosteroids, though a leak of some preliminary results at the '99 Tour suggested that race leader Lance Armstrong had a trace amount—below the limit established by the test—in his sample. The news triggered a brief scandal that further soured the already bad relationship between the eventual Tour winner and the press—until it was revealed by the UCI that the drug traces came from a topical skin cream to treat a saddle sore.

While the new tests unveiled in 1999 marked some progress, the big goal was still the development of some means of detecting EPO. The task was formidable, since EPO is a recombinant form of a naturally occurring human hormone. The Amgen-produced version of that hormone is essentially a clone of what the body produces on its own.

Nonetheless, several researchers have pursued the effort with some success. As part of the $25 million budgeted to the anti-doping effort, the IOC awarded millions in research grants to two competing efforts to develop a foolproof test. In Australia, the Australian Institute of Sport was pursuing the development of a blood test, based not on the direct detection of the presence of the drug, but a broad range of measurements of its effects. The approach was a sophisticated and far more complex means of detection than the simple hematocrit test used by the UCI since 1997. In that test, the UCI merely established an upper limit of 50 percent for the allowable proportion of red blood cells in a rider's blood sample. Though not proof, the hematocrit test was an indicator of EPO use. In the absence of proof, no penalties could be applied, so riders were simply ordered to "rest" for two weeks and then given a second test (which would have to register less than 50 percent before they could race again).

Australian researcher David Martin—part of the AIS group—explained that the body reacts in a number of very distinct ways when artificial EPO is introduced into the system. "Try to imagine the receptors that respond to erythropoietin as doors in a hallway," Martin said. "Under normal conditions, the body produces erythropoietin as needed. Normally, you would look down that hallway and see a small number of those doors open at any given time. Introduce EPO and look down that hallway and every single door will be thrown wide-open.... Nothing else will do that."

The Australian test measures the drug's effect—comparing a set of variables including the presence of young red blood cells (reticulocyte hematocrit), the levels of serum erythropoietin, levels of free iron in the blood stream, and a standard red-blood-cell count.

In a paper published in the June 2000 issue of the journal *Haematologica*, the Australian researchers, using the first of two methods developed, were able to repeatedly identify 94 to 100 percent of exogenous EPO users for up to two weeks after injection. There was, however, one false positive reported in a group of 189 tests conducted. Using a second method, researchers were able to identify just 67 to 72 percent of EPO users for a period of 12 to 21 days after injection. While less accurate, the second method did not produce any false positives.

It was that presence of the single false positive in the study results published in *Haematologica* that caused the UCI to hesitate in its support of the test.

"Can you imagine the consequences of a false positive?" UCI medical director Dr. Leon Schattenberg explained. "The liability issues, the moral question of publishing a false positive, the impact on a cyclist's career.... It's incomprehensible."

Instead, UCI president Hein Verbruggen moved hurriedly to embrace a promising urine test developed by Françoise Lasne and Jacques de Ceaurriz at the French national anti-doping laboratory in Châtenay–Malabry, near Paris.

The test, said de Ceaurriz, could detect EPO for up to three days after injection, by isolating subtle differences in the electric charges of natural and exogenous erythropoietin.

On May 25, 2000, Verbruggen and Tour de France director Jean-Marie Leblanc held a joint news conference in Geneva, Switzerland, announcing support for the French test and predicting that it would be ready in time for the Tour, just over a month later. Verbruggen noted that if the test met certain standards, it would be used at the Tour.

"All sections of the cycling movement have agreed to accept the test as long as there is a validation of this method before June 20," Verbruggen explained.

One of the conditions Verbruggen listed was for the test methodology to be published in a reputable scientific magazine. That condition was met when the team published a brief summary of their findings in the journal *Nature* a few weeks later.

The second condition, requiring the laboratory to carry out a series of blind tests using 220 urine samples with the results submitted to an independent panel of experts, was met as the French team coordinated its efforts with the AIS group.

Finally, the work was to be reviewed by a three-member independent panel. The next day, as he arrived at the Giro d'Italia, Verbruggen expressed confidence that all three conditions would be met. His confidence proved to be a bit premature.

The panel—that final hurdle—issued its report on June 22, just nine days before the start of the Tour. And though expressing confidence in the methods, the panel declined to endorse its use for the Tour, suggesting a need for additional review.

The hoped-for EPO test wouldn't make it in time for this Tour, at least. But within a few days of the report, Verbruggen surprised many when he announced that he had enough confidence in the test to order that urine samples taken during the 2000 Tour de France be frozen for later testing, when and if the French method received final approval. The message, of course, was to dissuade riders and teams from using the drug during the Tour. The effect of that deterrent may have been proven—although in cynical fashion—on the morning of the Tour's start on July 1.

On the eve of the Tour de France, it is now tradition for the defending champion to hold a news conference and to discuss the upcoming race. At Futuroscope, Lance Armstrong fulfilled his obligation and fielded a series of questions about whom he felt might be his biggest challengers, about his take on the course and, as expected, about the role of drugs and drug-testing at the Tour. Armstrong was clearly annoyed. The problem of widespread drug use in cycling, he said, was "a myth" unfairly perpetuated by the media. And, for the time being, the assembled reporters seemed almost in agreement, perhaps tired themselves of constantly writing about allegations that were nearly impossible to prove. But then came another practice that, too, has become a tradition of sorts at the Tour de France.

On the morning of July 1, seven groups of medical officials from the UCI fanned out to go to all the hotels of the 20 teams that were starting the 2000 Tour later in the day. With about 30 minutes' of advance warning, the medical squad—commonly called the "vampires"—visited the nine riders on each team in order to draw a blood sample for a pre-race hematocrit test.

It was about nine hours before the start of the Tour's first stage—a 16km individual time trial around the futuristic theme park of Futuroscope. But before they could even warm up on their time-trial bikes, three riders—Russian champion Sergei Ivanov of Farm Frites, Italian Rossano Brasi of Polti and Slovenian Andrej Hauptmann of Vini Caldirola—were ejected from the Tour for exceeding the UCI's imposed 50-percent hematocrit limit.

It was a record of sorts. At no other time, since the blood test was first imposed in 1997, had so many riders failed it on a single day. Given the three-day detection window of the French urine test, some believed that many riders simply "boosted themselves to the limit" in the days leading up to the Tour. The ability to manipulate hematocrit with a high degree of accuracy had been refined in recent years, particularly after the establishment of the 50-percent mark. Perhaps, the ejection of the trio signified more than just a failure to monitor. It may have been a sign that some were taking the threat of the EPO test seriously.

Either way, the news was a shock to the three affected riders. At 10:30 that morning, medical officials contacted the directors of Farm Frites, Polti and Vini Caldirola to inform them that their riders were facing expulsion. None of the riders had any indication that there was a problem until their teams were contacted. For example, just after breakfast, Ivanov was at the Farm Frites mechanics' truck, going over the particulars of his time-trial bike with his mechanic. The 25-year-old Russian was proudly wearing the broad red-white-and-blue stripes of his national championship jersey that he earned only the week before.

An hour later, Farm Frites team manager Jacques Hanegraaf received a telephone call from the UCI informing him that Ivanov had recorded a hematocrit reading higher than the allowed 50 percent. The news was especially difficult for Ivanov and the Farm Frites team, since this was the squad's first appearance at the Tour since 1998 when, riding under the TVM-Farm Frites banner, the entire team left in protest after being subjected to police interrogation during the infamous Festina scandal. It was for that reason, and the arrest and indictment of the team's former director, Cees Priem, that the Dutch squad was specifically not invited to participate in the 1999 Tour.

The UCI chief medical official at the Tour, Martin Bruin, a Dutchman, said, "I was a bit disappointed. And I am very surprised. Everybody knew. The whole world knows that at the beginning of a major tour—the Giro, the Tour, the Vuelta—that everyone undergoes a hematocrit check on the morning of the start."

Bruin said he was very confident in the integrity of the tests conducted that morning and convinced that medical officials left no room for error. "No, no, no, this test is 100-percent sure," Bruin said. "This test is certified, the machines are calibrated. We wouldn't come here without that level of certainty. This is exactly why we are in a position that we have to wait for the finalizing of the urine test for EPO. You see the significance of what can happen if there were a false positive. That's why we are quite certain of this result."

As insurance, Bruin pointed out, the tests already allow "a one-percent margin of error," adding that penalties don't kick in until a rider's sample is certified to have a hematocrit level of at least 50.5 percent. Hanegraaf concurred, saying that the UCI even tested the three higher-than-acceptable samples an additional six times before reaching the conclusion that the riders were beyond the permitted level. "We don't doubt the controls," Hanegraaf said as he walked hurriedly toward race headquarters to meet with Tour director-general Leblanc.

Bruin said he had no explanation as to why riders closely monitored by team doctors would find themselves in such a position. "You have to ask them," Bruin said. "I am simply the medical inspector doing his job. I can't imagine how or why someone would come to the Tour and fail the hematocrit test. They knew that the test would be conducted."

But asking the riders what happened proved difficult as each of the three quickly left Futuroscope that day. Brasi was immediately suspended by his team pending an explanation from the rider. According to team sources, Brasi had undergone two tests earlier in the week, each of which was "clean."

Polti team director Gianluigi Stanga quickly issued an apology to Tour organizers for the incident. The immediate fates of the other two was less certain. A stunned Ivanov was seen leaving his team hotel that afternoon, on his way to the railway station in nearby Poitiers. From there, he took a train to Paris, where he joined a connecting train back home to Brussels. Ivanov would eventually return to the squad, with Farm Frites vowing to stand by its beleaguered rider.

The young Slovenian Hauptmann was devastated and insisted that he had done nothing to boost his hematocrit level. "When I left home, I told my father that I would return with the white jersey (of best young rider)," Hauptmann said. "Now I've been kicked out of the Tour. What do I tell him now?"

———————————————— ❁ ————————————————

Not long after the Tour, a group of reviewers impaneled by the IOC issued its report on the status of EPO testing for the Tour. The panel granted conditional approval to both the Australian and French tests—allowing them to be used at the Sydney Games, but only in conjunction with each other. Athletes attending the 2000 Olympics would be subjected to both tests, and shown to be positive only if they failed both.

The immediate impact on the Tour was minimal. The IOC report prompted the UCI to issue a statement applauding the decision, adding that the frozen samples would be tested, but only once the French test could be certified as valid without being run in conjunction with another test. It would be a while before the samples would be tested.

One test that had already been certified and was used at the 2000 Tour was the means of detecting corticosteroids. First employed in 1999, the test was there to measure the presence of a drug that had been rumored to be in wide use among riders. Corticosteroids are banned because they allow a rider to compete at a level that would be impossible without their use. Their general effects on recovery and their euphoric effects are well-known and help explain why they are banned. Banned, that is to say, except for those instances in which a rider can offer a doctor's prescription for the drug—most often for the treatment of asthma and related symptoms, or as a skin cream to heal abrasions or saddle sores. That prescription must be presented prior to use—and certainly prior to detection. The UCI, in the interest of riders' privacy, does not reveal the names of those who have such a medical certificate.

In early August, the UCI issued a press release happily announcing, "all the anti-doping controls carried out during the 2000 Tour de France have proved negative for banned substances." Within the body of the release, however, there was a note that "the presence of substances, whose use is subject to certain restrictions (e.g. glucocorticosteroids, beta 2 agonists) detected in some urine samples, were in fact justified by medical prescriptions duly noted in the rider's health record booklet, in accordance with the Anti-Doping Control Regulations."

It was the use of the phrase "some urine samples" that prompted the French Council for the Prevention of and Fight Against Doping (CPFD) to issue its own report, noting that 45 percent of the 96 urine samples tested during the Tour had shown such traces. The CPFD is a pseudo-governmental body established in response to the Tour scandal of 1998 and authorized to oversee anti-doping efforts in France. After a somewhat bumpy start to the relationship, the UCI began working in cooperation with the agency, going so far as to adopt its policy of medical controls for the 2000 season.

The 96 tests in question represented samples provided by 71 riders, with the overall leader, the stage winner and two randomly selected riders tested at the end of each stage. In addition, 12 random tests instead of the usual two were carried out at the end of the 16th and 20th stages. CPFD president Michel Boyon said that in 28 cases traces of corticosteroids were detected. In 10 of those cases, there were traces of salbutamol or terbutaline, which aids respiration and has anabolic effects. In five other cases, there were traces of both corticosteroids and salbutamol.

French cycling federation president Daniel Baal, a man who had taken a strong anti-doping position after the 1998 Festina scandal, said the results were unnerving. "The fact that 45 percent of riders controlled had traces of corticosteroids or salbutamol in their systems poses a serious problem," he said.

Leblanc warned against anyone jumping to what he called "premature conclusions" and queried the timing of the release of the news by the CPFD.

"We can question the reasons which led the CPFD to disclose this information before the regulatory procedures laid down by the Union Cycliste International were completed," Leblanc said in a statement. "Whatever happens we will abide by the decisions and, should they occur, the sanctions which the UCI or French cycling federation might take if these doping cases are proved to have been as a result of the 2000 Tour."

Verbruggen and the UCI were not cautious in their criticism, calling Boyon and the management of the CPFD "intellectually dishonest" and predicting an end to the cooperative relationship that had developed in preceding months.

"There was not a single case of doping using banned products," the UCI announced in a statement issued a few days after the CPFD report. "The discovery in certain urine samples of substances whose use is restricted, was justified by medical prescriptions, previously entered in the riders' health records, according to the anti-doping regulations."

The UCI, however, did concede that the "case of two riders, neither of whom in fact finished among the leading group in the final standings, but who used substances subject to certain restrictions, are actually the subject of further investigations."

The statement went on: "The CPLD communiqué gave the impression that 43 percent of the dope tests in the Tour de France revealed instances of doping. That is not correct, it is quite false and one has to ask if one were not talking about a certain intellectual dishonesty."

The UCI statement concluded: "If their intention was to get themselves known, then they can consider they have achieved their aim. On the other hand, if the goal was to display their competence and objectivity, they have not succeeded to anywhere near the same degree. Unfortunately, once again the world of cycling has been used and abused for reasons which have nothing to do with a fair battle against doping."

The issue was far from settled and a few days later more fire was added to the flame when the Italian press reported similar results from the 2000 Giro d'Italia. Of the 80 tests that showed positive results for corticosteroids, 20 were submitted by riders who had no medical justification for using them. None of the riders found to be positive could, however, be suspended since the corticosteroid tests had not been announced prior to the Giro.

Far from a season in which one could prove that widespread doping was a mere "myth," 2000 again had given rise to questions on how drugs had seemingly permeated the sport.

Facts and Stats

Number of starters: 177 (three DNS due to inapt hematocrit levels).

Number of finishers: 127 (14 fewer than 1999).

Only team with nine finishers: U.S. Postal Service.

Average speed: 39.569 kph (third fastest in history).

Top sprinter: Telekom's Erik Zabel (a record fifth green jersey).

King of the Mountains: Kelme's Santiago Botero (by 36 points over teammate Javier Otxoa).

Top team: Kelme-Costa Blanca (by 13:42 over Festina)

Best rider 25 or under: Banesto's Francisco Mancebo (by 17:48 over Guido Trentin).

Most aggressive rider: Rabobank's Erik Dekker (by one point over Botero).

Top cash winners: U.S. Postal Service $363,000; Telekom $263,000; Festina $207,000.

Top stage winners: Dekker (3), Tom Steels and Marco Pantani (both 2).

Yellow jerseys: David Millar (3 days), Laurent Jalabert (2 days), Alberto Elli (4 days), Lance Armstrong (12 days).

About the Authors

John Wilcockson visited the Tour de France for the first time as a fan in 1963, riding his bike 200km a day, and managing to catch sight of the race on key mountain climbs, the time trials and several finishes. Five years later, he reported the Tour as a professional journalist, and has now followed the event 31 times. Prior to joining *VeloNews* in 1988, Wilcockson was the editor of four other cycling magazines, and for 10 years was the cycling correspondent of *The Times* and *Sunday Times* in London. He has written six books on cycling, including *John Wilcockson's World of Cycling*, which is available from VeloPress. He is currently the editorial director of *VeloNews*, and lives in Boulder, Colorado, with his wife Rivvy Neshama.

Charles Pelkey has followed the Tour de France four times, and this is his third year of co-authoring the VeloPress book on the Tour. Pelkey is a former amateur bike racer, and has enjoyed a long and varied media career—working as a political reporter, a U.S. senate press secretary, and even a late-night jazz disc jockey. He has been the technical editor of *VeloNews* since 1994, and lives in Golden, Colorado, with his wife Diana Denison and their children Philip and Annika.

Bryan Jew made his Tour de France debut in 2000—covering the race from start to finish as the lead reporter for velonews.com and driving the *VeloNews* press car. He has also covered the Giro d'Italia, Vuelta a España, Paris-Roubaix, Liège-Bastogne-Liège and the world road championships. Jew is the senior writer for *VeloNews*, and lives in Boulder, Colorado, with his wife Kori.